EDWIN T SCOTT

oceans
OF
Champagne

THE RAMBLINGS OF A
FUNCTIONING ALCOHOLIC

Mereo Books

Mereo Books 2nd Floor, 6-8 Dyer Street,
Cirencester, Gloucestershire, GL7 2PF

An imprint of Memoirs Book Ltd. www.mereobooks.com

OCEANS OF CHAMPAGNE: 978-1-86151-958-0

First published in Great Britain in 2020
by Mereo Books, an imprint of Memoirs Books Ltd.

The address for Memoirs Books Ltd. can be
found at www.memoirspublishing.com

Memoirs Books Ltd. Reg. No. 7834348

Typeset in 11/17pt Sabon
by Wiltshire Associates Ltd. Printed and bound in Great Britain

Other Books by Edwin T Scott

Contract Bridge (W Foulsham & Co Ltd, 1992)
Freezing In The Heat – a poetry selection

contents

ABOUT THE AUTHOR

Edwin Scott was born in Suffolk. He attended Northgate Grammar School in Ipswich and on leaving, chose to pursue a career in variety entertainment. This endured in a full-time capacity for twenty years. By the 1970s, he had moved into management and was appointed Entertainments Director with P&O Cruises, engaged on both the Oriana and the Canberra. During this period he started to play bridge seriously and reached moderate representative standard. Edwin qualified as an EBU Teacher in 1985 and passed further assessments of confidence in 1987.

In 1996, having retained over 200 bridge students annually for seven years, he was privileged to become one of the first ten lecturers in Great Britain to be accorded the status of EBUTA Professional. In this capacity he was invited to help formulate 'Standard English' as a small part of an esteemed group chaired by former Ladies World Champion Sandra Landry.

Edwin has three daughters.

ACKNOWLEDGEMENTS

My sincere thanks to my friend Will Johnson for his considerable help in reading through the manuscript and helping to supervise the complex process of editing and design, and to Sue and Paul, who helped to type up the manuscript.

CHAPTER 1

FAMILY MATTERS

My name is Edwin Scott, more usually known as Eddie. I was born at the beginning of the post-war baby boom on the 22nd June 1946 at Ipswich Maternity Ward in Lower Brook Street. My mother told me many years later that three and half hours after I entered this world of rationing, my father came to visit, took one look at me, said 'I wish we hadn't got him' and then left.

To mitigate my father's behaviour, both my parents were subject to the whims of the patriarchal Victorian values held by their parents. It was they who decided who their progeny would marry. Feelings and desires were ignored. Some rebelled but most, reluctantly, accepted that their parents knew best, and so it was with my parents. Both of their fathers were past masters of the Freemasons and members of the same Masonic Lodge; this suggested to them an ideal association.

Both my grandfathers were successful in business. My mother's father was Ernest Edmonds, who was born the same year that his father Harry started his own furnishings and fittings business called Edmonds and Son. In 1898, when Ernest was fourteen, he left school and was apprenticed to his father to earn 6d for a sixty-hour week. His father suggested that if he promised to save his wages for something special, he and his mother would give him a penny each week to spend on anything he desired. My grandfather told me that before his father's offer he had coveted the most wonderful bicycle he had seen in a town shop, so he agreed to the deal. Seventy-five weeks later, for £1 17s 6d, he took proud possession of a brand-new bicycle and could now cycle to work. The bicycle boy eventually became a master cabinet-maker.

Edmonds and Son was very much a family business. Ernest's sister Gertrude (my great aunt) looked after the books (extremely well, apparently). His younger brother Harry worked with loose furnishings, and by all accounts was very innovative. This was until, quite suddenly, he descended into alcoholism. Tragedy also hit another member of the family, Edwin (my mother's brother), who was expected, on the completion of his public-school education at seventeen, to join the business. (He had wanted to be a cricketer and was much talked about at Ipswich School as a fast bowler of extreme promise – no chance.) However, he felt severely demeaned by his Aunt Gertrude, who belittled him for his enthusiasm and bringing fresh ideas into the business, so he stormed out of the establishment, got into his Austin 7, drove to Henley, a village near Ipswich, and crashed it straight into a lamp post. He died a week later, on December 10th 1931, from his injuries. His sister Eileen (my mother), was just ten years old. Shortly afterwards my Great Uncle Harry (long before his descent into alcoholism), booked the remnants of my mother's family on a six-week cruise to South America. Being at home for Christmas would have been unbearable. It was as good as it could have been under the circumstances.

One evening during the cruise my mother and her mother were playing the piano in the lounge. As they finished, Sir Henry Wood, a highly-respected conductor of the period, stood and clapped his hands above his head. He then said, loud enough for all to hear, 'We'll see you at the next promenade concert!' He was only one generation out. My sister was to play at the Royal Albert Hall on many occasions.

Sir Henry was known kindly as 'Timber', which many assumed was a reference to his surname. He in fact loved woodwork, especially the heavy hardwoods. When my grandfather happened to be approached regarding a damaged rocking horse in the children's playroom, Sir Henry asked if he could come and watch the 'cabinet maker' at work. That evening my naughty mother came into the lounge, kissed her mother and father goodnight and turning said 'Goodnight the pair of you, whoever you are!' Sir Henry roared with laughter, unlike his humourless wife. Sir Henry and Lady Wood were travelling to the West Indies for Christmas and just before they were due to disembark, mum asked if they wouldn't mind if she took their photograph with her Brownie camera. It was windy and rough. It took over half an hour! Our family still have that photograph.

My father's father, Thomas Bertrum, was a survivor of the First World War who had fought and survived the Battle of the Somme. He was a popular and sociable man and had many friends. He played bowls for Suffolk (winning countless trophies), was a member of the Masonic brethren and was the owner of the Emperor Inn, a public house in Ipswich, where his friends regularly gathered. His wife described him, with not a little angst, as 'a man's man'.

On a rook shoot in May 1932, he was standing close to his colleague, a Mr Juby. Mr Juby's gun was duly pointed towards the ground when quite suddenly it exploded. A bullet ricocheted from the turf and up into the back of Thomas' head. My father, who happened to be there, travelled with his father in the ambulance to the hospital. Thomas died nine hours later. (There was an inquest but the outcome of that was accidental death; it took twenty minutes.) My father was eleven. The funeral cortège was a quarter of a mile long. The Masonic Brethren bought his wife Florence (my grandmother) a three-bedroomed house and paid for my father's public-school education.

In the 1930s, my mother's parents became the centre of the social lives of their friends and family when they had their back lawn transformed into tennis courts. Everyone congregated there, and tennis parties were frequent. My grandmother (whom I was never to know) welcomed the friendship, energy and enthusiasm, as she found them a comfort after the tragic loss of her son Edwin. In November 1943 my grandparents' house was bombed, and the back of the house was completely obliterated. My grandmother died less than three weeks later, partly due to shock but mainly because of the chronic asthma she had suffered since a young girl. She was a brilliant pianist and songwriter, and had played for silent movies. She died at just fifty-five.

My mother loved dancing and was accomplished in four disciplines. She started her own dance classes in the back room of the family home, teaching ballet, old time, tap and acrobatics. Had the war not intervened she could well have made it her profession. My father also had artistic leanings and from an early age had a gift for drawing and painting in both watercolour and oils (I still possess some excellent examples). Alas, this was a gift neither my sister nor I inherited. In 1938 my father joined the Territorial Army. I cannot think why, as he hated even the thought of war and he, like many left-wingers, had resented the education with which he had been provided.

Unhappily for both my parents, they were married in 1941. My father left the very next day to join the Eighth Army in the Signals Corps. The marriage had not been consummated. Whilst he was away my mother would receive letters (mainly blacked out). My father would sign them Private Scott, and then a subsequent letter would be signed Lance Corporal Scott and then the next one back to Private Scott again; he seemed to be playing the game by his own rules. He rarely talked about his wartime experiences and I think perhaps he should have been a conscientious objector, but that demands a kind of bravery I'm not sure my father ever possessed. His hero at this time was Josef Stalin, the Soviet revolutionary and politician, and he remained far to the left until he died. Years later, being a left-winger, he was at his most vituperous at any mention of Margaret Thatcher. Another reason may have been that at the time he was battling secondary brain cancer, a battle he lost on June 2nd 1989, the same day that Li Peng mowed down his own people in Tiananmen Square. His death at sixty-seven was horrendous. I was telephoned by the hospital and told to come and see him and to expect the worst. At his bedside, while he was fighting for his life, I reached for his hand. I soon realised that he was being restrained and strapped to the bed. Neither pre- nor post-mortem was there any semblance of peace.

* * * *

In September 1945 my father was demobbed to the comfortable three-bedroomed home that Ernest had bought for them. My grandfather registered it solely in my mother's name. My father and his family protested, being of the view that it should be in joint names. Their claim was rejected. It was hardly the basis on which to restart a marriage. My mother wanted to start a family, but my father did not.

The upshot was that after my parents' first physical association, I made my entrance into the world of rations; my mother had her way. From that moment on my father took it upon himself to save every penny he could, purely out of spite. By this point he had taken up a position in education as an art teacher, after passing the emergency teaching exams. He was an excellent teacher, as I can attest having observed him a few times towards the end of his career. However, he didn't like the word 'profession' because it wasn't working class enough.

My sister Catherine was born three years later and as a family we managed to have some enjoyable times: we saw the travelling Bertram Mills Circus, visited the Science Museum and London Zoo, and went to see locally-performed pantomimes. We also had an annual week's holiday, but it had to be cheap. Even though father was a non-believer he discovered the good financial value of the YMCA! There were several hotels dotted about the country and we stayed at one in Lowestoft. This was not far from our home town, but that insured that the travelling expenses were kept to a minimum. It was indeed very good value and Catherine and I looked forward to these holidays, and thoroughly enjoyed ourselves.

As the breadwinner my father held the purse strings; he allotted my mother the absolute minimum subsistence that he could for a family of four. An example of this miserliness was when my sister needed new shoes. My mother returned from town with a perfectly fitting pair of shoes for her, only to be ordered back by my father to order the next size up, his reasoning being that although they would be uncomfortable, they would last longer.

The purse strings relaxed a little when my sister reached school age. She was encouraged by my father to have ballet and piano lessons and given a promise that if she failed the eleven-plus he would pay for her to have a part-paid place at Ipswich High School for Girls, a dichotomy of sorts. On the other hand, I was told that if *I* failed the eleven-plus I would be sent to the local comprehensive, because the school uniform would be cheaper.

It might seem, patient reader, that I resented my sister; I did not. I was deeply fond of Catherine from the moment I saw her. When first seeing her in the bath I exclaimed, 'Mummy, Catherine has got two bottoms!' It never entered my head to resent her. Sixty-five years later I still feel the same filial affection for her.

The atmosphere at home was normally miserable, although it must be said that there was never any violence. Rows often came out of nothing and I would try anything to come between them (I'm told I was known as Mr Loyal). Deflecting one argument and anticipating the next had a bad effect on me, both mentally and physically. I began to find eating difficult. My father never played with me in a 'rough and tumble' way. At moments of togetherness when father would give Catherine a kiss, I was allowed to shake his hand. In fairness to him, he gave up smoking at the end of the war and never resumed, and he only drank a couple of glasses of port on a Friday when he spent the evening with his mother, who only lived half a mile away.

* * * *

In 1952 when I was almost six (and at school) and my sister was nearly three, I was parcelled off to my grandfather's, to stay with him and his new wife Mona. She was my gran, and I was very fond of her. My sister has no memory of this time and my mother (now ninety-seven) will divulge nothing. It turns out that my sister and I were sent away because my parents were having a 'trial separation'. The local GP, damn him, had advised that they should 'stay together for the sake of the children'! If my parents had permanently separated I know it would have been devastating at first, but in the long run I would have been better off, and because my sister was so young I'm sure she would have coped even better than myself.

I remember clearly going, two or three times, in mum's car to the Esplanade Gardens in Westcliff-on-Sea, where my great-aunt Floss (who was born in 1878) lived. I say 'mum's car' because she was the only one who could drive; dad didn't start lessons until the 1970s, after my parents' divorce.

In those days the journey involved driving throughout the sleepy hamlet of Hadleigh, long before there were trunk roads, let alone dual carriageways. I particularly remember mum screeching, 'Broom, broom, toot, toot, broom, broom, toot, toot, we're on our way to Westcliff!' while Catherine and I, in the back of the car, were parroting along with her. There were no seatbelts in those days and my sister and I jumped about in the back, a forerunner of the bouncy castle!

The journey seemed to last forever. Eventually we reached Esplanade Gardens, our haven for a few days. I'm sure the interlude proved a necessary break for both mum and dad. My memories of these trips are crystal clear. The first was the television; my great-aunt had bought one in 1948. (On both sides, my forebears were wealthy people, but they found a way of 'playing down' any suggestion of it. They all played the part of being Mr and Mrs Ordinary.)

The second memory really did seem to go on forever. It was the coronation of Queen Elizabeth II on the 2nd June 1953. My great-aunt, as happened in many homes, opened her house to friends and relations. Chairs were rustled up and some brought their own. The time came with everyone seated and ready for the coronation procedure to begin (not my words). For me, it was the long haul which began. Great-aunt's lounge was very large, large enough for forty!

My last abiding memory of the coronation was of my great-aunt's 'daily', who was determined to leave the room despite the chair she had been offered. In the end she was persuaded to stay as long as she was close to the door, so she would be ready if needed.

Another memory of that time I thought was much more exciting than coronations. At the bottom of the garden was the rail terminus (I think for Southend), with steam locomotives. I had been put to bed, but quietly got up, breaking the rules. It was one of those truly wonderful, unforgettable experiences. The locomotives steamed into the station, were turned around on the circular turntable, and steamed out so the next locomotive could go through the same process.

Eventually, the door opened and in came mum, expecting me to be tucked up fast asleep. She wasn't very cross. 'Come on Edwin, you've been a bit of a naughty boy.' I thought it was best to be subservient. She tucked me up and I went straight to sleep.

A final memory was of mum taking us down the road to Southend, where there was a better beach. We went to the long pier where they had a train (sadly not steam) in its yellow and green livery, which took you right to the end of the pier. I still really enjoyed it.

Shortly after we returned home, when all the news was about the Queen's flight to Canada, my sister, not quite three, piped up, 'She's gone on a stretcher cruiser.' Apparently I responded, 'She's gone to Confoundland!'

* * * *

When my sister Catherine and I were still at junior school, Grandma Scott said that Aunt Emmie had invited us to tea. Aunt Emmie was a distant relative of grandma's; they had a relationship which had endured for many years and were never out of touch. Emmie was born in 1886 and Grandma Scott in 1891. They had enjoyed each other's company whilst Queen Victoria was still on the throne.

Being invited to tea was a treat in itself, but after a ten-minute chat about this and that Auntie Emmie turned to us and asked if we had ever taken part in a treasure hunt. We looked at each other and I answered that we didn't think we had; Cathy nodded in agreement.

'Well' said Auntie Emmie, 'in the lounge, the back room, the kitchen, the cupboard under the stairs and in the upstairs bedroom which has the door open are little surprises. It won't be difficult because I have wrapped yours in blue Edwin and yours Catherine are in pink. Off you go!'

I suggested to Cathy that we shouldn't open them as we found them but save that for grandma. (After all I was three years older.) For at least twenty minutes it felt like Christmas time and wished it could last longer. Eventually we gathered our goodies and carried them in our cardigans to Grandma Scott. She told us we were lucky, and I asked her, 'can we open them now?' We had a half an hour like we'd never had before. I don't remember what was in all those wrapped wonders, but I can recall a lovely old-fashioned doll (Cathy's eyes were out on stalks). For myself, there was a young boy's cricket ball which looked the same as a real one. I was beginning a lifetime affair with cricket, which has not diminished 65 years later. We also had a big packet of sweets each.

We had a lovely tea with Auntie Emmie; sandwiches, cakes, jelly and blancmange and chocolate slices. We also had a choice of orange or lemon squash. When it was time to leave for the long journey home, we didn't need grandma to tell us to say thank you. What a wonderful lady, and what a brilliant day.

Almost a year later we waited to be invited again. It would seem as the day got closer that we were both thinking the same, would she or wouldn't she? We need not have wondered. She did, and it was just wonderful.

At about the same time, we were invited to tea with Uncle Eustace and Auntie May. May was Eustace's second wife, as his first wife had passed away after a long marriage.

Eustace, born in 1885, was Grandma Scott's nearest brother; his garden was 100 metres long and 25 metres wide. He was a millionaire. All my forebears, as I mentioned before, were wealthy, but behaved as if they were very ordinary.

Also living with Eustace and May was Miss Bertha Carter (born in 1884). I'm not certain who she was related to, but once again she was a long-time associate of Grandma Scott and Auntie Emmie. She was most likely related to Eustace's first wife. What a difference to Aunt Emmie. Bertha, on this occasion, had decided on the utmost formality. She had never accepted Aunt May, who was apparently easy going, gentle and polite. There was a brief moment of peace before she said 'Mrs Goddard, will you pass the jam?'

'With pleasure, Miss Carter.' Followed with a grunt.

'Miss Carter, would you pass the mustard?' Followed by another grunt as the mustard winged its way to the other end of the table.

There was no treasure hunt. It's not that we expected it. No wonder Uncle Eustace was in his garden throughout; he kept away.

To conclude, many years later, at the beginning of 1976 (several years after Grandma Scott passed away), I overheard my father speaking of Auntie Bertha being in a hospital home. At the time she was moving towards 92. I had a chance to say to someone special, thank you. I duly phoned Aunt Emmie after mum kindly said I could use her car. I asked Emmie, 'Would you like me to take you over and see Aunt Bertha?' She was really up for it, at 89. I picked her up and our journey was a pleasure. We found Bertha's ward and bed, and there were no grunts or formalities. At this stage Bertha was blind, but their reminisces were a sheer delight. Within a few moments

I stopped thinking I should join in and just listened. I listened to them talk of something that happened in 1908 – they were in fits of laughter!

Eventually the time came when Bertha was carted off for a blood test. Aunt Emmie and I returned to the car. She turned to me and said, 'It was so good to see Bertha again. When you get to her age you don't know how long you're going on for!'

* * * *

My father loved his football and was an ardent supporter of Ipswich Town FC. He had turned out in all weathers, even before they were promoted to the Football League. I have to say that this gave us our closest association. He took me to my first game when I was eight and looked after me assiduously. We always walked to the ground (which was not far) and he, without question, paid for my ticket. He even brought a box for me to stand on so I could see the action. I can remember to the very moment, with the score at Ipswich Town 1 – 1 Swansea Town (as they were then called) with about ten minutes to go I said, 'Dad, I don't think there will be any more goals'. Dad looked down on me (despite the box) and placed his fingers on his lips and said 'sshhh old boy, those Swansea players may hear you!'

Although relations within the home were no better, (mum was in a permanent state of depression), the tensions I could not avoid were lifted on those Saturdays when Ipswich Town were playing at home. There were championships, league titles, European involvement and the FA Cup. I felt a more positive atmosphere, although this in itself was not as strong as the negatives which persisted.

CHAPTER 2

GrowInG up

On my first day at junior school, in the playground waiting for the whistle that would beckon us to class, a boy punched me with seeming hatred. Having had no such experience before, this momentary aberration decided my fate for the next seven years. I burst into tears.

I joined the church choir, which to my surprise, considering his atheistic leanings, my father welcomed. It cost nothing and although my father and I didn't realise it, it was a useful earner. Weddings, funerals and a thrice-monthly stipend depended on my attendance. My first pay came before I even realised it was my due. Two sixpences were proffered as the vicar caught me on my way out from a wedding. (My first luxury yacht would be next!)

I thought this might ease the fear of the bullies, but the word had spread: *he's a cry baby, he's a coward.* With the unhappiness of my estate never to be voiced, I was alone. My parents were oblivious to my plight for all those seven years. Two teachers let it happen when they could have stopped it.

In later years, when I was blessed with a good marriage and three wonderful daughters, my first concern when they attended the Ipswich High School for Girls in Woolverstone, long before the considerations of their education, was to check on bullying. When I discovered that two of my daughters (along with other students) had endured bullying, I wrote to the Headmistress, who responded superbly. Her unconditional threats that they would be expelled were such that the bullies spent the rest of the time before they left looking over their shoulders.

* * * *

Christmas was in general a happier time. Catherine and I had exciting stockings which we opened in the morning. On one occasion at about two o'clock in the morning (so we were told), I woke, felt my stocking, which crinkled invitingly, woke my sister to say Father Christmas had been and put the light on. Then we began to open our goodies. This was the first Christmas when Catherine took less **notice of the wrapping and more of what was inside it. The commotion brought forth a slightly bleary-eyed mum and dad. I honestly remember the** incident (I was five and a half). **They did take it in good** part, **but firmly put us back to bed and put our stockings on the floor where we could not reach them. (Having heard mum frequently complain while I was growing up, she asked me when I was about six and a half, 'What have you got in your stocking?' Apparently** I retorted, 'a ladder!')

The usual routine was to have breakfast and to look forward to Grandma Scott coming and enjoying our Christmas Day roast with us. Afterwards we opened our main presents. At half past three we set off on the short walk to Grandad Edmonds' house, where we would spend the rest of Christmas Day and in our formative years, the night as well.

Before moving on, I have one final memory of Christmas. I fortunately managed to pass the esteemed eleven-plus. (The alternative would have been awful – at least ten of the choir bullies would be going to the same secondary school.) Despite my father's protests about the cost of the uniform he realised he had no choice but to accept the inevitable, certainly as far as the strength of family opinion was concerned. He busied himself trying to find the least financial expenditure; would it be bus fares or a cheap bike? It was a close thing, but the bike would be the cheapest; he bought the one that cost £12. But my father had not taken into account the ever-darkening evenings which started closing in during the months after September. My bike had no lights, so he bought a cheap dynamo and fixed it to my bike. A few weeks later I opened my main Christmas present from mum and dad. It was my dynamo! Dad had removed it from the bike to present it to me. It was duly refixed to my bike to continue its function.

* * * *

My lack of interest in gardening first became apparent when on a Sunday (following Saturday football), my father asked me to help in the garden. We had quite a large back lawn, split into turf and 'allotment', where dad successfully grew all the vegetables we needed for the year (he also had enormous success at growing tomatoes). I followed him onto the lawn, where he handed me a bucket. I was instructed to pick up stones. This was to remain par, before even I guessed the times to absent myself.

My sister passed the eleven-plus, which was a relief to both my parents, especially mother as she knew there would be no backlash regarding uniform. We both enjoyed sports at school (built side by side in the same complex. In the middle was a swimming pool which was used very sensibly, on alternate days). We were not exceptional, although Catherine became a more than competent tennis player (she played for Suffolk Juniors). I played basketball for the school, was in the tennis squad and played hockey for the YMCA, second eleven.

In my early years at school, I struggled. After year two, the Headmaster did me the biggest favour possible by keeping me back a year (repeating year two). He had given me the chance to consolidate. When the results for year five arrived (in those days O-levels) came and I had succeeded in passing five (out of the six), he included within my results his personal printed logo 'Congratulations!' Obviously, we both knew that the action he had taken had mutually borne fruit. When I went up to year three, he was awarded the OBE for his services to education.

Catherine went into the top set (lower 3A), but dropped back to lower 3D. My parents were slightly surprised, as she was a hard worker, if not inspired. But we were all (including a touch of sibling rivalry) bemused when the school indicated that she was to be demoted to D. She was 21st out of 28, so fair enough to drop her to B, at the very worst to C, but D? She reacted in the only way she knew; she never failed another paper. This despite the fact she was now in an environment with the 'also rans', a different type altogether, boasting of all their boyfriends.

Catherine, with enormous fortitude, passed all nine O-levels, and then the two A-levels she took. Not surprisingly she had been absolutely determined to show the school what a spiteful decision they had made.

Her relief at passing Music changed the rest of her life. She was accepted at Goldsmiths College in London, but she was not happy there. She approached the University of East Anglia; she was accepted and never looked back. Her instruments were the oboe and cor anglaise. She had also kept up her piano and received her letters. She approached the BBC National Orchestra of Wales, succeeded and prospered.

Having enjoyed her situation for about two years, 'Second Oboe' began a relationship with 'Principal Cellist'. This turned, in the fullness of time, into a happy marriage. Her husband John is a special man. I could not have wished for her a nicer person. When Cathy realised that a little one was on the way she had to give up her full-time musicianship. She did however stay on call, and when Principal Oboe was away, the leader of the orchestra was happy to promote her rather than bring in another oboist. She continued her association with the BBC right up until her husband retired after thirty-eight years with the orchestra.

* * * *

My O-level results gave me the option of staying on at school to do A-levels or to leave and apply for professional jobs that might be available, an example being at a teacher training College. I did stay on at sixth form for eight weeks, and when I had a free period, I used it to cope with my English Literature, History and French; I felt I was just coping. Then the school took the free period away so I could learn Russian! I think this bypassed the Headmaster but that was the last straw, and I left. I had been cast in the sixth form as Antonio in Gilbert and Sullivan's *The Gondoliers* and much to my surprise I was welcomed to return for rehearsals and the performance. I got an office job at £4 17s 6d week.

* * * *

In conclusion, I managed to get my parents into trouble. I was six and I could (basically) read and wondered why Catherine could not, so when she was three, I taught her myself. On her first day at school it caused an uproar. Mum was summoned to the Headmistress, who made it clear that the *school* did the teaching.

My first memories were early. The first one, which I am 99% certain is genuine, occurred in the back room of grandma's house. I was in my pram and crying, dad came into the room and softly placated me (nobody is all bad). This was when I was twenty months. My second, when two and a half, was at London Zoo, I was lifted up at the penguin pool and I wondered how they could order blue water. I didn't quite realise that the pool was painted blue. From three I have many memories of sitting on the same chair in the back room to hear *Listen with Mother*. Each day I was given a little paper cone in which were assembled six little dolly mixtures; I could make them last for an hour. On one occasion I got cross with my mother for turning the wireless off before the theme tune which finished the programme had ended. The theme tune was the *Berceuse* from Gabriel Fauré's *Dolly Suite*. This was my introduction to classical music, which I have loved ever since.

* * * *

Apart from a YMCA holiday at Eastbourne and a cheap disaster in Bournemouth, we always went to Lowestoft YMCA (Claremont). This gave us tennis and a putting green just a minute away from the hotel and the beach a mere three minutes. Over the years we experienced mixed weather conditions, but dad always paid for a weekly tennis ticket which he made sure would be of good value rather than overpaying each time. Luckily, we all loved tennis, but it was morning noon and night!

I spent most of my saved holiday money at the eighteen-hole putting green. The turf was over 350 years old and would have graced any of the top golf courses in the world. My totals gradually came down over the years and when I was fourteen I putted my first par (thirty-six) for a round (sixteen twos, one one and one three). Towards the end of that same week, I was delighted to card thirty-five. I was approached by a married couple who had been watching me; they were in their late middle-age and were successful golfers (according to them anyway).

The lady carded a thirty-five (seventeen twos and one one), her husband carded a thirty-four (sixteen twos and two ones). I was behind until we came to the last five holes. Some power seemed to course through my veins; hole fourteen was a good one and hole fifteen a 'gimmie' two. The last three holes seemed to be played by someone else. Sixteen and seventeen were both ones and as I approached the eighteenth I knew it would be a one (a sixty-foot putt, only two holes were less than fifty feet). Down she duly dropped. I had managed a round of thirty-three.

The couple disappeared very quickly; they didn't want to shake hands. I went to the reception, where an old gentleman I had known for years would occasionally give me a free round. I handed him my card and he said he would put it in the window, but it was not a record. That privilege belonged to Bobby Jones, who had carded a thirty-two.

Several people suggested that I should approach a golf club; in due course I did just that, but I must say I never got near membership. I couldn't drive without lifting my head; my iron work was even worse. I could still putt, but by the time I had the opportunity I'd taken nine or ten shots to get there!

* * * *

From year four at Northgate Grammar there coincided the comedy of Tony Hancock, Peter Cook and Dudley Moore and *Steptoe and Son*. I found I could do impressions, and on top of that I could tell a joke with reasonably good timing and make the class laugh. This ended any semblance of bullying. I did get into trouble sometimes, but it was worth it. I would spy a master laughing. I am not alone; several comics have used the same ruse to avoid the bullies.

I saw Jimmy Tarbuck on television on *Sunday Night at the London Palladium* (he played the clubs 'up north' and could easily have audiences crying with laughter for hours at a time). On the *Palladium* he told a few jokes and introduced the stars of the show. I said to myself, I could do that – stand aside Jimmy T, Eddie is on his way! Little did I know, but they say ignorance is bliss.

* * * *

My last visit to Lowestoft YMCA was in 1964. I was eighteen and still had a small car, and I had left school for a boring office job. During that last holiday I met a small group of people who had travelled together. They were kindly and encouraged my efforts. One of the gentlemen told me there was a talent competition at the Sparrow's Nest theatre, which was not far from our hotel. He volunteered to drive me there because parking might be difficult. We arrived, but the gate was closed. Obviously I was disappointed, but he said, 'I can get you in if you stand on my back'. He was right. I thanked him profusely and he wished me luck. I was just in time to register.

It was a lovely day and the stage and microphone were set. The judges were the four dancers who appeared in the review. Most people there were out to enjoy themselves. There were seven or eight participants; I was the third act on. The lady before me went on and on and on, and sang at least twenty choruses of 'I'll take you home again Kathleen'. I went on eventually and I felt my little eight minutes went okay, but I did not think I would win. The female judges did laugh a little. I was genuinely surprised when the judges gave me the nod – I had won! The lady who had crucified 'Kathleen' was livid. She ranted and raved, 'I am the most talented person here, I always win these competitions, you must have made a mistake'. The judges didn't budge, and the lady was left complaining to all and sundry about her great talents!

A very nice lady who I thought should have won came up to me. She made no fuss and said to me that if I ordered *The Stage* newspaper I would find at the back all sorts of adverts for talent agencies, variety management etc. She wished me luck and I thanked her for her advice.

I ordered a copy of *The Stage* as soon as I got home. Glancing through the pages I saw articles by and about the household names of the time. I eventually reached the back. On the page before last there were lots about employment in London and northern clubs, but there, towards the end, was an advert for cabaret artists by an agency in Clacton. I contacted them, and they invited me to come down to the address given in the advert. This was another example of my good fortune.

I parked outside what turned out to be a private house. I introduced myself to the two gentlemen there and discovered that they worked at Butlins in Clacton. Len Rooker was a pianist and band leader, and this was his house (I also met his wife and daughter). Tony Dennes was the camp comic. I told them what I had done (which didn't take long), and I think they pencilled me in as a Butlins Redcoat. However, in the meantime they gave me a couple of gigs in Colchester, for which I was paid £2, which went okay. I also performed at a Boxing Day special, for which I was paid £5. Unfortunately, it was a bit of a disaster; my inexperience showed, little things went wrong, then they became bigger things. They say, 'you've never lived until you've died'. Very much a performer's insight. Much to my surprise, I took it on the chin and was determined to learn from it.

The top billing act on that Boxing Day show had the worst stammer I had ever heard. At the bar it was embarrassing to hear, but once on stage he was a changed man. He was an all-round entertainer and word perfect throughout. He brought the house down! I thought he was brilliant. I was, for the first time, experiencing life 'in the raw', and I still had not drunk alcohol.

* * * *

In 1965 I exchanged one boring job for another. However, working in the drawing office in this company was someone whom I'd known all my life. John Cooper and his family lived opposite our house for many years. We were never close, but only because he was seven years older than me. When I joined Eastern Counties Farmers he took me under his wing. On one occasion he told me that he and Jack Downey (also in the drawing office) went out for a drink on a Wednesday and Friday, would I like to come? 'Don't worry about transport, I'll pick you up' he said. I agreed with pleasure.

A fourth joined us and we had a very enjoyable time (this relationship continued, on and off, for many years). Obviously, I was keen to have an audience for my jokes and impressions. They seemed willing enough to listen, even to repeats. The laughter was loud and other patrons in the pub would stop talking and start listening and bought us several drinks.

The first time was the best. I had two pints of bitter, and with it the tensions I had come to accept as the norm dissipated. I suddenly felt better than at any time in my memory. The same thing happened when I made the numbers up for ECF cricket against local villages who had their own cricket clubs. Afterwards I had two pints of bitter and felt the same freedom from tension as before. I didn't know I had a problem, but alcoholism didn't rear its ugly head for many years.

At this time (October 1965), a letter arrived from Clacton asking me to keep December 4th available. That was exciting to read. Butlins did several winter breaks and I was required to do a ten-minute spot before the main cabaret. When I arrived, Len Rooker told me that the camp manager was coming down to see me. I felt it went well enough to deserve the quite generous applause I received. I walked to the bar and Len introduced me to the manager, Larry Knight. He said, 'My God, son, you really have an awful lot to learn!' I was pleased with my riposte, 'Yes sir I know, but I'm willing to learn'.

He gave me a wry smile. 'How would you like to be a Redcoat next summer?'

'I would be delighted, sir.'

He then bought me a coke and left. I turned to Len. 'You've done this for me and I am so grateful,' I said.

'Don't forget the manager's words – a lot to learn,' he replied.

'I won't let you down, Mr Rooker.'

In some ways I always felt I'd embraced entertainment for the wrong reasons, to show the bullies what I had achieved. I badgered the press and local radio, who much to my surprise, seemed to take the view that it was a case of 'local boy makes good'. When I later approached them as a Redcoat, they wrote a lovely article. Before I left they told me to contact them when I had further news. I was determined to show those b*****ds who had made my life such a misery.

CHAPTER 3

GOOD MORNING CAMPERS

As life moved on, we reached 1966, World Cup year. I was still bored with my day job (which was mainly filing), but I had Butlins to look forward to. Eventually, May 19th arrived, the day I was expected. I jumped into my new car (even smaller than the last) and drove the thirty miles to Clacton. I was duly registered, given my chalet and most importantly my red coat! I was to share with three others. All of us greenhorns were given a brief guide to the camp and left to our own devices.

(David Croft and Jimmy Perry, the writers and creators of *Hi-de-Hi*, amazed me. Though it was based in the 1950s, it was still accurate in 1966. A children's entertainer who disliked children, a camp comic played by Paul Shane who had a birthday every fortnight, a tyro wanting to 'get on' [Jeff Holland and me] and a hostess [Sylvia] of long standing looking frayed around the edges.)

The first campers would be arriving on Saturday, so we still had a couple of days to go. I remember vividly a member of the Highland Trio (one of the established resident acts who, apart from Sunday, performed at all the main review shows in the enormous theatre). He had five or six of the company of Redcoats in stitches. He was gay and his style was like that of John Inman in *Are You Being Served?* He was hilarious to everyone except me. A lot to learn? I didn't like anyone else getting the laughs. However, looking back, accepting that someone else was in the 'chair' took me longer to accept than it should have done.

With four or so others, I was deployed to meet the trains as they arrived at Clacton Station on Saturday morning. A cheery word and smile were required, as well as showing the campers where they needed to place their luggage for collection, assuring them the system was reliable and that they would be reunited with it as they arrived at their chalet. We then helped them into the coach that would take them to the camp. Other Redcoats would be stationed in reception, again greeted the campers with a cheery word and a smile and help if they had any sort of problem.

Settled into the chalet they could relax, knowing that drinks and smokes were their only outgoing expenditure. Everything else was included. If they had a baby that they had settled before their evening out, they could relax, as the chalets were patrolled. If there were any sounds of crying, it would be relayed to the entertainment areas within minutes.

I had my first jolt towards the end of that first week. I had been instructed to introduce the acts off stage, during the compère's day off. On that Wednesday evening I duly did as I was commanded and introduced the acts, which included the

Highland Trio. The next day, that brilliant raconteur whom I in my ignorance had resented, had lost a gold cigarette case, which had been given to him by his present love. He had told friends it was the happiest time of his life. That same day, they found him hanged in his chalet. On the Friday I was backstage again (the compère was 'unwell') and, talk about early experiences, I introduced the Highland 'Duo'.

* * * *

The memory of my words to the manager on that last winter break reverberated, and I tried to live up to them. Some of the male Redcoats were prancing around during the day and acting like peacocks in the evening at the disco, trying to 'pull' or 'wheel in' a different 'bird' every evening. After all it was the 'Swinging Sixties'.   I was no good at chatting up girls and did envy them. However, I instinctively felt this was not my approach. I needed to make myself popular with the campers, which meant talking, smiling, being prepared to be the fall guy and to still laugh at myself when I was thrown in the pool (something I organised myself when I knew it would be busy). I would surface with a pretend fist while laughing my head off!

I had good opportunities very early on in the season, when I was put down to be a 'second' with a bucket and sponge. The chief Redcoat was on the microphone. This was wrestling with professionals; wrestling was *extremely* popular at the time. I was six foot one and weighed just over nine stone. I was early into the ring and once again I was the fall guy. They never actually hurt me, but I enjoyed acting as if I was in agony. The public room was all set up and packed with campers. The chief looked at me and called over his loud speaker 'What shall we call him?'. Before anyone had a chance to speak he said, 'I've got it, we'll call him Lurch!' And Lurch it was throughout the season. I had an old top hat and painted it with my new soubriquet.

The next approach was to always talk to the children, especially if they were alone. This of course was long before you would automatically be assumed a paedophile. So why? Firstly, he or she may have been disorientated by the myriad chalet lines; with that sorted I said,

'I'm Lurch, what's your name?'

'I'm Johnnie, I've been on the rides.'

'Excellent Johnnie, are you coming to the sports this afternoon?'

'I think so.'

'Well, if you can make it, come and see me on my stage with my microphone and I'll sort out the best things for you to join in.'

'Thanks Lurch, I'll see you later.'

What has been achieved? Johnnie goes back to his chalet, tells his mum and dad, they see their little one full of it. Johnnie's happy, mum and dad are happy.

Finally, I thought, the campers see me all day but not so much in the evenings. I decided to try and solve that by coming out of the public room (usually the ballroom, I could dance a little) at 11 pm. I then walked round for three quarters of an hour and said good night to all the campers going the other way. I hoped that with a little banter along the way, it would give me a little 'street cred'.

Six weeks into the season, the camp comic was given two hours to pack and leave. He had sexually assaulted a waiter, who reported him. The King is dead… The next day my top hat was emblazoned with 'Lurch'. It was resented for a day or two by the other Redcoats, but I held on and they soon put their emphasis on the 'crumpet'.

The Butlins' Camp Comedian was a major part of what was known as the *Butlin Movie News*. This was shown on a Friday for much of the day. The central figure had been swept away! It needed a new figure for the rest of the season. The movie camera man approached me and explained the situation, and with regard to the *Movie News* he said, 'Most people know you, would you help me out?' I said 'I'd be delighted'. This entailed walking from my chalet to breakfast having 'forgotten' to put my trousers on. A few ladies are seen pointing and laughing at me. At the end of the news I'm seen going into the main toilets, then after waiting a few seconds I ran out like crazy with half a dozen women coming out branding brushes, brooms and pails etc (subtle stuff). This *Movie News* was just another example of my good luck, which never seemed to end.

****

We had one day off a week and mine was Thursday. It was a perfect time in the week for me. Five days for the campers to get to know me and a return for the Gala Farewell Evening Show. Having my small car, I realised it was feasible to leave the camp at 11:30 on the Wednesday night, when everything had been done. I got home at about midnight and went to bed. I had all day Thursday and went to bed setting the alarm for 7:15 am. Then I made the journey back to Clacton, arriving in time for breakfast duty.

As for drinking, I took very little. As mentioned before, because I could dance, I was nearly always given the ballroom duty and I believe there was no bar. If I had worked in one of the pub bar venues, I would frequently be offered drinks. However, several campers did offer me drinks and I always had a half of bitter, costing less than the old shilling. It was sacrosanct amongst campers that they would not accept (politely) a drink from a Redcoat, because they knew what we were paid.

Tuesday was *our* night. The Redcoat Show! I remember a lot of rehearsals which I quite enjoyed. The theatre band were very good, and patient. Some Redcoats did not perform but took up the duties that go with being 'backstage'.

I was given a chance to perform. I could sing a little and started my act with Bernard Cribbins' song *The Hole in the Ground*. I then did an eight-minute spot with impressions and a closing joke. It seemed to go very well, but I had forgotten that the Butlins' campers knew Redcoats were beginners and would always take every opportunity to encourage.

I would like to think that as the season progressed, I became more polished and a touch ruthless with the material I used. It must have been reasonable because the compère, Bobby Hayes, invited me to perform on his own Wednesday late show. I was thrilled to be asked and although there was only an audience of about a thousand (the Gaiety Theatre held 2,200), it was still good. I felt for the first time I would be judged on merit.

It was one of my two most memorable performances (the other one was to come). It started well and got better. When I left the camp at 11:30 for my day off, I drove home on such a high, feeling I'd had one of the best days of my life. Show people had even come along with kindness and encouragement and Bobby Hayes gave me the thumbs up. Obviously the euphoria didn't last. It was soon back to the norm.

One day we had a remarkable snowfall – in August! I was on tennis duty and arrived the statutory ten minutes early. The tennis courts were covered with snow and I thought that anyone thinking of playing must have known it was a non-starter. I waited five minutes and then left. Five minutes later one man turned up. He reported my misdemeanour to the management. I was duly hauled in and got a right roasting from one of the assistant managers. He threatened me with the sack if it happened again. So much for the camper's Lurch!

A similar thing happened towards the end of the season. As I left the office for Gaiety Theatre duty, one of the under managers asked me to pass a message on to fellow Redcoat Tony, who was doing the same duty at the other side of the theatre. Apparently a message for him to telephone his family urgently had just come in. I knew we were not permitted to talk on the same duty, but I considered this exceptional. I crossed the theatre, imparted the message, and returned to my station. I was called to the office immediately after my duty was complete, and once again threatened with the sack. Butlins' way of paying was a pound suspended until the season's end, when an £18 bonus would be paid. Billy Butlin was notorious for visiting all his camps in the last week, and finding any excuse to sack Redcoats so he wouldn't have to pay the bonus!

Returning to the entertainments office, I was told I would probably be sacked when it was cleared by Mr Larry Knight, of 'much to learn' fame. I got out of my pram. I said to this underling, 'I might be Lurch out there, but I can be as ruthless as you in here. Any sign of the sack and I will sue you. I have all the details with regard to your colleague and his instructions.'

Collapse of stout party!

I enjoyed theatre duty because I hoped to learn from the professionals. The resident comedian and top of the variety bill was Reg Dixon. I learnt so much from his performances. He is hardly remembered now, but during the 1950s he did three command performances. He did appear on an episode of *Are You Being Served?*, but even that was a long time ago.

Many household names started as Butlins Redcoats. They include Jimmy Tarbuck, Des O'Connor, Charlie Drake and Roy Hudd. During the season I was pleased, nay honoured, to meet Bud Flanagan, Tommy Trinder, Jon Pertwee and others, including the unique Linton Boys.

The season ended in early September and I duly received my bonus. I was told next year's pay would be a rise of fifty pence (£7 10s to £8 only). Come September it was time to say farewell to Butlins, with my bonus intact (just). I am told by various sources that I was missed at Butlins, but I'm sure there were 'freshers' who would soon overtake Lurch.

Some readers must wonder if I was to leave Butlins as a virgin. If you thought I would be, I have to disappoint you. I'd learnt much on a higher level, beyond being a Redcoat!

I decided early on to save when possible. I could not afford to be in a precarious profession and spend just because I might have money to squander. My grandfather Ernest had some finances he wished to 'lose' in an effort to reduce death duties. He gave my sister and me £500 each. This was quite substantial in the early 1960s. Catherine and I decided to open separate bank accounts in which we deposited our windfalls.

Back in Ipswich I scoured the pages of *The Stage* and found an advert for a 'shop window' show in Liverpool. These were events at which agents would be present and decide if any of the acts were worthy of consideration for signing up. The acts did not get paid. It seems impossible to believe, but I decided I would journey from Ipswich in my small car and show my 'star quality'! As I look back I shudder at such audacity.

I was a chorister at our local church and just happened to mention to the rector my plans. He suggested I see him after the end of the service. I took his invitation and he asked me to sit and wait for him. He went to his desk and wrote an introduction to take to a rector he knew in central Liverpool; what luck!

I set off on my long journey north and reached the Everton area. It was a good time to telephone the manse to find my bearings. I had journeyed with a small case and a wallet containing £11.50. I was given clear instructions to proceed. Four miles on, my heart missed two beats. I had left my wallet in the telephone kiosk. I backtracked in a panic and found myself at the kiosk with a lady inside. I had little hope, but she saw me and opened the door. She looked at me as if recognising my distress and asked me if I had mislaid a wallet. I resisted the temptation to give her a big hug. What luck!

Within a half an hour I arrived and received a welcome from the rector, who had read the letter I had been given. The charge was £4.50 weekly, which I considered very reasonable. It included full board. I had two weeks on account and felt confident that I would be able to keep my head above water, even if the show didn't work; the heady wine of youth!

The first thing was to open my wallet and find the telephone number of the club. (That would have been lost but for my luck on having it returned.) I was assured that I was expected and to arrive early.

The principal agency was a threesome. The leading light was one Billy 'Uke' Scott. In clubland he was considered the best ukulele player ever. His technical prowess was beyond all, even though the star was George Formby. In the 1940s and 1950s Billy was a regular on the wireless and then on television.

I duly arrived as requested and was ushered to a seat next to the great man. I introduced myself. I think he was fascinated to observe such a presumptuous and callow youth. Billy Scott told me I was next on and I was given a kind introduction. The club was full, and I hoped for the best. I was on for twenty minutes.

From the start the audience was on my side. The laughter was genuine and loud. The applause was deafening. I felt the same euphoria as I had on the Compère's Show at Butlins two months earlier. However, this was certainly the best; what luck, again.

As I came off the stage Billy Scott welcomed me and pointed to the space next to him. He just said, 'We'll talk when the show is over'. I watched the other acts do their business. Some were very good, but not all of them.

Mr Scott was as good as his word. He talked to me for an hour and gave me great guidance. He certainly didn't, in that hour, give me unqualified plaudits. The things he thought I would need to become a regular recipient of applause were hard but fair. At the end of our time together – by then the club was nearly empty – Mr Scott said to me, 'I would like to give you a chance. I will give you shows on Saturday and Sunday nights. You will be paid £8 at each and at your earliest you will bring in the commission to the office in Lord Street.' He gave me his card, we shook hands and he wished me well.

When I look back, I am amazed at my downright cheek. I was twenty and had the nerve to think I could go to the centre of Lancashire comedy, assuming I would make the experts laugh whilst competing with the most experienced. It beggars belief. But back again to the luck; *The Stage* to Redcoat, contact Liverpool, deserved to lose my wallet, a comfortable billet, show case success, two shows a week. How could this go on?

* * * *

The next day, the good people of Liverpool were devastated to hear of the Aberfan disaster. It may have been the closeness despite different nations; they were still near. The tragedy and the aftermath are forever in their hearts. (There is in my hometown of Ipswich a thoroughfare called Silent Street. The children, sometimes as young as nine, who laughed and played raucously, enjoying that short period of time before work started. The Great Plague decimated their lives, hence the street name.)

After my lucky start in comedy, I thought I should try to fill my weekdays with gainful employment. It was mid-October and I thought the big stores would be taking on extra staff for the Christmas period. I approached the emporium T.J. Hughes in Lord Street, close to the Billy Scott agency. I spoke to a lady in reception who put me through to the personnel manager. I was given directions to his office.

He was very welcoming and asked where I had worked in the recent past. I told him I had just finished a summer season as a Butlins Redcoat. He thought for several moments and then asked me if I had worked with children. I spoke honestly when I told him I was not a children's entertainer, but I had much time in my capacity to give children the best possible holiday. The personnel manager hesitated and then 'eureka!' he cried, 'I don't think a store Father Christmas has to be fat and eighty. How about you doing the job, I have one vacancy?'

I immediately agreed and thought, more luck! I couldn't have been offered a better job. My pay would be £12.50 a week. Suddenly any thoughts of bankruptcy were forgotten! It turned into a wonderful experience and I repeated it twice more at the Ipswich Co-op, as was, at the end of the 1960s.

I shared the job with a cheery old gentleman called Sid. He was seventy-eight and weighed at least sixteen stone. Our changing room was directly behind our 'throne'. We had just a curtain to change in and out of costume. We decided with the help of the photographer that when the change was due, he would say, 'Don't worry children, Father Christmas has just gone to feed his reindeer.' (Eyes lit up).

On one occasion we had the pleasure of a seven-year-old wide boy. (I'd put money on him, if he's still alive, being in prison). Everyone involved tried to 'move him on' but he kept coming back. On this particular day it was my break and he was standing close to the curtain when the photographer did his extra duty. 'Father Christmas … feed his reindeer.' And then out came Sid. At the top of his voice, this feral boy yelled out, 'Feed his reindeer? He looks as if he's eaten the bugger!'

A gentler experience was when a little lad aged four (wonderful age) came to see Father Christmas with his mother. He sat on my knee and took over the conversation. I just listened. In the end his mother looked towards me and cocked her head towards the exit. Our discourse was nearly over. I said to him, 'Time to go now David, but just one thing more, it would be very kind if you could leave me a glass of sherry and a carrot for Rudolph by the chimney.'

'Of course I will and I'm going to the shop near where I live, and I'll get you some fags.'

* * * *

I was organised with my weekend routines. The shows achieved very mixed receptions. I didn't have a run of bad or good responses; it was so variable. Billy Scott, on one occasion, told me that he had received a negative call from one of the concert secretaries about my performance. I had to say I was disappointed and I said I would work hard to make them successful. He told me he would review the situation. As I said before I may have become a 'comedian' for the wrong reasons, and I had only just begun.

One of my bad shows started with the concert secretary spitting into the microphone, 'Good evening ladies and gentlemen, I'd just like to say we are sorry to Mrs Jones at table six whose husband dropped dead yesterday. Now I shall introduce the next act. What's your name son?'

I believe the late Paul Daniels had a similar introduction, but at the time he was in his late thirties; I was twenty. However, making no excuse, Paul handled it beautifully. He came on stage and looked round the room and said, 'Ladies and gentlemen, we should first send our condolences to Mrs Jones, and I think she deserves a round of applause for coming out tonight with her friends, (much applause). This show is not for me, it's not for you, it's for Martha and Harold Jones.'

Paul brought the house down. I hadn't realised the depths true professionals will go to. How did he know their names?

When he arrived, he would have ask the concert secretary if anything had happened of interest. Probably nine times out of ten his question would have a negative response. That night he picked number ten!

Returning to my experience, it was one I had never encountered. The result was that I never had a murmur from start to finish. I left the stage to the sound of my own footsteps. Talk about a contrast; the previous night at Dunlops, the best show I had ever done, I was given a standing ovation. This was just three miles away from where I left the stage on that Sunday at the South Liverpool Football Club. I said to myself, at least it can't get any worse. But I had not allowed for the confounded Concert Secretary. There was an old crackly loudspeaker in the dressing room. A vocalist had been introduced and I could still hear a lot of noise. Eventually I was privy to the secretary back on the microphone, he yelled out, 'If you lot don't shut up I'll bring that bloody comic back!'

* * * *

The last week before Christmas, I started to pack. Someone took my Father Christmas uniform to hang it up for next year, and I said my farewells to the rector with many thanks. It was Christmas time and I was going to enjoy being at home. As far as my drinking was concerned, I had enjoyed, at the 'weekend show time', a pint before I performed and sometimes a pint afterwards. On weekdays I had no more than two pints on the evenings I went out.

I don't remember the journey home. I must have thought about the wonderful experiences I had enjoyed, what luck! I might also have thought about my act. Most great comics have an original style which propels them to the top. I was a Max Miller fan and didn't think beyond variety. I believe it was gradually going out of fashion. It was at this time in the mid-sixties when for comedy, the world moved on. David Frost, John Cleese, *Fawlty Towers*, *The Goodies*, *Monty Python*, Peter Cook and Dudley Moore and others changed the face. Apart from my figure (9st. 3lb), which I used as a sympathy vote on stage, I was nothing to do with modernity. However, as my story unfolds, the reader will acknowledge I was not quite finished yet.

* * * *

I don't remember Christmas '66 at all. I'm sure I enjoyed it. The one memory which is absolutely clear, happened two days before twelfth night on January 4th, 1967. Donald Campbell CBE was live on television attempting another world record on Coniston Water. Suddenly the speed boat took off. His remains and those of his boat were not discovered for another thirty or so years.

Within a couple of days of that disaster I was struck down with the worst dose of flu I have ever endured. I quickly decided that a return to Liverpool was out of the question. I informed Billy Scott and thanked him for all the help he had given. I contacted the local agencies when I felt better, and I had a few gigs as before. I also, for the first and last time, signed on the dole.

In the early spring of 1967 I received a call from an agency in Norwich asking me if I would like to be a Pontins Bluecoat. I was told the weekly wage would be £12. I didn't feel much loyalty to Butlins – a fifty pence rise and having been threatened with the sack twice! The 'Redcoat' became through my eyes antediluvian, and I happily endorsed the 'Bluecoat'.

Pontins, Pakefield, like Clacton, was only an hour away, so I could do the round trip with two nights at home on my Thursday off. May was the time a new summer season would begin. I had packed the night before so I could make an early start.

When I arrived, my first impression was how clean it looked. It was also well appointed. The grassy areas were obviously looked after by a groundsman who enjoyed his work. As I drove through the main gates I could see the reception in front of me. I parked my small car and looked for someone in authority. There was a young lady behind the main desk. I introduced myself and she gave me the clothes of my trade, and the key to my chalet.

It was Thursday and she told me to be ready for work on Saturday morning. She pointed to a door and said, 'That's the Entertainments Manager's office, the rest is on the card.' She smiled, and I thanked her and went chalet hunting.

* * * *

During the Butlins days I met a chap who was a waiter and, because he was good, sang regularly in the bars. He performed an excellent yodel. He told me that the next year he would love to be a member of the entertainments staff. Why shouldn't he? He was very personable, so I gave him some telephone numbers, including Pontins. It was still a surprise when he turned up on the Friday morning; Terry was to be my 'sharer'. I thought, better the devil you know.

The next morning was the first meeting with Jack Pound, the Entertainments Manager. It was well under way. Terry was late; very late. The meeting was almost over. He was told to wait outside until we were released. Saturday morning, he didn't turn up to the meeting at all. He was as good as frogmarched to the General Manager's office and was warned he was on his last chance. Sunday morning, still no Terry. I had tried to wake him. He was given an hour to pack and leave. (Shades of Peggy from *Hi-de-Hi!* in a way, but hers was a much more deserving cause). I had a chalet to myself.

Jack Pound was hard but fair. I never thought he liked me. He was easy going with my 'Lurch' character, which I had hoped to retain, and never questioned my Prince Monolulu character 'get up' during the Donkey Derby (I gotta horse!) Even Topsy-Turvy (transgender) night was acceptable. Two of the Bluecoats were dancers and had just returned from a cruise. (They spent their first week at Pontins saying 'I'm off to my cabin'.) One of them I really fancied, but she refused kindly. Someone had got there first. She and her partner were makeup experts and gave me different characteristics weekly. It was a lot of fun, but I was a trifle uncomfortable when it came to the last waltz. My boobs were enhanced with two tennis balls, which I took out and juggled.

* * * *

I at last feel it's time to say more about drink. At this moment it is not very exciting. One of the few times in my life when I was drunk was the eve of my 21st birthday, when the General Manager invited all who were part of Entertainments. He bought the first round and left the rest to us. I think we all put a few bob into a kitty. What I didn't know was that my drinks were being spiked. Eventually, I am told, I performed a total pirouette before landing on the floor. To be honest several of those at the party, especially the girls, were not happy about what had happened. Two of them managed to help me back to my chalet.

It seems strange, but I woke up at the normal time, well enough to be on breakfast duty at 8:15. A few moments after I arrived, the General Manager did the same. I am sure he wanted to catch me out. I have never seen a greater 'double take'! I was glad to have the opportunity to put one over him.

* * * *

One week our Sports Manager/Organiser was asked by a spokesman for the campers if it would be possible to make up a team of Pontins staff to challenge them. Barry was a good all-rounder who had played semi-professional football. I offered to play if they wanted a goalkeeper. No one else offered, so after we had had a couple of training sessions I was given the nod.

Jack Pound didn't want me to play. As the game unfolded he may have been right. He couldn't stop me because I had finished my duties until 8 pm.

I loved being a goalkeeper, not only football but hockey also. The Ipswich YMCA were in four divisions and (as previously mentioned) I played in the 2nd XI. I was quite good until I was about fourteen. Good because I was close to the ground. In the next year I grew seven inches! Suddenly the ground seemed a long way off. My ability in the air was less than moderate. I came onto the pitch and took my position between the goal posts. I tried to look confident but had been told moments before that the campers were fielding an Irish International!

It turned out to be the best I had ever played. We were winning 1-0 when the ball went out, but the referee hadn't seen it. I raised my hand to try and get his attention – just at that moment the ball was crossed to the edge of the penalty area, where our Irish 'friend' was waiting. He let fly from fifteen yards and he caught the fingers of my raised hand. I knew I had a fracture and gathered the ball in my other hand and kicked it into touch.

I called Barry and went behind the goal. Some kind camper offered me his chair. An ambulance was called, and I was taken to Gorleston Hospital, about three miles away. I remember waiting for ages when eventually I was plastered (unfortunate word). It was a severe Colles' fracture. I heard on my return that the final score was Campers 5 Pontins 1. (I had held on until the seventieth minute.)

I was brought back by ambulance and dropped off at the entrance to the main ballroom, which catered for nearly seven hundred people. The previous dance was over, and the campers had returned to their seats. I came into their view. Suddenly I found myself in the midst of a standing ovation. How long it lasted I cannot remember. But I shall never forget…

Reading this again I feel somewhat boastful. In mitigation I have told it exactly as it happened.

* * * *

During that summer season I was given more latitude as far as being on stage was concerned. I met a great act known as the Jones Boys, and compèred for them frequently. One of their members was Fred Mudd, who had been one of The Mudlarks. I realise few would remember them now, but during the 1950s and early 1960s, they were very popular with many wireless and television performances.

Towards the end of the season they approached me with regard to next summer season. They did some agency work, and when Clem, as was his name, spoke to me he offered me work on the Isle of Wight. It would pay £35 weekly less 20% agency fees - £28 a week – double what I was receiving at Pontins. Soon after I was invited by Jack Pound to come back next season, with a raise of £1 to £13. Memories of Butlins. But I was ready to move on; I enjoyed Pontins (I met Fred Pontin, a cheerful man, who signed my plaster after my football fiasco).

As far as my drinking was concerned, I'm sorry – it was still moderate. Regarding my fractured wrist, I was once again extremely lucky. Had I broken my left, driving would have been extremely difficult.

* * * *

That 1967 season reached its conclusion. The week after I was one of eight Pontin's Bluecoats drawn from around the country to perform at the Royal Albert Hall. This was just a basic marching number, a prelude to the crowning of the winning 'Pontins Grandest Grandmother'. The successful contestant was an Indian lady. She looked twenty-eight and was the most beautiful lady I had ever seen.

We were told we would get expenses, but they were not

forthcoming. The hostess I was with suggested we go for a drink. By the time we left and returned to the station the last train had already left. We dossed down on the platform and waited for the 05:30 to Ipswich. I doubt if that ever happened to Sir Henry Wood. Eight hours separated us from the Royal Albert Hall to the milk train!

Having arrived home, I telephoned the agencies and decided to contact the Ipswich Co-op for day time work. I was pleased when they offered me 'filling in' periods within a variety of their capacities; some for a week, some for longer. During that time, I worked in the warehouse, delivered funeral flowers, was a petrol pump attendant, delivered provisions to outlying country parts of Suffolk, cashier and accounts clerk.

Early May was the time to begin a new adventure. I drove south in my small car towards Southampton and took the car ferry to the Isle of Wight. I can't remember where the landing was, but Colwell Bay was the nearest to the leisure centre, which was also close to Totland Bay (near to the Needles). I quickly reached my billet for the summer. I was given keys to the club room and also my room within the complex, which was somewhat superior to those of my chalet days.

I was given a couple of days to acclimatise myself. On the Friday I drove in my Austin A35 to the Totland Hotel and introduced myself to the Manager. I told him I was a 'comedy act' and would be interested in a twenty-five to thirty-minute slot on a Thursday. What luck again – he said it would be a good day for him, and if I was free tonight I could do a spot which he said would be like an audition, so not to expect payment for it. I said I was content with that.

The show did go well, and I was beginning to find that 'seaside' efforts were much better rewarded than Working

Men's Clubs up north. The Manager came to my dressing room and handed me a fiver!

'Very good son' he said, 'The Thursday night shows will be £8 if that's all right with you?'

I shook his hand and told him, 'I shall enjoy these evenings'.

I thought, what luck! It nearly covered my agency fees. I do not wish my attitude towards money to appear miserly. It went with my opinion of a precarious profession.

That summer season was a wash out. It didn't affect me that much because we always had the club/dance hall. I settled down quickly and had great fun with the children. As far as I was concerned 'the twist' was still up there for fun. How I had the energy I don't know, but when I got them on the floor it was incredible mayhem. I would suddenly run to another corner of the dance floor and continue twisting. It was like an exultation of larks! Wherever I went they followed. We're talking of up to forty of them. The parents were genuine. One said, 'Marvellous and they're getting tired!'. It was just like Butlins – concentrate on the children and the parents have a better holiday.

* * * *

I now turn to the 'Mussel Shoot'. Jack Pound introduced this at Pakefield on the Saturday night introductions. Apart from the usual 'what's a Mussel Shoot?' he kept a straight face but didn't take it any further. I thought there was much more mileage in it as long as two other principles were adhered to.

The first thing was money. Although I mentioned the cost per head, I never took any money. If it was offered I just said politely that the Harbour Master would deal with all that on the night. I also had the freedom to cancel it, if I felt that there were elements who would not take the scam in good spirit. On two or three occasions, not more, I had to take that view. I just used to say that I had phoned the Harbour Master and that prevailing westerly winds had made it impossible to bring the boats round.

When I tried this out for the first time I didn't expect the result to be anything like it turned out to be. I was back from my gig at the Totland Hotel, and thought I had made good time having prepared for the Mussel Shoot participants, assuming they would probably drop out. After all, I thought the midnight call would be too late for them. (Just to be clear, my room was within the reception complex and I had asked them to assemble there.)

At about 11:50 I heard people talking and laughter – the noise kept increasing. I came out and could not believe the sight. They were all kitted out – two were dressed as pirates – and it was just like a pantomime. One fellow had brought a fishing net, and binoculars made out of two milk bottles sellotaped together. I was shaking and was sure I was going to corpse! Somehow I held myself together and said to them, 'There are babies not far from here, so if you can regulate the noise please. I must just count you. I need to phone the Harbour Master so he can organise the boats required.'

There were forty-nine campers! I told them to make their way to Colwell (which was very close). I said, 'And don't forget we have left as well as right-handed mussel guns. I'll be down with you in a couple of minutes.'

One or two held back. I got one highly suspicious look, but old 'milk bottles Bill' shouted, 'Come on, Lurch (I still used the name) will be with us soon'.

It had been a very long day for a day off. I washed, cleaned my teeth and went to bed. I had so much fun with the Mussel Shoot. I even looked for the lads who had joined in, but naturally they wanted their revenge. It was decided that they should throw me in the pool (the clothes I was wearing would soon be washed and dried). However, as I explained, 'if you throw me in now, there are so few people it will be effectual'. I suggested we should make a loud speaker announcement saying that revenge on Lurch, that dastardly cheat, would take place at 11:30 around the pool. Come and make your point!

So, I was brought to book. At the appointed time I was frogmarched to the pool kicking and screaming and shouting, 'It's not fair!' The lads had to be careful, and some weeks I couldn't be sure that would be the case, so I defused the situation by cancelling.

As far as I was concerned all that was required was me surfacing with a smile, a big one. One week I did a ten-minute spot while still in the pool. It started when I said, 'It's not fair!' By the time I got out of the pool, I was distinctly chilly! It's not difficult to believe that my final two days of that week would be a sheer delight, I got them and they got me.

Soon after that I put a big sheet on the notice board, 'Mussel Shoot night – Thursday – No money required until the day'. This particular 'advert' encouraged 164 people!

On one occasion when the Mussel Shoot was in full swing the 'shooters' walked down to the Colwell Bay beach, where there was a very old boat which had obviously been dumped. However, about twenty campers, convinced it was their transport to the rocks, sat in it for at least twenty minutes before exiting with as much dignity as they could muster (so I was told).

When asked how we shot mussels, I explained that there was a very large breakwater where the mussels gathered. When we had been given our guns (left and right-handed), we would aim and shoot just above them. They would shriek with fear, stick their arms in the air to surrender and then fall off the breakwater into the buckets which would be provided.

In conclusion, I resurrected the Mussel Shoot from 1980 to 1983. It was a success for the first three seasons. My final camp year was an absolute unmitigated disaster. It was always going to be, because the General Manager would not trust my judgement. He insisted on doing my things his way. (On a much happier note I was to have other fish to fry in the new year.)

* * * *

Towards the end of my summer season on the Isle of Wight I had a strange experience. For most of the season, Diane, the wife of one of the bandsmen, made it perfectly clear that she wanted me. It was so obvious that even I could read the signals. In the last weeks of what seemed like an eternity of rain, she started coming to the club at the time I was there to introduce the band, and started flirting with me openly. She was twenty-seven and had two children. The husband seemed very annoyed with me, which was unfair because I always tried to extricate myself without losing my temper.

* * * *

Up to now you might well be getting the impression that I was an innocent party. But as the story unfolds, I had much to be ashamed of.

On the last Thursday before the end of the season, Diane caught me while her husband was setting up the microphones. 'Come back to the house' she said, beckoning. She was attractive, and I succumbed. First, I introduced the band at 7 pm; that would give me three hours before my last show at Totland at 10 pm. Then I rather unsubtly got straight into my small car for a two-mile drive. This was new; I was twenty-two and this was a new experience, I was not 'worldly wise'.

I had been with her for three quarters of an hour when there was a squealing of brakes followed by a deafening smash of windows. I just had time to put my trousers and trainers on; I lost my jacket and shoes and nearly my keys. I met him on the stairs. He hit me with a 'south paw' (he was only 5' 6' tall). He grabbed my keys, but with luck I held onto my car key.

I went to Totland and did my last show, which all things considered was a miracle; it went okay. I decided, as Diane's husband had threatened to kill me, to leave the next morning. I packed overnight and was ready to go when the Assistant Manager knocked on the door, telling me to come and answer a phone call. I did as requested, and not surprisingly it was the lady.

'I've left him' she said 'I need to see you. Please come to the Links golf course; look out for my horse.'

I knew exactly where she meant as I had played golf there once during the season with a couple of friendly campers and made my usual apologies! (I am not suggesting the lady would ride all over the golf course, she knew the slope would make it easier to see her.) She begged me to stay with her. I told her, 'I'm sorry I can't, I've booked my car ferry for 10:30 am'. What a coward!

I gave her a long embrace. She was crying, I could have stopped all this, If I had decided not to scramble into bed with her.

I duly joined the car ferry with a sense of relief, (what would I have done without the luck of retaining the car key?) For once, it was fine and warm. Then the ferry docked to pick up foot passengers... you can guess the rest! We booked into a hotel near Southampton and talked a lot without fuss. I said to her that I must return home the next day, and there was no protest – just tears. This was not my finest hour!

I briefly returned to Pontins in 1967 where I met a lovely girl, also called Diane. We had an intimate relationship which stopped 'short of'. She had decided that marriage emphatically came first. I respected her decision. We were in touch for the next two years. (She was Miss South of England in 1964). In 1969 she would introduce me to Hughie Green when I was on *Opportunity Knocks*, more of which later.

The last time we met I was at Champneys in Tring, probably the best-known health farm in England. (If I am keeping the reader away from my drinking, I am sorry, it will come.) My doctor was worried about my weight (too low). I was the only person there to gain weight and made a few fellow travellers quite envious as I tucked into fillet steak while they had to make do with a few lettuce leaves!

Returning to Diane, we dined at the Bell in Aston Clinton. She told me she had met someone and they were moving towards a permanent relationship. I was thrilled for her. I wasn't ready to be married, and to be honest, I wasn't *in* love with her. Apparently the wedding was a wonderful day for all. I was invited but had to decline because I had a family wedding the same day. Diane's husband was a musical genius;

some readers may remember the radio show *Name that Tune*. He was almost unbeatable.

In the early 70s I received a letter inside a Christmas card from Diane's mother Val (she was a lovely lady and we still exchanged Christmas greetings.) The news was awful; her eldest daughter (Diane's sister) had been murdered by her husband. The following Christmas this was compounded; Les, Val's husband, had severe Alzheimer's disease. Then the next Christmas she wrote to say that Diane had inoperable cancer. She was given two years to live. No wonder many people doubt their god.

For each of the next four years I received an agonising letter/card. I sent one back trying to find the right words – impossible. The next year I did not receive a card. I felt only relief that perhaps she had been released from her hell on earth.

* * * *

Having had my life threatened once, it was threatened again in totally different circumstances. About a five-minute walk from our reception office were some stables. There were about eight horses, and a 'husband and wife team' were doing their summer season, well-advertised, to teach all ages how to ride.

At Colwell Bay we always had many children and I asked, during the first band break in the clubroom, if any youngsters would like to take part. The response was more than encouraging and it was agreed that we would book on the Tuesday (and continue this throughout the season). I contacted the organisers and they were pleased to pencil us in. Their costs were moderate.

After two or three weeks they invited me to join one of their classes, without cost. They insisted, saying I was helping them. Wednesday at 4 pm was ideal and for the next five weeks I went through, walking, trotting and lastly cantering, which was my absolute maximum. I have to say I found it very difficult to stay on.

One week they asked me to come on the Thursday, as they had had a family bereavement. I was on the last horse – without a helmet! My horse lost all the others and galloped at such a pace it was a miracle I stayed on. I couldn't control the horse (I had dropped the reins) and could only hold onto the front of the saddle with both hands. This lasted for two to three minutes. Then Georgina (the horse) caught up with the others and slowed down. I had no feelings in my hands whatsoever for over an hour. Without a helmet I thought I would die. Health and safety had not been invented. Not surprisingly I have never again sat on a horse.

* * * *

As the reader will remember, I ended my Isle of Wight adventure in ignominy, but I must press on…

Two families who came to the Isle of Wight (they were mussel shooters) invited me to come and visit at the end of the season. They lived in Watford and I got on with them all extremely well. I took them at their word (I was still Lurch) and it was great to be so accepted. Virtually everything they did I was encouraged to join in.

I had luck again. I was given the chance of a shop window show with the agency who had funded my Isle of Wight adventure. I didn't hold out much hope, as news leaked out that I wasn't in the ballroom for the last Friday night. There was talk of me being charged for it. Quite reasonable I thought, but it was not pursued. I hope it was due to a few nice letters from the guests and their children.

As it happened it didn't really matter. I gave a poor performance, by the standards I had set myself. It was very much a case of 'don't call us we'll call you'.

I had called bingo in my last two seasons. (Not in Butlins as they had a full time Redcoat caller). Still from my base in Watford, I drove my small car into Kilburn, where they had a Top Rank bingo hall. I enquired at reception if they ever had jobs for callers. The receptionist returned, pointed to an area with chairs and said, 'The manager will be with you shortly'. The manager duly appeared and sat down next to me. He enquired about my recent employment. I told him about my seasons at Pontins where I called bingo, and the Isle of Wight, recently finished as Entertainment Manager, where I was also calling bingo. He took a few notes and told me there were five Top Rank bingo halls, all quite close to central London. 'We need a caller in Kilburn' he said and offered me the job. The wages were £35 a week, so I agreed with alacrity and started the next week. I could stay in Watford (paying my way of course) and did so for six months. I enjoyed it and kept working on my comedy act. I practised while out for a walk.

* * * *

The previous year I had an audition for *Opportunity Knocks* in the Woolwich Arsenal at 9:30 am. It went very well. There were several other acts setting themselves up and they stopped and laughed. Roy Mayo, Hughie Green's auditioner, shook me by the hand and said, 'You'll be hearing from us'.

When I eventually received a letter, it came with the date they wanted me on the show and a cheque for £36. It was for early April 1969. I was dreadfully nervous, especially on the day when they chose to adjust my act. It was more to learn 'on the job'. As it happened it didn't go badly, and I was placed third (of six) on the clapometer, and in the postal vote. A young group won, a decision I completely agreed with, as they were excellent.

But here we were, in yet another example of extreme luck. I applied to the Caister Holiday Centre rather late, after the involvement with *Opportunity Knocks*. The manager of the centre said to me, 'Come by all means, but we do think we have got our Entertainments Manager. We just need to see him perform.'

I informed him that I would come along on the off chance. Would you believe that the other person was first on, and his performance was like mine at the South Liverpool Football Club three years previously.

I was introduced, and it was just like that Shop Window Show I did for Billy 'Uke' Scott! I was offered the job and was invited to close the show. Top billing for the first and last time. I was remembered by so many campers for my display on *Opportunity Knocks*, which I saved for being called back. And every week, I was. Luck? Has anyone had so much?

It continued. My deputy, Steve, was a likeable chap and a budding magician. He used to come along to my hut in the mornings, so I could inform him of his duties for the day and explain mine. He was a year younger than me; I would like to think I divided our work fairly. I must say when he compèred the Sunday show, he did it well and always gave me a generous introduction.

One morning he came into my hut, in extremely high spirits.

'Did you score last night?' I enquired.

'No but this is much better. I've written to P&O for a job.'

'Why do you want to work at the Post Office?'

He looked at me as if I had had a lobotomy. 'No, P&O the shipping company.'

'Oh, why do you want to be a steward?' I was quite pleased at my knowledge.

'Not a steward' Steve said, as if conversing with an imbecile. 'An Entertainments Officer.'

'Where did you see it advertised?' I asked.

'I didn't. I just thought I might enquire.'

'You're joking, you'll never get a response.'

About three days later when we had the usual get-together he came in, like Chamberlain in 1938, waving a piece of paper at me. He had received a very courteous letter from P&O head office. In short, they thanked him for his interest and said he would need to be twenty-five (Steve was twenty-two) as you would start as a Senior Officer, but he should keep in touch. I thought to myself I was a year older than Steve and had that extra experience. I decided to communicate with P&O.

Less than a week afterwards I received a letter, similar to Steve's in style; keep in touch when you are twenty-five, contact us and we'll arrange an interview. I duly did as requested. I sent updates and continued interest.

The last letter I wrote was close to my twenty-fifth birthday. P&O duly kept their promise and invited me to head office for an interview. I did think it went quite well. The Personnel Manager wrote (S/B) at the top of the page and then just said, 'Goodbye, thank you for coming. We'll be in touch.'

I felt very unsure of being received. However, a week later I was asked to attend a selection board (hence the S/B). There were five of us for two appointments.

The evening before I had been out for a drink with my father. (We tried to put any resentfulness behind us.) I asked him the phrase which was bugging me – pleasing to the eye. Aesthetic, he said. I nodded and put it to the back of my mind.

When my name was called, I thought I had done my best regarding presentation. I wore a smart suit and tie and responded evenly to questions asked. Suddenly a voice from the hierarchy said, 'I wonder if you have the experience to cope with speciality nights?' I responded that I had no experience of 'dressing a tableau'. However, I said, 'I think I have a reasonable aesthetic eye and would make sure I gave it my best possible efforts'. (Thanks dad).

I was down to the last two. The next thing was a basic medical. I was sitting next to one of the five and we hardly said a word. After an agonising ten minutes one of the board members arrived, He looked at us with a smile and said, 'Congrats lads, you've got the jobs'. We shook hands and I waited for the medical, aware I might have to tell a fib or two.

I actually had duodenal pain which, if not actually causing dreadful pain, hung about. It seems remarkable how a short letter that Steve shared with me would make such an impression on my life. At the end of the 1969 season, Steve and I said our farewells. I never saw him again and he never did work for P&O. I felt something of a cuckoo.

* * * *

Returning to 1969, the season progressed very well. The Mussel Shoot was as popular as ever, and the show was successful. A late-night sing song was a pleasure, as I had several songs, some from the old days, some from the previous three years. I decided not to go home for my day off. It was a longer journey and I had been fortunate to get a twenty-minute spot at Potter's. They offered me £8. This was the same as the Isle of Wight and I was perfectly happy with that.

Throughout the season, the shows went well – it was an ideal room for comedy. The campers obviously realised I had been on *Opportunity Knocks* a few weeks before. (Brian Potter has been a highly popular and successful entrepreneur. Most readers will have remembered and may still see the World Indoor bowls. He has also done an awful amount to help the success of darts.)

I must be getting old; it was Brian's father who booked me!

* * * *

Now we will look to my drinking and lady friends. When you gain even a modicum of localised fame, you find the girls who used to say 'sorry, I have to wash my hair' take a lot more notice. That season I had about twenty-five 'lovers'. The drinking became rather 'loose'; particularly towards the end of the season. When the General Manager, his tongue firmly in his cheek, made mention of it, there was no admonishment; he seemed rather amused.

After the Sunday show when I arrived at the bar, there were suddenly two or three pints already set up. I did my best to enjoy the company I found myself within. The only downside was that everyone, at all times, needed to tell me a joke. I am sure I am not alone. I listened and laughed. This was how it would have been at Butlins. Some of them were very good!

Had I by now become a functional alcoholic? I think at this stage, no. I woke up as well as ever and had no yearning for the bottle.

At the end of the season I returned home and almost immediately realised I had fallen into a deep depression, the likes of which I had never had to endure before. My parents were separated on the 23rd December, and our family cat Binkums died at 13 years on the way to the vets. It saved the decision to put to sleep.

I was given a bottle of tablets, one a day, and was told they would begin to take effect in ten to twelve days. The doctor was spot on. I kept on this medication for at least six months. Unlike Valium, it was not addictive. I also used alcohol, in moderation, which helped numb the pain. Better than being told to 'snap out of it' or 'there's always someone worse off than you' etc etc.

I contacted the Ipswich Co-op to see if they had a full house of Father Christmas's. They seemed pleased to be able to tell me that they had a vacancy and could I 'look in' the following morning. I was very happy to accept.

On the first day I met a lady who was a toy demonstrator near to my Santa's Grotto. Her name was Myrtle and she had recently married Clive Goodall, a bon viveur. Throughout the next forty years we remained firm friends. Myrtle disliked her name and I started to call her Caroline. 'Why do you call me that?' she asked. I told her she was like Caroline of Ansbach (the Queen Consort of George II), who was a real beauty in her day. Several years later, just before I left P&O, I heard she had changed her name by deed poll. She was now Caroline Goodall.

Clive and Caroline lived just outside Ipswich, and they invited me to join a small gathering for drinks and a buffet. As it happened there were just five of us, but they went out of their way to make me welcome.

The buffet was finished (the drinks were not), and I was beginning to feel better as the medication had kicked in. They were setting up a table to play cards. Clive approached me and asked me if I played bridge. I told him I had heard of bridge but had never played. He asked me if I would feel left out as they and their friends would always play towards the end of the evening. I told Clive it was no problem and I would enjoy watching. I quickly began to realise what a wonderful game bridge was.

As the evening was coming to an end Clive said, 'do play one Eddie'. I had a good hand with about six hearts. Ray played as my partner and we went to four hearts. If I made it, it would have been game. Four hearts worth 30 points each 40 x 3 = 120, 30 x 3 = 90 points, not game. I did my best, but I ended one off. Disappointed? Not likely, I was smitten. A wonderful evening, which became the first of many.

* * * *

It was an amazing season at Caister (£30 a week), but the wanderlust was still with me. I saw in *The Stage* an advertisement for an Entertainments Manager at the Majorca Holiday Centre. I applied and by return was offered an interview. I was aware that the job was not actually in

Majorca, but with a firm from Yorkshire who had purchased an established holiday centre on the Suffolk/Norfolk border. The interview seemed to go well, and the General Manager said, 'You're in the frame. I've still got a few interviews, but you will be hearing from me.'

True to his word, he wrote offering me the job at £40 a week. I accepted there and then.

I had a hostess, a male deputy and of course the bands. We seemed to get on very well. I'm ashamed to say I cannot remember the hostess's name (it was nearly fifty years ago), but we were inseparable, despite the platonic nature of our relationship. (Eighteen months later, at sea, I was to have the same relationship with my hostess Pam. Suddenly my 'sepsis mind' has stood aside, the one I had forgotten was also Pam!)

In May 2013, I was in hospital for a routine procedure. I picked up an infection and developed sepsis. My wonderful daughters did everything to keep me awake. Hannah, my eldest, was told by the surgeon that there was little hope, but he accepted her entreaties to be with her sisters in the ward. By keeping me awake for three days they enabled me to pull through. They have already given me six more years of quality life.

* * * *

The Yorkshire management had established a relationship with the television world, in that household names appeared as the celebrities to talk to campers, and to give a brief chat as to their lives both professionally and (within reason) privately. The third week we had two *Coronation Street* stars, both of whom were delightful. Doris Speed played the publican Annie Walker in the early days of the street. Annie was a right harridan but not Doris, who was a lovely lady. She gave everyone she met a warmth and an interest in what they had to say. She was also a keen bridge player; in fact she was playing during her last week, when she passed away at the age of ninety-five. Eileen Derbyshire was unusually like the character she played (Emily Bishop), warm and friendly despite a certain reticence. I knew the holidaymakers liked her because they told me so. A fortnight later it was Dick Emery. He did a solo spot, but didn't seem happy.

In conclusion, we had as our last celebrity guest Alexandra Bastedo, star of the television show *The Champions*. She was a sheer delight. Like Dick Emery, she died in her sixties.

Something rather worrying was happening at the 'Majorca'. The company was financially 'going to the dogs'. I was told the night before that all departmental heads were to be sacked. I had been given time to work out my strategy.

After breakfast (about 9 am), over the loudspeaker system came the words, 'Would the Bar Manager please attend the General Manager's office at once'. The guillotine fell for the first time. Within less than ten minutes, 'Would the Catering Manager... at once'. Second guillotined head in the basket. 'Would the Entertainments Manager... at once.'

I arrived at the General Manager's office and he repeated his sacking spiel. I told him that I had heard the rumours last week. I had taken my day off on Thursday and took my contract to my solicitor. I explained how I had been booked for the season. I told the General Manager the parts that were pertinent. I didn't even have a contract! In the end it was decided I could stay on, working three nights for £20. I felt I had got away with enough, so I hesitated and then accepted. The Manager gave his deputy the job of Entertainments Manager. The next two weeks were an absolute disaster. I was reinstated.

I left 'Majorca' in time to take up a position in Penzance, Cornwall. I had been offered an introduction fee, to be paid for the first two weeks and then raised to the fee as advertised (perhaps I should have smelled a rat). Those two weeks went well, with the exception of a children's afternoon which included quite a few disabled, five of whom were severely autistic. They spent their time just running around the room nonstop. Others were disabled in various different ways. It was absolutely impossible to organise anything formal. I'm convinced even a fully-fledged children's entertainer would have found the situation impossible. Used to bright children at the holiday centres, I found it harrowing and whilst talking to one of the mothers I could have wept. She had no life. I received no criticism at the time. (The reader will know I talk of the good times, but I do make mention of the bad.)

I went to the office to collect my pay and promised rise. The 'patriarch', who treated his staff like serfs, told me I could stay but only at the lower level of pay. 'You didn't do very well with the children,' he said. I rarely lose my rag, but I gave him an earful, something I doubt he had ever experienced. I took the 'dime' I was due, went back to my room, packed and left.

He was standing on the shingled drive and put his hand out. I stopped, and he was almost speechless. He just said £13 a week was generous. I drove off without feeling it necessary to speak; my look was enough.

Reading this back, I seem to be awfully defensive. All I can do is tell you how it actually was. The cynic in me wonders if that tragic children's get-together was a put-up job.

Eventually my small car did the 400-mile trip to my home in Ipswich without incident. I had agreed to contact the General Manager of a camp near Kessingland, north Suffolk.

He, quite understandably, felt a bit put out that I had treated him as 'second best'. I think he was right and I apologised profusely. I promised him I would give every effort to make sure it would be a good season for entertainments. Having apologised to him, I never mentioned it again.

The season had a disrupted start when I went down with a dose of flu, so it was two weeks before I could start. The day after I had a panic attack. I was having a shower when my whole body seized up. I can remember using my hands to try and move my legs. Once I had started moving I could not stop; instinct told me that if I did stop I would collapse.

The resident nurse on the camp prescribed Valium and told me to take a letter she had written to the GP, who would probably continue the treatment. On my next day off, I drove to Ipswich and managed to make an appointment to see my GP. He decided to continue the Valium and said, 'Don't come to me, we will keep a repeat prescription for you. Do however take them only when you feel you need them.'

Those last eleven words saved me from serious addiction; after all it was 1971 and the problem was in its infancy. I do still have a mild addiction. When doctors hear of it, particularly the young ones, I have at times been severely berated. Rest assured I lambasted, at least two to three times, those greenhorns who had the temerity to think they knew it all.

I stabilised and got down to work. I knew my deputy because we had worked together at another camp; the hostess was unusual. She was a country girl in her sixties. Her main occupation apparently, had been laying out deceased women. The children loved her, so I left her to it.

The Mussel Shoot was still very much to the fore, except when a camper, one of the few staying for a fortnight, spilled the beans. I was annoyed, but he was most apologetic, and he really was a nice guy, the sort who would always support the entertainment staff unequivocally. He even made me a mussel gun! It was a wooden revolver covered with mussel shells. He asked me if he could present it to me during the first band break in the ballroom. What could have turned into a negative happening was happily defused.

* * * *

One thing that can make a new Entertainment Manager's life difficult is to follow someone who has done four or five seasons running in the job. I met him once in the early part of the season – after my flu fortnight. I liked him and although our styles were very different, he must have been good at what was an important occupation to last for all those years. Whenever campers spoke about him I relayed the knowledge that I had met him once, and automatically took a liking to him.

'I've got a lot to live up to haven't I? I will do my best to make your holiday a happy one, just as he did.'

If any reader thinks 'YUK!' I understand but I don't care...

* * * *

From the beginning of June 1971, I was approached by the camp photographer, who wanted to pay for the use of my small car. He offered to pay me a 'rent' which was twice as much as I would have expected. It seemed surreal. I never really got to the bottom of his reasons; perhaps he was doubling up.

All I can say, finding it difficult to eat, at the end of giving my best in the ballroom, I bought a pint of Guinness and joined the photographer. He had also 'found' a pint of Guinness –

and his daughter. I don't remember much more, except for the fact that wherever he went, he came back with two pints of Guinness! I've always wondered why I didn't chat up his daughter. I suppose she had made it quite obvious, without any words, that I was 'not the answer'. I'm not handsome.

* * * *

I enjoyed the season in Kessingland. I knew I had something special to look forward to. 1971 brought me to the age of twenty-five, when having kept in touch with P&O cruise liners, my interview was set for early October.

There were two other interludes before I pointed my car to London.

Over the years 1966-1971 I was expected to communicate with children. As previously mentioned, I could be admonished (as a Redcoat or Bluecoat), if anything got back to management to suggest that I had ignored a child. As well as giving autographs to the youngsters, I received at least four or five letters each season from children. Let me share one with the reader:

> *Dear Lurch,*
>
> *We had a lovelly holiday with you and Mum and Dad send a hello. We hope to come next year but Dady has lost his gob Roten cumpane I think. I love dady and I must help. Yesterday I brought him a bear to drink.*
>
> *Love From Diane XXXX*
>
> *P.S I've just had my brakefust. It was corflakes!*

Finally came the last but one Friday, when the ballroom was now closed and the vast bar area was ready for business. I organised the sing-song, told a ream of jokes, introduced campers who liked to perform – a sort of karaoke before it was invented. I needed to go for a 'Jimmy' and noticed two couples sitting at the back of the ballroom. I passed them on the way back to the bar,

'You don't look very happy,' I said.

'No we're not. It's the worst holiday we've ever had.'

'Why don't you come into the bar? There are 160 people having a great time.'

'The chap who did your job last year was much better than you.'

You certainly can't win them all!

I had access to cash for two summers before 1971, and I can honestly say I never took a penny (after all I had been a choir boy). 1971 was different; the ethos was such that two campers would take a collection from all the holidaymakers and then present it to the Entertainments Manager. It was straightforward; a really good week would provide more than a mediocre one. It had been understood over many years that the Manager would take a half, and the deputy and hostess would each take 25%. This posed no problems to my team. I double-checked backstage to be certain that the division was absolutely fair and above board. As it turned out the situation at sea was very different...

* * * *

I salvaged my car from the photographer and passed my thanks to the Camp Manager and his wife, (she had given me great help when it came to prize giving). They were kind with their acknowledgement. That last week I had been with a lovely Indian lady, Arinda. We came back to Ipswich – she knew about my new job. It was not an easy time, especially for her. I had managed to tell my grandfather (aged 87) that I had managed to get the job with P&O. This was my last memory of him – his thumbs up in the air. He passed away a week later.

Suddenly life became chaotic, especially for my mother. I had to take Arinda to London – the first time I had really felt like a rotter. I couldn't even attend my grandfather's funeral. I had to sell my car and rely on mum to drive me to Southampton with all my luggage. Looking back, I flinch. I didn't realise at the time just how much I 'used' my mother. I have tried to make up for my selfishness. As I write she is in her 98th year.

CHAPTER 4

A LIFE ON THE ocean wave

Iarrived at Southampton as a supernumerary. It was on the P&O ship SS *Oronsay* that I made tentative efforts at coping at sea. Management sensibly put on board most joining Senior Officers, who would have the opportunity, with no responsibility, to get their bearings.

I certainly needed it. With little or no idea, I was not only at sea, I was all at sea. I got to the stage of looking for a ball of wool to tie to my cabin door. I could let it all go in the one direction, helping to return it to the first. That apart I only had one queasy night, cruising through the Bay of Biscay, so I felt able to join in with the entertainments.

* * * *

It was 11am when the telephone rang, I answered, 'It's Ronnie Owen, Tourist Entertainment Officer, would you like to come up for a chat?' I explained to him how difficult it was for me, because I couldn't find myself, let alone anywhere else on the ship. He told me to get to a lift, go up to level four, and he'd look out for me. He was as good as his word; he invited me in and pointed towards the bed (there was only one chair), 'They do these 'extra number' cruises with nerds like you in mind.' I liked him already!

'Would you like a drink?' he threatened.

'It's early still, can I have a Coke?'

'No you bloody can't!' he said, his broad northern dialect at full throttle, 'They cost a fortune. You'll have a double brandy and I'll join you.'

We chatted about the cruise. There were events I would be happy to share with him. He talked about the Pub Night and the Old Time Music Hall. I was ready to go; I did love performing. There was nothing special on the third evening, so Ronnie suggested I come to the ballroom after dinner. We could have a drink and discuss forthcoming events.

The upshot was a Pub Night that lasted from 9:30pm to 3:15am. The Captain stayed until the end. I don't think he could believe it, there were fifty people still there when we 'drew stumps'. We were buddies for life. Neither upstaged the other – it felt like we'd been a double act for years. I will talk of Ronnie again, but at the time of writing he is eighty-three and was married this year to a long-term partner. And for me, it suddenly feels like 1971 all over again.

When, later in the cruise, we had rehearsals for the Old Time Music Hall. Ronnie decided he would like me to be the Chairman. The cabaret artists we had on board did their own spots and the cruise staff came up with an appropriate 'pastiche'. Ronnie had the comedy roll of the pot man, frequently supplying the Chairman with pints in a trick glass. I don't know who enjoyed it more.

In the couple of years before P&O '71, I had discovered the writings of W. Somerset Maugham and very soon had the full opus. I particularly enjoyed the short stories, compressed into four large volumes. We sailed to Australia via the South Seas (soon I would be travelling in the Federated Malay States, as they were then, taking in Singapore, Kuala Lumpur and Penang etc).

During this voyage on *SS Iberia* we visited Fiji, Tonga and Pago Pago, the latter being where one of Maugham's most popular stories, *Rain,* was set and made into an excellent film starring Rita Hayworth. Fiji was lovely and in Tonga we played football against the locals. The King's Palace overlooked the pitch and His Majesty sent us 'royal watermelon' at half time. We lost 3-2, but of course we were playing away! Maugham had written about all these places – déjà vu?

* * * *

I believe I mentioned being still in touch with three people from nearly fifty years ago; there is a third one, my first hostess on SS *Iberia*. Her name was Pam and we developed a remarkable and rewarding platonic love for each other. We have kept in touch for nearly fifty years with Christmas cards and letters. We nearly always went ashore together.

I had arrived on board *Iberia* two days before sailing. I found my cabin, just thinking of that letter Steve had shown me two and a half years previously. It had led me to the fact that I was nearly on the way to Australia. I was sitting on my bed in a mood of euphoria. I had only one concern – the niggle in my duodenum…

I'd had a large delivery of drinks to my AC (alcoholics cabinet). I poured myself a largish brandy and returned to consider my astonishment at such good fortune. Nearly fifty years on, the memories of that moment are still vivid.

I awoke from my reverie as a loud knock at the door heralded company. Would they want to take my duty free with them? Perhaps they were bringing me a girl for those quieter moments? Now that was a long shot! I opened the door, 'Are you Mr Eddie Scott? I'm the Shop Manager, Cyril.' He was a doppelganger of John Inman ('I'm free!') from the television series *Are You Being Served*? I was stupefied. He sashayed up and down my small room, and said, 'To provide you with prizes for the cruises, each cruise is allotted £160. I can do you a beautiful selection for £60. This enables us to share £100 50/50. Now isn't that good?'

He looked at me hopefully. I faked an expression of delight and offered him a drink. Without any comprehension of such working practices (I mentioned that in the years of holiday camps I frequently found myself in charge of money, holding the key of the strong box), it never entered my head to reduce the wherewithal for my own benefit. But this was different.

I unscrambled my brain and told Cyril I had only just arrived in my cabin, but if he could give me half an hour I would no doubt finalise positively his suggestion. I agreed to give him a knock. I sat back on the bed and within a moment came the next 'knock knock'. 'Come in' I said. It was the Bar Manager, a stalwart Scotsman named John. He was of a type I had always found difficult to communicate with. Usually they looked at me as if I was an unfunny joke.

This was a different situation, I knew I was 'doing his will', so he knew the status quo was safe. But when he was on duty at the Senior Officer's cocktail parties he looked after my needs like a Dutch uncle. When I arrived, or when I was 'hosting', he was like Jeeves of Jeeves and Wooster fame, he was at my shoulder and said, 'Your usual sir?' and the brandy was duly served. As I finished he was there again to pass the tray and my usual was what he poured me.

All the time I was at sea, when he was Bar Manager it was the same. (I was only in my 20s). There was a mutual respect. There must have been.

John chatted as much as Cyril had danced. I asked him to give me twenty minutes, and to point out his office. 'I'll be there,' I said.

I was about to climb back on to my bed when 'knock knock', in came the Entertainment Leading Hand. He was a senior 'non-officer' who was in charge of four Goanese lads. They did all the setting up, especially for the theme nights and for other functions, (tables, chairs, dais, microphones etc.) His name was Gary and he filled me in with regard to gambling events – horse racing, frog racing, casino nights, bingo and bedside bingo (more of which later).

I had had time to realise this was part of ship lore. I had (with personal reservations) made up my mind. I said to Gary that I would be pleased to keep things as they are. He seemed happy and said that he would gladly make himself available for any meetings we might call on general activities.

He was a breath of fresh air, always smiling; I sensed he loved his job and loved life. I could on the 'pecking order' have taken over Freddie (fox, the box) for non-cockneys, but

I thought I would give him a chance to see if I considered first allotment was fair. It was fair – very fair.

I had quickly made up my mind. If I refused to be a part of the 'organisation' – just one of many on board – my life would have been made a misery. As mentioned, I was top of our pyramid. The atmosphere would have been unbearable. I doubt if I would have reached Australia.

I crossed the deck and knocked at the Shop Manager's door. He answered, and I just said to him, 'All systems go'.

'Glad you've come aboard' Cyril exclaimed, 'I'm sure we'll have a good relationship'. I drew the line at that!

Just in time I got back to John and said I would be pleased to retain things exactly as they were. However, he interrupted and pointed at the drinks in my cabinet and said,

'Already paid for, if you just sign this it's sorted'.

I offered an expression which suggested disbelief, and he gave me a quizzical grin. This system on board gave me the opportunity to become a wealthy single man. After all my luck I could not expect to escape the 'equal and opposite' syndrome.

* * * *

Two weeks at sea I nearly caused an international incident. In the role of supernumerary officer just three weeks before I decided I would like to hold a lunchtime 'pour out'. Yes, that is what they called them. I approached Ronnie for advice, he told me to have up to sixteen; eight of the younger junior officers, equal boys/girls, and the senior officers. However, he told me not to invite the Captain as 'he hates these lunch times'. I thanked Ronnie for his help and it turned out to be a very enjoyable get together.

Fast forward a month and I was preparing my first 'pour out' on *Iberia*. I was fixated with captains, rather than one particularly and didn't send our Commodore an invite. Yes, the Captain/Commodore of the fleet. I heard that there had been a meeting of senior deck officers and the purser. It had come to a break and the Staff Officer said, 'It's time to go to Eddie's pour out.'

'I've not been invited,' said the Commodore stentoriously.

'Oh, but you must have been,' said the Staff Captain.

'No, I must not be wanted,' the Commodore said with a gimlet eye.

The Chief Officer rang me. 'Did you invite him?'

'Yes,' I lied.

'He sent an invitation sir,' the officer told the Commodore.

'If you're sure,' he said doubtfully.

Nevertheless, people arrived and drinks were poured. I looked up and there framed in the doorway was our Master.

'I trust I have been invited.'

'Oh yes sir, I can only think your invite went astray.'

A large gin was ready, and he was in his element. Equilibrium reigned. Two hostesses sitting on the bed moved to allow the Commodore to sit between them.

* * * *

SS *Iberia* had left dock on November 6th, 1971. It was her final voyage. She died young. After a brief stop at Octeville (Cherbourg) we stopped at Lisbon. I've loved Portugal since that day.

It was special in that we were invited, including Pam, to one of our Band Leader's favourite spots. He (Johnnie Graham, who had a trio, and jolly good they were) suggested we catch the train to Cascais e Estoril. Lovely day, lovely trip, lovely food, lovely beach. It was magic; what a lovely day. I recognised a film star, George Sanders, eating alone. A year before, as he predicted, he would take his own life.

We next visited Gibraltar and can you believe it – I could never invent it – the first people we met (on the long walk towards the 'Rock') were my next-door neighbours! Pam and I did the usual things – cable car and having a chat with the monkeys.

The next few days were at sea, organising deck quoits, deck tennis and enjoying the cricket. Florida was wet, but Pam and I had booked a trip to Disneyland. I have two abiding memories. The first, and many readers will have done this, was the 'Pirates of the Caribbean' ride. I considered the eight to ten minutes my most incredible experience. It was a water chute into the most amazing tableau. It made you feel so much a part of it, a wonderful pirate ship shooting at everything. The 'pirates' were so lifelike, I didn't think I would get out alive!

The second experience was the Matterhorn rollercoaster. I've never been so frightened. In fact I would never experience that again. (Many years later when I went with my family, I was still petrified, and for the day I was called 'chicken' by all!) Several sea days later we reached Los Angeles, land of billionaires and smog. We avoided the latter and enjoyed a trip to Bel Air, seeing some of the enormous homes owned by the biggest stars of the cinema. Name a star of the thirties, forties or fifties, that's where they lived. As the reader would appreciate, our coach did not stop!

We returned to Grauman's Chinese Theatre, and the footprints of the 'stars'. Opposite was a famous restaurant called the Brown Derby (as in the hat), Pam and I had lunch there, and I bumped into a wonderful character actor called Pat Buttrum. He was starring in a television programme called *Green Acres* alongside Eva Gabor. He was delighted that I had recognised him.

Our next stop was San Francisco. Having travelled so extensively, it became my favourite of all. It started soon after we docked. It was a lovely day, and all there was between us and Fisherman's Wharf was the Sir Nigel Gresley, 4472, Flying Scotsman. On the footplate stood Alan Pegler, the first owner; he had salvaged her from destruction. Some readers will remember Alan, his daughter Penny and the wonderful five years they enjoyed before the 'wheels fell off'. Alan had done the majority of the driving (he loved it), and was also a pilot, in service towards the end of the war.

We became friends/associates. Before we left he opened up, telling me he had gone bankrupt and at that moment he did not know how he was going to get home. The banks in America also might not release the locomotive, using its worth as part of the debts. I sent the others on and got to Fisherman's Wharf just after they closed. We chatted for a while and I stuck my neck out.

'Would you have the wherewithal to lecture on your wonderful railway experiences?'

He told me he had five films of railways including the Ffestiniog Railway, of which he was Chairman. I returned to the ship and approached the Commodore to see if he could make room for him, with his assets. The Commodore agreed. Obviously, there were things to sort out, but this turned out to be a positive just in time. The USA decided they wouldn't prevent the return of 4472 to the UK. That was tidied up when the Chairman of McAlpine, Sir Bill McAlpine, decided to buy her. With all its ups and downs, 4472 was saved.

Having missed lunch in Fisherman's Wharf, I made up for it in the evening. A young lady I was truly in love with, Donna Snow, came with me for dinner at the 'Top of the Mark' (The Mark Hopkins Hotel). This revolved, twenty storeys up, showing a continual panorama of San Francisco at night. Tony Bennett was the cabaret. Yes, the very same Tony Bennett as nearly fifty years ago and still working – as was Charles Aznavour, until his mid-nineties!

It was one of several situations, when I felt strongly, only for her to reciprocate, showing strong affection with which I could not cope. Donna Snow was a lovely girl, and I was determined not to let my ludicrous feelings spoil the evening.

I asked our waiter, who was excellent, where he would recommend for the rest of the evening. He suggested a jazz club called Earthquake McGoon's. It boasted a remarkable atmosphere, such that everyone was made to feel inclusive. All in all, it had proved an extraordinary evening. And Donna could really dance!

We even managed to fit in a helicopter flight over the Alcatraz Penitentiary, before a boat trip which took us onto the rock. We saw where Al Capone had been incarcerated, during a long 'tenure' for tax evasion. Apparently, he had been unofficially diagnosed with syphilis. No action was taken because he was due to be released within weeks. After this had come about, he was similarly diagnosed. (He died from complications caused by the illness in 1947, aged forty-eight.)

Despite this stark realisation I was determined to return to San Francisco, independently if necessary. I rejoined the ship to await the visit to Vancouver, where Donna was due to leave the SS *Iberia*. Although I was destined to enjoy many visits to Vancouver, I regret failing to see more of Canada. Perhaps I may have another chance. This is somewhat dependent on my lifestyle!

Having departed Vancouver we sailed towards Hawaii, the jewel of the west, America's 50th state. I was still loving the journey despite the niggle with my stomach, which I have to say was not getting any better. In fact, for the first time I had decided I wouldn't go ashore, and told Pam.

One of my fellow compatriots was Martin Carrigan. I really haven't said anything about him. We were very different, but I rather admired him. He had been a professional ice hockey player in Canada. We had been together that day at P&O selections, when we both received the mutual 'good news'. Martin prised me away from feeling sorry for myself. He persuaded me when he told me that he would like to go to Pearl Harbour. Amazingly, it was the day before the thirtieth anniversary of the Japanese attack, on December 7th ,1941.

It was an amazing vista. Flowers were festooned with so much colour. The American ship USS *Arizona* lay in twelve feet of water in the harbour, still revered as a USA war grave. It was a chastening experience. Martin said he had been there before and explained that there was a large room/bar. He led me to it. There were no passengers and at that time we were virtually on our own. He ordered a gin and bitters and asked me what I wanted. I replied carelessly that I would have the same as him. We found two chairs and a table, and we chatted about our variable pasts. We were close to a runway and watched the landings and take offs.

I really don't remember how many gins we had but I was beginning to see double – 'one of my eyes were both the same!' Martin got the message and suggested we eat. He claimed two menus and we ordered. Halfway through I excused myself, found a lavatory and had a complete oral evacuation! It was the best thing I could have done, and I started feeling better. How we got back to the ship, I shall never know. I was however on time for 9 o'clock bingo!

We then visited in quick succession Pago Pago, Tonga (Nuku'alofa) and Fiji in the South Seas. Beautiful islands, so fresh, so warm, so colourful; they made you feel as if their land had just come back from the cleaners.

It might be the time for an update on my alcohol intake. The first thing I must say is that I loved my job; there was no way I would allow it to interrupt my first responsibility. I was drinking spirits and wine. I enjoyed it, but I had one more ambition and that came before drink. During my seven and a half years at sea I only had two days off and that was a totally freak situation, with sunburn! It was an indictable offence (at sea) to suffer sunburn. There was no excuse, no back door. It was immediately placed in the hands of the Captain, who could take what action he would choose.

I was lucky the master was Joe Chapman, my favourite Captain. Where most Masters died in their early sixties, at the time of writing I recently phoned Joe, who is ninety-one. I visited a few years back, but I am semi-disabled now and a journey from Ipswich to Truro would be unwise for both of us. My phone call lasted three quarters of an hour; it was something special. He was frail, but his excellent mind was undiminished. Joe could have taught Classics at Oxford or Cambridge, but he always wanted to go to sea, so it was their bad luck.

Returning to my 'walking the plank', Joe took a different view. I had explained to him that I had taken two towels to protect me from the scorching sun of Aruba. However, they didn't cover the sides of my skinny legs. Instead of the forty lashes, he drew a cruel cartoon of the red and white parts of my body – and sent a copy to all pertinent departments! (Joe was also a brilliant artist – eat your heart out Oxbridge!)

I spent two nights secluded, then returned to my duties. How different this could have been.

That was nearly it. The duodenal discomfort had become a permanent pain. The surgeon on board gave me medication but told me to return to night surgery. I was hospitalised until we reached Fiji, in case of complications.

On my last day in hospital before Fiji, I had a visit from my Goanese steward. He couldn't read English so a 'No Visitors' notice was sidelined. They were lovely people, loyal and kind and nothing was too much trouble. He was mortified when he saw me and the tears rolled down his cheeks.

'Oh Saab! Yesterday you well, today you ill!'

I reassured him and one of the surgeon's nurses gently guided him to the deck.

I was taken from the ship by a stretcher to an ambulance on a short journey to the Colonial War Memorial Hospital on Fiji. I was diagnosed, having endured a barium meal, with a duodenal ulcer. The doctor was very pleasant and cheered me when he said, 'Don't worry old boy, it will take a few weeks but then you'll be as fit as a fiddle'.

I returned to the ship and was told to rest. As the x-ray showed no complications I was not returned to the ship's hospital.

Throughout the voyage we had cabaret artists who entertained the passengers, one of whom was Roy Waterson. He had an excellent tenor voice and proved to be very popular with the passengers. (But the times they were 'a changin'; this trip was one of the last 'voyages'. From then it was 'cruising' all the way.)

I contacted Roy and told him of my plight. He told me I could go and stay with him and his wife and son as long as I didn't mind contributing towards expenses. I informed him that I wouldn't have asked had I not realised that this would be a natural prerequisite. We fixed a cost that was mutually acceptable.

I had to have early nights (9pm), plain food and no alcohol. I thought this quite reasonable. I really don't think the drink caused it, but it did aggravate it. I was told there were no complications, so I sorted out with Staffie (Staff Captain) my arrangements with Roy. I was to join him on the second night in Sydney.

* * * *

When we docked in Waitangi, North Island, New Zealand, we joined a small queue for a ten-minute flight in a Grumman five-seater seaplane. Pam and I were together and a Deck Officer friend with an officer (female) in the purser's department. The cockpit had two seats at the front – pilot plus one, then two more behind them and one at the back. The girls were very sporting and told us to toss for the front seat. I was the lucky one, and having not been beyond the Isle of Wight, I had my first-ever flight sitting next to the pilot (in New Zealand)!

As I'm sure the reader will remember, my grandfather's passing away came within a week of my sailing to Australia. My mother put his house on the market; it comprised two large rooms: the lounge and the withdrawing room, kitchen, receiving room and scullery. Upstairs were four bedrooms (one for the live-in servant, the 'ways' of 1928 were very different), a box room and a large bathroom. It was put on the market for £12,500 and the highest bid was accepted – £11,000. I could have bought it! Two years later it was worth £130,000 – hey ho!

I looked at a couple of properties which would be well within my budget, but I declined, partly because I was concerned I would be away for the most part. Had I done my homework correctly I would have realised it was perfectly viable. (Awaiting me was a tax bill for £21,700! More of which later).

Then the Australian government decided on a whim to offer a deal to the electorate to share a promotion regarding Sunshine Coaches. These cost $20,000, and it worked out very well. If the individual would offer $4,000 the government would pay the rest, $1600 approx. I decided to take advantage of the promotion (a little slave of conscience). I was invited to the unveiling and a splendid time was had by all. It was a Down's Syndrome coach for a day centre. The joy on the faces was wonderful to behold.

* * * *

I have always loved cricket as much as I do steam locomotives. My great regret is that as with golf, I was no good as a performer. I do though have one good memory: I turned into a better player of deck cricket. It was very similar to the indoor cricket of today. We were out in the fresh air. It was on the largest open deck and netting was used to such an extent that no recalcitrant ball could sneak though and end up overboard. This had been the routine since the second-ever match was played. I was told that on the first game they hadn't used the netting and apparently they had lost 49 balls over the side. No, I didn't believe them either!

The Officers v Passengers match was played weekly. The basic rules were that when batting you should play until you were out or had reached twenty. The bowlers moved on after one over, to the left. This gave all the players a chance to be part of the proceedings. It was good for me to be involved. I was always asked by the Officers' Captain if I would be available for the next game before I left the deck.

The umpire during the SS *Iberia*'s last voyage was one George Pope, who had played for England. He and his brother played for Derbyshire in county cricket for many years, and were a fine pair of fast bowlers. It didn't enter my head that he and his wife were travelling to meet English expats in Australia.

When we arrived in Sydney I went down to dinner in the regular way. We were after all staying in Sydney for five days. The restaurant was less than half full and looking round I saw George Pope with guests. I recognised two of the most esteemed cricket players in the world – then and now. (I would ask readers to indulge me. I know these names will mean nothing to some of you, I will move on as soon as possible.)

I had my 'invitation to a party' cards with me and excusing myself to the passengers at my table, I invited the esteemed table to join me for drinks in my cabin. I did not think I would receive a positive, but five minutes later came a card, 'We would very much like to join you'. I was in my eighth heaven!

At 8:30 precisely the protagonists of the body line series, captained by Douglas Jardine, entered my cabin. Harold Larwood, rated the best fast bowler in England and the world, and Bertie Oldfield, the Australian wicket keeper, considered to be in the same league as Larwood, was there with his wife, as was George Pope. Concluding, there was also Sir Jack Hobbs' son Len, who was a first-class cricketer. He was advised by his father to have a business career and to play the game for enjoyment. (Sir Jack Hobbs in his best year earned just £500.) This was a wonderful evening for me, I poured the drinks and just listened as they reminisced.

* * * *

The voyage towards Sydney, until we were almost, there was eventful for all the right reasons. The varied entertainments 'menu' seemed to please the passengers. My hostess Pam must take much credit. The ports we travelled to were all fascinating in many ways.

Just before I went ashore in Sydney on the rest cure, I had enjoyed the cricket company, and the night before I joined Roy and family, I played bridge for the first time in a competition. On the voyage there were many bridge players – most of them good. They were very kind to me, and if I was off duty they insisted on me joining in. They taught me so much and persuaded me to come along on the afternoon sessions in the card room. I didn't see this as skiving as afternoon was zizz time, and to be honest I didn't really feel tired. (Cricket and bridge – so lucky.) I believe my partner and I came eighteenth out of forty.

We arrived in Sydney for that wonderful gathering of esteemed world-class cricketers. The next day Roy Waterson collected me from the ship. I had my luggage, everything ran smoothly and we returned to the bosom of his family in the district of Balmain.

I made sure my 'keep' money was up to date and stayed within the doctor's restraints with no difficulty. We must remember I was still twenty-five. It is not far beyond the likelihood that at the time I was not an alcoholic. Be patient folks, it will come.

Roy was bisexual, though I had no problem with that. He never made suggestions of a personal nature, although he wanted me to sleep with his wife. Somewhat different to the Isle of Wight! In the fullness of time this did happen, but it was no big deal for either of us. It did not have any repercussions. The son was a truly nice lad; he spent as much time with his friends in Balmain.

Roy for many years had been the proud owner of a Rolls Royce (1930s). He was known as 'The Tenor with the Rolls'. He was sure it had brought him gigs he would normally not have expected. At the time I stayed with the family, he had, five years previously, sold it. But he didn't tell the agents.

'Where's the Rolls, Roy?' He had a plethora of responses, 'It's in for a service,' 'It needs new tyres – so difficult to find them,' 'I've lent it to the RR Society for a public showing,' etc etc. Five years on, they still believed him.

One thing we found we had in common was Tony Hancock.

In 1968, when he was at his lowest ebb, Hancock went to Australia to film a series of *Hancock*. But it was something of a disaster. About this time during a row with all those who loved him, he drank a whole bottle of brandy in five minutes. The television company had made about fifteen minutes of three of the shows and aimed to make it into one show. (This was just after the 'lad' had committed suicide in his room. He was forty-four.)

A meeting of the production team was convened, and one member said, 'We obviously need a link man, I have a feeling Roy Waterson (you know, the one with the Rolls. Sorry couldn't resist), is about the same size.'

The unanimous decision was made; they spoke to Roy's agent and another meeting was established. It was remarkable in that they were exactly the same height (5'7'), had the same hat size, weighed the same and both could be lugubrious at times. The contract was signed the next day. Roy asked me if I would like to watch what had been salvaged. 'It would be a privilege,' I said.

Australian television in 1968 was much like British television in the 1950s. Roy was not a 'star' in the way it was, by then, in Britain. Though I must stress he was an excellent tenor. I went to several of his shows during my time in Balmain. He always went down well (unlike me at South Liverpool FC). He made a good living doing the thing he liked best.

He phoned Channel 9 and said he had an acquaintance who was a Tony Hancock aficionado, and would love to see our efforts. A private showing was arranged, and I was given VIP treatment. It was tragic; Hancock had lost all sense of timing and the best thing was Roy's linking work. Had it not been for him, even the one showing would have been worthless.

I considered it a privilege and it was very memorable, even though it was awfully sad.

I read a lot and slept even more. I had been given a prescription and took the recommended dosage without fail. After three weeks the symptoms started to recede, and a week before I returned to the ship I had a hospital check-up, which I passed with flying colours. I returned to the ship after I had said my goodbyes with many thanks to Roy and his family. I was not destined to meet them again. We did send each other Christmas cards for several years. I was able to follow his son's progress, which indicated how well he was doing at school including sports.

* * * *

An Australian entertainer had filled my empty seat, and he stayed on for a couple of weeks to give me a chance to regain my sea legs. For the next month I stuck to whisky and milk. I must have got the taste for the whisky, because I hated milk!

I felt so much better and enjoyed the return to Southampton. I was to have one more slight bout four years later, but I chose the time when I was on leave and soon recovered.

I can honestly say P&O treated me exceptionally well. There was never a whisper of frustration, or anything like it. They were pleased to hear of my progress and never once gave me anything but encouragement.

Until 1973 the Entertainments Officer reported to 'staffie' (the Staff Captain), who was senior, second only to the Captain/ Commodore. Towards the end of 1973 the Entertainments Officer became Director (three stripes, as opposed to two and a half). This was when the new, disastrous intake were introduced. The other Conference Officers resented this intrusion and made their complaints very vocal. They needed reminding that the person who gave them their jobs was the same person (in head office) who was responsible for the Entertainments Director's employment. There were three very sulky old hands who demanded four stripes!

The pathetic saga was eventually sorted, but about eighteen months late. In the meantime, they might have gained much more had they thought of the dictum 'Softly, softly, catchee monkey' (or 'give them enough rope'); they would have had more pulling power.

*** *

I did not know at the time much detail of the intake which turned into such a farce. The Entertainments Manager in London was Alan Davy; I also knew him as a friend. I have not changed my views, in that his judgment was excellent and sincere. In the latter days of my tenure, when on leave, I was invited to be a part of the selection boards. I saw again his ability. So what went wrong? I cannot say, but one by one they 'walked the plank'.

I was at the time Deputy Cruise Director, and Alan, as I said, responded to my letter with a negative, for now. He was absolutely right. My 'boss' Chris was a year older than me; he had been a Butlins Redcoat the year before me.

In the period I was with him, I saw a man carving out a department. He took no truck from anyone. He was twenty-eight, but if he considered a fellow Conference Officer was trying it on, even if he was fifty-five, he got the same salvo as a Junior Officer who had been late for a duty.

I learned so much from him, I began to feel more equipped to take the responsibility; a situation which then, I was not capable of handling.

* * * *

There was a surgeon called Ross Wheatley who I always looked out for. If he was on board the world seemed a better place for it. He was a Surgeon Commander and Honorary Physician to the Queen. He was an army man but when he retired (compulsory), he decided against staying at home and applied to P&O for employment. It was a win-win for everyone as he was accepted.

When we had our 'Pub Night' I was told he would appear, sharing his musical talents as long as he was asked. I was told he would come even if he wasn't asked, but I played it by the book. He'd bring his 'dots' (sheet music) for the band and prepared by blowing into the microphone. (No wonder the Ents. Departments had no spare cash for emergencies!)

Ready to rend; he directed the band and took a deep breath: '*Let's all go down to Alice's house!*', a popular music hall extravaganza. His arms were flying in all directions; he must have brought the wrong dots because not one note was the same during his recital (memories of Les Dawson). It was always the same and he brought the house down – always. I can honestly say I was usually in tears. He was given the same ovation every single time (some standing).

When you were due vaccinations you had to be ready for bed in the afternoon. They were also always at 12 noon. I arrived on the dot. Ross turned to me and said, 'I'll just give us a glass of sherry each, because you shouldn't drink after the vaccinations. Incidentally, did you note how I harmonised with the band last night?'

We drained our glasses and he ushered me into his surgery. 'Did that hurt?'

'No' I said.

'That's good! We'll have some gin!'

I was lucky if I got away before two thirty! It was then I made it to bed, having asked for a wakeup call!

One of the changes come 1973 was an influx to the ships of the new intake of potential Cruise Directors, to establish themselves in a senior capacity. As mentioned, it proved to be less than successful. I actually applied for the position and received a very generous response from the Entertainments Manager in London. He said I was already in their thoughts, but they felt I needed a little more experience. And, like my headmaster years before, he was absolutely right.

This coincided with one of the new boys coming to his baptism. The 'going on leave' Cruise Director was Chris. He taught me so much. I have often wondered if Alan Davy (London) put me with him deliberately, because he was able to fight his corner so well. I really took that on board.

Mike, who was replacing Chris, was a sheer delight, although paperwork was not his thing. (I spent the first week handing out the pertinent paragraphs of our administration – and he spent the next week handing them back!) However, he was very witty and good as a front man and very popular (except when he was attempting to emulate the Duke of Edinburgh). His gaffes were hilarious.

The situation changed, and we all settled down. Mike was

happy for me to have the box and I erred on the side of caution. The others further down the line all had what they had hoped for and Mike took over the front man's responsibilities.

We did come together during the Pub Nights and Music Hall, and we worked on the musicals, which we co-directed. I was always aware it was Mike who was Cruise Director, so I would not interfere in aspects of which we didn't agree. I would just accept and get on with the next challenge.

Casino Nights were when a group of the crew were invited into the public rooms, took various single gambling posts, such as Crown & Anchor, Spin a Six, Find the Queen, Black Jack etc. We knew they were taking a little off the top, and they knew we knew. The Casino Night always made a profit. They didn't get greedy! At risk of sounding patronising I considered they were comfortable with the passengers and enjoyed the evening. Rarely, if ever, at cashing up time did the casino register a loss.

* * * *

The time came when I was due for leave and I was duly repatriated. I think the break was good for me, and I caught up with good friends. I left behind Capt. Wacher, who wanted me to know that he had contacted head office to let them know that if one Cruise Director went on planned leave before his replacement arrived, leave would be handled by Eddie on this ship; he was happy I could professionally take the part of Cruise Director in an emergency.

I received a call from Alan Davy with regard to my whereabouts at the end of my leave. He said he wanted me to join Chris Chapman on one of the Princess cruise ships. I can remember when *Arcadia* passed the brand-new *Spirit of London* underneath the Golden Gate Bridge in San Francisco. I was on the bridge with Alan Peglar (still with us).

I was delighted to be with Chris again. He was 100% gay and because we were able to totally cope with each other's predilections, the time we had together was always a hoot. (For someone who is actually 100% not gay, I must have been in more gay bars than was good for me!) I hasten to add Chris was brilliant. He was always aware, and if necessary he would put those who doubted him to the sword.

This might be a suitable time to include examples of some people's amazing thought processes, one or two seemingly impossible to believe. The purser was very often the recipient.

Twice a week during a cruise, the ship would borrow one of the public rooms to put on an alternative lunchtime 'deck buffet'. They were *so* good. Two long trestle tables were demanded much of. They were groaning. You name it, it was there, together with red and white wine. It did not matter if their plates were empty, the passengers were welcome to replenish (and again). (The Catering Deputy Purser was a friend and in the fullness of time we would work together in different capacities.)

However, that was not enough. After every cruise came the complaints: 'Why did you put the deck buffet on at the same time as lunch in the restaurant? We couldn't get to both!'

Then came the time when the train robber Ronald Biggs was being extradited back to this country. A passenger was overheard saying, 'You mark my words, the police will put him away for a weekend and then they'll let him out on patrol!'

I saw a man queueing with an American one cent coin to have it changed for a Canadian one cent coin, because he was disembarking at Vancouver. In similar circumstances I heard two of my table companions, both Methodist Ministers, arguing ferociously over the seven yen one owed the other. At the time it was ¥700 to the pound!

Finally, if you doubt the veracity of the aforementioned, try this one for size. It occurred as we were leaving port. The purser heard a hammering on his door. This was a very busy time for a purser, without interruptions. So, he pointed to a junior officer, and when that failed the Deputy Purser invited the woman into his office. She was shaking with what appeared to be fear.

'Tell me madam, how I can help you?' he said.

She didn't seem convinced but decided to battle on. 'If, young man, if, the ship sinks and we have to take to the lifeboats, can you guarantee me a non-smoker?'

Ah, the human comedy.

CHAPTER 5

cruise director

During my P&O days I worked with some wonderful people. (Really, I'm not name dropping, in fact I was chatting to Prince Charles about this just last Thursday...). Some of those readers may have heard of are Craig Douglas, Mike and Bernie Winters, Joan Regan, Edmund Hockridge, Freddie 'Parrot Face' Davies and Al Read (megalomaniac). More about some of them later. I was gratefully informed that Al could be awkward. Quite right. At the end of our introductory get together he stayed until everyone else had left. He told me he rarely did cruises but on his last one he gave the Cruise Director his own programme. 'You'll find it the best way'. Forewarned, I just said that he either accepted my programme or left the ship at the next port. He dissolved and left my cabin.

In 1980 I joined a group of like-minded people in Ipswich, where experienced Samaritans – managers and directors – were there to help us understand the ethos of the Samaritans and the ways we should disport ourselves as Samaritans.

One aspect was how to cope with 'presenting problems', people who said one thing but meant another. For the 'drones' like me it seemed incomprehensible. It was also made clear that we did not contact them in any circumstances. We also learnt about silent calls. Instead of putting the phone down, we should reassure them, just say 'I'm still here' and similar short phrases. We were also told that when answering a call, we should wait for three rings. This would be the most comfortable for the caller.

At the end of the seminar I really thought I'd been over-busy asking questions and didn't think I would be accepted. However, about half of the group were invited to join and I think I must have got in via the back door!

I had a difficult call early on. I was confronted by a situation not covered by the training. A lady phoned up in hysterics, because her neighbour had gone out in her car with all the accoutrements to kill herself by carbon monoxide poisoning, which she had threatened to do for several weeks. 'Can you help me?' she asked, I asked her to give me the telephone number of her neighbour; and put myself into a personal muddle.

One of the excellent aspects of the 'Sams' was the fact that 'foot soldiers', like myself, had a double hierarchy to go to for help. I phoned the day leader and explained to him the situation. He said he would phone the Director and would come back to me. I thanked God for that. In due course the leader phoned me and told me that under such circumstances

I should follow it up. I rang the caller, who was much relieved, 'She's in one hell of a state but I'll give you her telephone number'. I duly phoned the lady and endured 44 minutes non-stop vituperation, learning a few new words on the way. Towards the end of the call, she calmed, and I just said, 'Phone me if you think I may be able to help'.

I had noted she had returned home alive. I immediately rang the day leader to explain where we were. He said we would proceed with caution. Starting at three times a week I was with her, gradually reducing, for six months; always under the direction of the leader. He was obviously concerned, and rightly so. But it was never a problem. In fact, I went with her to the doctor's on that first night. He had just shrugged and said, 'I can't stop you committing suicide'. However, she recovered, remarried and soon re-learned how to smile.

Another situation that occurred in my last few weeks gave me a challenge. The doorbell rang and three young ladies, aged about 14, informed me that they had wet their pants. I invited them in, but they ran away. A moment later – yes – the bell rang, I repeated my procedure and yes – the same response. I persisted and the fourth time they came into the centre. There were lots of giggles and I suggested that it wasn't about the pants and asked if I could help. Eventually they stopped giggling and one said, 'Actually we sniff glue and want to stop'. Progress had been made.

My time with the Samaritans coincided with a new life. By 1986 my wife Judith was caring for our two daughters, born only two years apart. As a Samaritan I had to offer one all-night session every week. That winter was bitter, and my wife was virtually living in one bedroom in our spacious 1499

Tudor house. I resigned, with many thanks to all concerned, trusting they would understand my predicament. It turned out to be a mutual and friendly conclusion.

Ladies of the Night

This will be short. If I had not reached the positions I did, I would probably have enjoyed at most four or five sexual partners. I'm not good looking but I do think I have a reasonable personality. Without that I might well have lived and died a virgin!

This was also the time of 'Flower Power' which lasted much longer in and around San Francisco (Haight-Ashbury). While you might think I am counting 'my times' in notches, I do have quite a memory for numbers. I was given a set of cigarette cards of the Kings and Queens of England. I was only eight, but before I was nine I knew the dates of them all. In fact, I did the 'act' in cabaret and in three shows scored 16 – 17 – 18 (out of 20). There was no trick.

I had about five partners in each of the holiday camps except Caister, where it was twenty. In all my time at sea I had seventy partners. And in the years before I married, twenty-five.

Do I feel guilty? They were all consensual, and I would like to think the ladies enjoyed it as much as I did.

My first sexual experience, when I was still nineteen, was a fiasco. I thought I would be highly embarrassed putting on a condom, whilst the young lady could see me doing so. I put the condom on at home and then dressed for the evening! I hoped it would stay on. As you can imagine, I had a very strong case of the droop.

I remember bumping into one girl and saying, 'I think I remember you from somewhere?'

'Right you bloody do!' she said. We had had a one-night stand about two years before. Oops!

Finally, I was on a plane from Heathrow bound for Sydney. There was an engine problem and the powers that be, quite rightly, aborted the flight. We all trooped off the plane. We had reached Frankfurt, where we would stay in a hotel overnight. I found myself sitting next to an Irish nurse. She was attractive rather than pretty, but she exuded enormous sex appeal. We collected our keys and I said I'd see her to the door. Her door number was B172, and she asked me where I was – I said 'B172'. She looked at me and smiled. We went in together. I'll never forget the next two hours.

On the airliner the next day we joined the mile-high club.

* * * *

After leave at home in the early spring of 1974, I was asked to join Chris again, this time on the *Sun Princess*. It would be a season of cruises with the ship based in Los Angeles. I was happy that P&O Entertainments in London were considering me for the future. I never doubted, especially as I knew they were putting me with Chris, who was the best teacher I could have had.

I was also with a hostess I loved to distraction! She'd let me kiss her but gave the distinct impression she was not joining in. Her name was Suzanne Jones – dancer per excellence. I wondered if she was gay. She was kind to me. Please don't think I mentioned the gay thing out of resentment. Two of my daughters are gay and I love them just as I love the third.

We were a week into the first cruise when Chris (in the process of concluding his staff meeting), received a phone call from the bridge. It was the Captain asking Chris to come up to his cabin and to bring me with him.

'Certainly Captain. My meeting is nearly finished. Is five minutes okay?'

I sensed a small grunt. However, true to his word Chris and I were on time. The Captain handed me a telex, which instructed: 'EDDIE SCOTT JOIN ARCADIA JUNE AS ACTING CRUISE DIRECTOR. REPLY'. I was five days out. This direction was 27th June 1974. I had always hoped I would be something I could truly see as success, after my difficult start in life. I gave myself until I was twenty-eight. My birthday, as previously mentioned, is 22nd June, so I had only just missed it. It was however, not going to be straightforward.

The Captain asked me to pass the telex to Chris, and I obliged. 'Well done Eddie,' he said. Then he added, 'Look I'm not having this season changed. We've got the team we want.'

Instinctively, I got the most important words of my life out into his domain.

'Sir, I don't think you have the right to stand in the way of my promotion.'

There was a long pause and then he turned to me with a smile.

'You're right, I haven't have I?'

'No sir.'

'It's very early, but could you manage a sherry?'

* * * *

I duly packed and was booked onto a flight from San Francisco, arriving in Juneau, the capital of Alaska; it was in fact quite a short journey. One of my cases was missing but I was told it would be on the next flight, before *Arcadia* was due to sail. All was well, and I paid Captain Hannah a visit. He was a captain whom I had sailed with in the past; I liked him immensely. We had some gin and he wished me good fortune, I now had to get down to work.

I had a very encouraging letter from Alan Davy waiting for me. He did however say that Alan Pegler (the first private owner of the Flying Scotsman), was involving himself with something quite illegal and to look out for it. This saddened me. I didn't want to delve any deeper, but the next day I found out he was still 'employed'. I was on my first day in the job and I had a job to do. I've already said I looked up to Alan and was pleased he had made initial success as a Port Lecturer.

Alan had been a pilot towards the end of the Second World War and had himself driven his beloved Flying Scotsman 4472 throughout Britain and most of North America. He had achieved a lifetime desire, and sold her to another millionaire, who in turn passed it to another – both just avoiding bankruptcy. She really was an expensive lady to please!

In the end she had the best possible outcome. The pragmatic Railway Museum bought her for the nation. It was for all who had kept her alive, privately. The best of all results. It is hoped she will carry on being brought out to do short summer seasons from convenient railway stations.

I saw Alan two or three times after we had both 'swallowed the anchor'. He was always good company for a bibulous evening out at some reputable eatery. He lived to be ninety-one.

I worked from early afternoon to plan the cruise. I had organised a cocktail party for all those involved in the Entertainments Dept. I pencilled a meeting with Alan for the next morning at 10am (after my own staff meeting). I didn't relish it, but it had to be done by me and only me. He was over fifty, easily old enough to be my father. It isn't very often that someone you greatly admire has to be severely admonished, but after all it was a gambling scam. I had to go in hard and had learnt enough from Chris Chapman to justify it.

I know I was lucid and met his eyes. I needn't have worried; he subsided. I made my point, we stood up and I shook his hand. In the nicest way I said, 'Don't let me down Alan, it's the last chance saloon'. It never needed saying again.

****

The cocktail party enabled me to meet all the Entertainments Dept. staff. This involved band leaders, speciality acts, flower arrangers, dance teachers, our hostesses and of course cabaret artistes. Max, my new deputy, handed out details of their days and times of appearances.

One such act was called 'The Gentry Brothers'; known universally as the 'Gentry Sisters'! They had done several cruises when I was a deputy. They were still at the party after only Max and I remained, and they asked if they could discuss their programme. I told them I could fit them in the next day, in my cabin at 10:30am.

'This should be interesting Eddie,' quipped Max.

'Yes Max, and I want you with me.'

I asked him to stay for a few moments and told him what I expected of him. It was one thing only, total loyalty.

'Our department will survive on that. Any tittle-tattle is unacceptable. If they [the staff] start trying to get to me through you, you will come directly to me. If you think they're justified, come directly to me, I can listen. I don't think this will happen, but forewarned is forearmed. And as you know, quite a few sailed with me before I was elevated! I think tomorrow may well be one of those examples... your turn?'

'It's all been said.'

The Goanese Stewards arrived and, on my nod, got on with clearing up the cabin. They were delightful people, throughout my life at sea.

Captain's meeting – my meeting – and then the Gentries. Max and I now awaited their entrance. I resisted the temptation to bow. They arrived on time and I seated them.

'Well gentlemen, what can we do for you?'

'Well Eddie', said one 'sister', 'We need to discuss the programme you have provided for us. It really isn't on; we have done our own programme and we are convinced this will be the best for us, and more importantly for you. It would be a shame if your start as CD should be thwarted by poor planning.' (I do not claim this was word for word, but it is certainly the essence).

Max did what he was asked to do; say nothing. He had certainly heard enough. Having listened, with some amusement, for their care towards me as a new Cruise Director, I just said,

'Like it or not, I do the programme. And that is it.'

They, as one, said they would leave the ship in Vancouver.

'I trust' I said, 'we will finalise everything by 2pm.'

I requested them to be in my cabin at this time. After the 'Gents' had left I told Max I wanted him back for that confrontation. I phoned the Captain and asked if he could give me five minutes towards a peculiar request,

'Try me Eddie!'

I arrived and explained what had happened. I said to the Captain, 'I'm not going to accept their nonsense as I'm convinced my programming is the best possible. The main reason sir is if you could authorise a telex to London to replace the act with another as soon as possible. I have another meeting at 2pm. I'm damned if I should put our season in jeopardy.'

Captain Hannah put on his thinking hat and suddenly his face was wreathed in smiles.

'Tell them they are not getting off the ship in Vancouver. They are getting off when we arrive in Skagway (one of the several 'wastes' in Alaska), and they can find their own way home.'

The meeting at 2pm was one of my most satisfying times. I did not gloat but awaited their reaction quietly. They seemed to dissolve; I handed them another copy of my programme. They took it and managed to stutter that they could work with it. I reminded them they were on stage at 6:30pm and stood up, as did Max. And so did they. I opened the door and they were gone. What a Captain; I never had cause to need his council again during that cruising season.

* * * *

I thoroughly enjoyed the Alaskan period. I had a girlfriend in Vancouver. We were docked overnight so I stayed ashore with her, returning on time for the Captain's meeting before we sailed. I also found myself responsible for all entertainments when it came to 'Comment Forms', or as the passengers called them 'Complaints Forms'. These covered everything from cleanliness of open decks, quality of food, daytime/

evening entertainments, assistance from the Bureau, medical treatments where applicable etc. etc.

From the passenger satisfaction forms a result is in the form of a percentage. I was quite pleased when the figure was 88%. I felt we were going in the right direction to be accorded that. I fact throughout that season of Alaskan cruises the percentage varied from just 85% to 92%.

I was sailing with my favourite Captain, Joe Chapman (David Hannah had gone on leave). He was always so supportive and on the rare occasions when we had a wobble, he was always there to encourage and fortify. Most captains were on the side of change; but not all. The days of voyaging were over, as it was no longer cost effective. Those were the days when the evening highlight was dressing for dining. There would be a piano lounge and a three-piece band every other day. Occasionally the passengers would come together and organise a fancy-dress competition, or perhaps an island night to add a little variety. In those days the ship's crew included a Liaison Officer, who would make himself available to passengers for added involvement, like a meeting of Masons who liked to organise a ladies' night or some such activity.

When I enjoyed my start at sea, my cabin had on the outside wall 'Liaison Officer'. Old habits die hard. This was in the early 1970s when suddenly the people who wanted to cruise had a change of priority. The quality of the entertainment was just as important as the food provided. It was not the refuge of the past.

I once asked a Senior Deck Officer of long standing how he saw the function of the Liaison Officer. He didn't need prompting,

'Well,' he said. 'He'd wake every morning with the shakes.

He would drink about three double gins and was then able to have a shower. He missed breakfast. He would then go on deck, chatting cheerfully with the passengers, who were only too happy to offer him a drink. 'I'll catch you at the bar when the sun passes the yard arm! I couldn't possibly take advantage of your generosity until then!'

'This would be followed with another walk around the passengers on the deck – always friendly; the life and soul etc. etc. He checked the sky and his perambulation enabled him to arrive back at the bar at noon exactly.

For the next two hours he would enthral his audience of passengers. The Bar Manager kept watch, knowing that soon he would have to make himself responsible, with some passenger, for helping to get the Commodore Liaison Officer back to his billet; where he would sleep until his Goanese steward brought bring him afternoon tea. He would repeat the process at 4:30pm, when he was brought a very large gin and tonic. He would then be able to get himself into the shower and deal with the 'soup and fish' at his passenger table. He did order a couple of bottles of wine at the beginning of the voyage, hoping the passengers would get into the habit.

He would then enhance the ballroom activities with detail of when he had been a professional dancer. By ten of the clock he was unstable and was helped by a couple of leading hands to his cabin. The same routine he was already looking forward to doing the next day, until he was away with the fairies.'

* * * *

This may be a good time to reappraise my own drinking, First, at that time (1974-75) I had reached a good position. I was thrilled to have the opportunity to stamp my personality on proceedings. A job I was so lucky to have achieved. Here I quote Winston Churchill, 'I have always used alcohol as my servant and *not* my master!'

There was absolutely no chance of me jeopardising the terrific position I had been accorded. I never forgot the responsibility of a staff of fifty-five. I obviously drank more than I should with regard to those pesky units. There were a few events which would make non-drinking as easy as having the whole ship's company sign the pledge! These were Pub Night, Roman Night and Island Night. Who could resist a Mai Tai?

I think looking back I was becoming a functioning alcoholic. But I was in good company. If I had questioned it at the time, it might have been a bad thing.

* * * *

One thing happened halfway through the season which was a touch of genius. Captain Joe Chapman was in charge. We arrived in Glacier Bay. The Radio Officer announced that the Captain had organised 'Brunch on Ice'. The voice continued that the other three Senior Deck Officers would join him, disembarking on the starboard side. All the passengers had jostled themselves onto that deck side, cameras at the ready. For the officers, two Goanese boys were in the boat to serve the food and drink. The table was set up silver service, cloths, serviettes and cutlery. It started with a drink: Champagne, Black Velvet (Champagne with Guinness), or Champagne Gold (Champagne and Brandy). (I don't want you to think I'm being patronising, but some won't have known of the derivations.) After a refill of drinks, the starters arrived, king prawn on avocado with rosemary dressing and brown bread and butter. This was followed by further drinks and a dish of salmon with the usual sides. The starboard side was still packed. The boat was gently raised back onto the deck and the 'power' of the ship were warmly applauded as they made their way back to their stations.

I returned to my cabin, well aware that the whole display would not have had a deleterious effect on passenger satisfaction. I was about to leave when my phone rang.

'Eddie.' I knew then it was Master Joe.

'Yes sir.'

'What did you think of today?'

I told him I thought it was ingenious and that my most recent thought had been that it did everything to aid entertainment satisfaction.

'How would you like, next cruise, and with your officers, a repeat of our efforts today?'

'I would be delighted sir,' I said. 'It can only be an additional aid to everyone's satisfaction.'

I then asked him if there would still be on board king prawns on avocado.

Passenger satisfaction (entertainments) on this cruise was 89%. What a delightful thing we had to look forward to on the next cruise.

The first person I asked was my Chief Hostess. I was well aware she had been working for P&O long before me. She was steady and reliable, and I thought she would willingly join the loyalty brigade if I said and did a few basic things. Having a reasonable knowledge of people, I felt the only thing she yearned for was to be treated with elemental respect. This was hardly a problem, as she was intelligent, and I treated her as such. I would have been stupid not to. Our association was very much the same as mine with John the Bar Manager, to whom I was returning with the same mutual respect, I asked my Deputy, Max, whether he would like to join the junket. I knew he was unsure but hoped it might have been the first opportunity to establish loyalty. He joined us and enjoyed it. My second hostess was delighted to be asked and I had told them all to try and make it as close as Olde Time Music Hall when it came to dressing up.

I was delighted to say to one and all that their efforts were as exactly as I had hoped.

The atmosphere around the ship's starboard side, was much the same as on the last cruise with the Deck Dept.

In Juneau during the Alaskan cruising season, the ship did not leave the berth until midnight. The Captain gave me permission to go ashore between eight and eleven and join the director and those passengers who had been invited by the director of the Juneau Bridge Club. The Captain qualified his support by saying, 'If you delegate well enough and there are no adverse comments, it will be all right.'

Juneau was a jewel in the crown as far as capital cities go; the food was excellent, as were the restaurants that served it. Many passengers stayed ashore to dine for a change of venue. I hasten to add that the food in the restaurants on board were excellent, but this was the only opportunity of the cruise to eat ashore. As the ship's stay was longer, passengers on board were sparser, so I gave the 'cabaret variety' a night off. We still had on board two bands playing for dancing, the piano bar always had a good following, general quizzes, the disco, prize bingo and 'Brain of *Canberra*'. (This was the first round and the passengers ashore would be given their chance the next evening.)

The team didn't let me down, but at the Juneau Bridge Club I did let my partner down. The final irony though was that when the Juneau Director announced the results, we had won! He certainly wasn't talking about me. (I've still got the sterling silver bowl.)

The evenings on board were programmed to the persuasions of the passengers. It was variable. The Disc Jockey appealed to certain young people, the piano bar to others – live and let live. Obviously, the cabarets were popular and were followed by many, dancing to a good band. One I had forgotten were the dancing pair, usually a husband and wife team, and they would teach a variety of dances. They were invariably very good at their craft and had a good following. Their skills enabled them to see the fruits of their labours later on in the voyage.

At my first introductions I would give cruisers a welcome to any of the social events on board that might appeal to them. However, I stressed to them that if they chose the 'quiet life' as a therapy, no one would be persuaded to join in a knobbly knees competition!

On disembarking at the end of that cruise, a man came up to me and asked, 'Eddie Scott?' I affirmed. He continued, 'On the first night of the cruise you said people who didn't want to be involved in the entertainments programme would be respected. I haven't seen you since, from that first night until now!' He stretched his hand out, which I took with respect.

He was, I found out later, the Hong Kong Chief of Police. After a workload to stretch the saints, he had been ordered to take a fully paid-for break. I knew where he'd been for most of the cruise. I saw him the first time purely by chance in the ship's library, the second, third and fourth by design. And I'm certain he wasn't reading crime stories…

Away from the library there was a dayroom; this was a comfortable room close to the library, with very comfortable furniture. In the evenings the room was ideal for music, quizzes and a variety of competitions that involved brain work. I had recently published a book of poems and every week or so, Vince Billington and I did a 'poetry recital'. I enjoyed reading poetry, as did the average audience. It wouldn't have worked without Vince.

Quiz nights were very popular. We suggested tables of six or thereabouts and the prize was a good bottle of champagne. The tables were numbered, paper was provided and having discussed and chosen the answer, a table representative would bring their answer to our table, from which it was transferred to the blackboard, and a successful result given a tick. We did have some wonderful answers; my favourite was the answer to a question about what the pangolin (an anteater) ate. This table had their own ideas. Their answer was 'pancakes'!

One of the most amazing situations I encountered was while holding a music quiz. The gentleman concerned was at my dining table with his wife, who seemed in awe of him. He was due to leave the ship before her, but not before the music quiz. I had devised twenty questions as generally as I could, particularly knowing the people who love rock and would be at the disco. This man sat on his own. I would be asking the questions, which I considered reasonably difficult. We put out the paper fillers and pens so they could bring their answers to the hostess, who recorded them on a blackboard. Before I'd finished the question he was up to the table, whilst the others were still considering their answers. He did this nineteen more times. He got twenty out of twenty correct!

So many good things, some unique, have come to me in my lifetime. I give thanks for them all.

* * * *

It's about time I reappraised you with an update with regard to my drinking. First, I was proud of my job; it was demanding, but I loved it. I had been so lucky; however, it is very possible that I had become a functional alcoholic. I can be truthful with the reader when I say I was totally oblivious to the fact. For no particular reason, I still never drank alone in my cabin, even if I knew I was going to be 'in' for a couple of hours (afternoons).

During my last summer season in 1983, I remember buying a bottle of scotch and hiding it in my dressing room. No excuses, it was just a rotten season, the only one I had to endure. I was totally shafted. A guy called Dave May along with his band had been there for four or five seasons. He had expected my job.

In July of that same year, I had two brilliant weeks, much to the annoyance of the band. Dave May returned from illness, as did the bad mouthing to campers he had met over the previous four years. In consolation, I was about to be married. It was confirmed by James Paget Hospital in Gorleston that Judith, who lived with me, was 'with child'. We had always said we would get married if that occurred. We managed to obtain a Bishop's Licence; the date was 24th August 1983.

It was a lovely day and there were just the four of us: Judith, me and a friend each as witnesses, and the Rector. We repaired to a hotel in Hadleigh and then the Red Lion in Southwold. The next day we drove back to Gunton Hall and both of us got back to work. Later, we did have a honeymoon. We booked a Christmas/New Year holiday on the Isle of Arran.

* * * *

The Alaskan cruises of 1974 sadly came to an end. I felt established, had total support from my team and the Captain. The last cruise ended with passenger support of 89%. It was time for a six-week break, which I spent at home in Ipswich. I was able to catch up with good friends, especially my booze buddies. Mother was kind enough to add my name to the insurance on her small car (I did at least pay for it), which gave me extra freedom when she was not using it. I read and rested, wrote a little and played bridge once a week. I also spent time with my father.

The first of these occasions was on my first night home. Ipswich Town FC were entertaining Sunderland FC. I was well aware I had come from a warmer climate and was now in a bitterly cold one. In mitigation I had put on many clothes, starting with long johns, several pullovers, two pairs of trousers and a thick duffle coat. I also sported an Astrakhan hat.

At half-time, the town, having played superbly, were 3-0 up. I began to feel extremely cold in a distinctly different way. I should have told my father, but stupidly decided to see the game through. I was later told that it was hypothermia. Never before had I experienced such a feeling. But, on location a few years later, we were in an airport filming a scene. We were given clothing, which was 60s casual, and were standing in the middle of this airport. I cannot think October, even when it's a sunny day, would be an ideal or particularly warm location.

The director showed sympathy and gave me the cup of coffee he'd just poured for himself. One of the actors, on the trip back to the BBC, held up the coach and bought me a half bottle of scotch. I am now told it's not much good, opening the pores and then closing them. I have to say that the scotch did little to make me think this was true. I do know that getting into a steaming hot bath does absolutely nothing. You continue to freeze, however hot the water. This is a particular subject I will return to in much more detail.

After a short recurrence of my duodenum trouble, I was sent to the SS *Canberra*, the largest P&O ship in the fleet. (Most readers will remember the Falklands War and the role the *Canberra* played as a hospital ship.) I was replacing one of the most popular Cruise Directors, Billy Allison, who had been on the *Canberra* for five years. He would be the first to admit that administration was not his 'bag', but he had an artistic gift given to few.

Pinpointing potential problems before my first meeting was essential. The other 'boys and girls' seemed ideal for their stations; personable, willing and bright. I would change things. I had set out eight hard chairs in a circle. In the past some seniors had acquired lounge chairs; I decided this was not to my liking. So just before the cruise staff were due to arrive, I set out the chairs, and in addition to that, I decided where the Deputy Cruise Director and Chief Hostess were going to sit. This was not in their usual places, as I had observed at the one meeting I had attended.

There was a knock at the door and eight members of the cruise staff spilled into the cabin. I waited less than a second before saying, 'Cliff, I want you next to me on the right side with Maureen next to you. The others should sit in the chairs provided, engineering yourselves boy/girl.'

It was a picture, and they looked completely lost; it was something like blind man's bluff! Eventually they settled down and Maureen looked at me with a face like thunder, but I considered I had won a small victory. The seating was never mentioned again. I am forever indebted to Chris Chapman.

The Christmas cruise lasted about three weeks. One of my priorities and main responsibilities was to invite and welcome all the cabaret artists, daytime lecturers, band leaders and port lecturers to acquaint them with their times and duties (day and night). I would include the Deputy Cruise Director and Chief Hostess in these gatherings. I very rarely had a problem. I always found that whatever the subject, the 'guests' were balanced, welcoming and constructive. Many had known me as a deputy. The vast majority were supportive and kindly.

This Christmas cruise the entertainment included Edmund Hockridge, Alan Shaxon (magic man), pianist Vince Billington and Joan Regan. Daytime activities included keep fit, shore excursions experts and an artist teaching those who wished to improve their efforts on canvas. A golfing expert taught how to swing to get the best of results (this was held on the biggest open deck with the netting round it, so we could still play deck cricket, giving the hardworking golf expert an afternoon off).

At the Captain's cocktail party, it was usual for the Cruise Director to welcome the passengers as they approached you and then to introduce them to the Captain. I had to have the passenger list to read several times before the party. I would need to know the Knights of the Realm, the Lords and the Ambassadors. Everything to make the truth of my introductions. The reason? All those higher echelon wallahs would never tell you.

On this cruise, I only half saw the next couple but heard someone say, 'Mr Kenneth Williams and mother'. I introduced them grandly to the Commodore, but I don't think he even recognised Kenneth and his beloved mother. Despite this, they were soon in the thick of things.

On the positive side I was happy in my work and handling staff, after a brief coup attempt instigated by my deputy Cliff Perry. I have dined out on this story many times. One of the passengers was a millionaire, having *twice* made top money on the pools. His forms had been filled in by friends. This rather sad person was persuaded to go to the Commodore with Cliff Perry to complain about how incompetent I was and to say I should be replaced by Cliff at the earliest possible moment. What a silly person he was. The pools winner was illiterate and had a vocabulary of about forty words. I am told they were ejected by the Commodore. I was called to the bridge, where the master welcomed me.

'Are you all right?'

'Yes sir, I am settling into a new ship. I feel good about it and really enjoy my work.'

'Good,' he said and then regaled me with his visitation. I was livid. The master said if I wished it, he would happily repatriate him, together with a letter suggesting he should be demoted. I thanked him for his support but suggested he should be given a last chance – reluctantly. I made sure everyone pertinent was warned of exactly what would happen should there be a repeat of such behaviour. I did break one 'law'; I did inform the team of the betrayal at our daily meeting. It was the price he paid for having been given a second chance.

Returning to Kenneth Williams (I was a genuine big fan), I walked past him on the deck. Seeing who it was, I turned, and he came the closest in accepting interruption. I asked him how he was enjoying the holiday,

'Mother's enjoying herself enormously, but it's not really my scene, dear boy,' he said with his wonderful drawl. We must have talked for a quarter of an hour, during which I noted his intellect and his classical astuteness, yet lurking sadness; I left him to his life. He came to our 'Olde Time Music Hall' in which I had sung *On Mother Kelly's Doorstep*. He caught me in the foyer and said, 'I've never seen more milking in my life!'

I just said, 'I had a good teacher!'

Finally, towards the end of the cruise I held a passengers' party in my cabin, I had invited Ken and his mother. I really didn't know whether they would appear. However, at precisely 7:30pm on the dot they were the first to arrive. They chose from the variety of tinctures. I was about to chat to Ken's mum when a knock at the cabin door heralded several of the invited. I returned to 'pouring out' while the guests made encouraging party noises. I left them to it. Ken was talking to some guests about the *Carry On* films; they were in stitches.

The dinner gong reminded us, as if we needed reminding, to dine. Ken and his mum were the first to leave, as they had been the first to arrive. I have no doubt that he was as punctual at work as he was on holiday.

* * * *

We were no sooner back from the Christmas break, than we were leaving the streamer ribbons behind us in Southampton. The trip would last 105 days and was the longest ever at that particular time. It would be something of an ordeal for the officers.

We took some of the original Christmas cabaret artists, Joan Regan and pianist Vincent Billington, together with a new group who were booked for the next three weeks. This was an excellent idea; no cabaret act can be expected to work longer than this to the same audience. The idea was they would be repatriated from a convenient airport and three or four would take their place, for the same length of time.

Daytime activities were essential and generally very well supported. Take an artist for example; passengers would bond with them, same as with golf, bowling and keep fit. These experts in their own fields were inclined to stay for longer on such a distance voyage. Hostesses would help out by bringing players together to play Yahtzee and other card games, whilst another would teach crafts.

As for the cabaret artists, we started with Joan Regan, Craig Douglas and Mike and Bernie Winters. We also had Vincent Billington, an accomplished pianist, who was with Max Jaffa's long-time radio show *Grand Hotel*.

Craig Douglas was a delightful fellow. He had had, from 1959 to 1962, seven top ten hit records and was the 'talk of the town'. After this meteoric success, top ten hits eluded him. It was obvious that he never resented the fact. He continued to entertain his many fans and he worked in venues long established for hosting household names.

Craig seemed to live a contented life; work on a luxury liner was not that easy to acquire. Joan Regan, a few years back, was stunning. Even then, in the 1970s, she was still very attractive. In 1955 she performed in a Royal Command Performance, the apex for any performer.

Mike and Bernie Winters, I sensed, were drifting apart as a double act. It was just a feeling. They were thoroughly professional, and their performances were of an extremely high standard. I was touched when Bernie called me 'Boss'. The name remained for the whole cruise.

There was one stopover and I was relaxing in my cabin, feeling a little rundown. The door suggested someone wanted to arouse me. 'Come in,' I said. It was Mike Winters.

'If you're just a bit run down it might be better if you came out and had a breath of fresh air, our treat.'

I took him at his word and did feel better for it. We all went to a bar and after a couple of snifters, I started to feel better. We found a local Chinese and had a meal. Then we wended our way back to the ship, stopping at the local bar, one for the road. I thanked them and hit the deck.

The next morning there came a knock at the door: Mike again.

'I've brought you your tab from last night.'

Their 'favour' cost me just over £20. I thanked him profusely for his kindness! The word 'pusillanimous' came to mind.

Burns Night, 1973

I was standing at the bar with Captain Joe Chapman. We both felt that the evening was going to be a success; I signed for the next round. We had good resident bands and without taking much credit, I had always, since my beginnings, had a resident band leaders' meeting in my office. Here I discussed overtime with them. I had one band who 'filled in' for one cruise. They claimed ninety hours overtime! I tried to offer a compromise, suggesting overtime claims afforded are not ungenerous, and if they claimed close to the figure which is acceptable to head office, we could both get on with our jobs in mutual harmony. This was invariably acceptable to the musicians and enabled both sides to continue with mutual goodwill.

On this night my band was one of the 'residents'. You would not believe how many Scotsmen had come along to celebrate, with their colourful immaculate tartan clothing and all wearing a Sgian Dubh, which had to be handed in to reception on embarkation. This was a security necessity, respected by all concerned and were available for collection after 4pm on the day of the event.

As Captain Joe refilled my glass the band called *The Eightsome Reel*. The floor was packed. I knew one of the revellers, Willie, who was at my passenger table where we dined and was 83 years old. He joined the crowded floor and gave it his all. The band excelled, showing how well they coped with international variety. Willie came towards us. I told him he was exceptional and introduced him to the Captain, who offered him a drink. He declined with thanks, saying he had one at his table waiting for him. It waited. As he turned back (within two or three seconds of leaving us), there was a loud thud as his portly figure hit the deck; he was dead. They moved him so he would be behind a curtain. The rest of the ballroom was in a state of shock. I went on stage and announced the obvious, suggesting we take a twenty-minute break and hoping everyone would stay. I quietly promised the band leader an extra hour of overtime. We did lose a few, which was understandable, but enough people remained, and the evening continued.

Was I callous? Should I have cancelled the rest of the evening? I've never really come to terms with my decision. It's still a moral conundrum 45 years on. And then I wonder if readers doubt my judgement or suggest I'm being insular. What could I do?

At the morning conference the next morning, the Captain turned first to our Surgeon. 'Not an easy one for you doc?' He then turned to me and said, 'Difficult one, fun maker?' I answered as best I could, 'I took a view sir'. The surgeon turned to the Captain (he was not prone to exaggeration), and said, 'He was dead before he hit the ground.'

* * * *

Eric Jolliffe (Australian cartoonist and illustrator) and his wife were regulars on the list of those who travelled on board as 'speciality daytime activities gurus'. Eric was the performer whilst his wife kept him in order. He was a truly wonderful man who I still think of with a special smile.

I am a technophobe (I am writing this book in longhand – involving over 1000 sheets of foolscap). When I was out with friends recently, one called Martyn was checking something on his Apple when Eric just slipped into my mind. I asked Martyn when he had finished if he could look up the name Jolliffe. He found it within two minutes. I discovered all the bits and bobs I already knew, but what was special was that he had lived to be 94. If anyone deserved to live a long life it was Eric. I prayed he had kept his mind.

We first met in 1976. The ship I was on docked in Sydney for five days (opposite the 'nuns in a scrum'). There were very few on board, even for dinner, so formal entertainments were pointless. I introduced myself to Eric and called the waiter over, and we both chose a gin and tonic. We must have been chatting for over an hour; the only break was his insistence to buy me a drink. I tried to tell him my 'on board arrangements', but he waved me away kindly and I demurred.

It was only then that he actually opened up. His story was far more interesting. He had left home when he was 14, and from then on he lived in the Australian bush, surviving for three and a half years. He told of how each day's mission was just to survive until the next. He made his own billycan and lived off roots (if he could find them). He had made his own boomerang, which after six to eight weeks trying gave him his first marsupial kill and the chance of proper food. He had developed an incredible sense of direction, as he had omitted to include a compass in his one bag! If that had happened to me, I'd have run for my life (and most probably would have lost it!) Eric became his own compass. By the time he was fifteen he could trust himself to judge the source of a billabong in three directions within twenty miles.

He talked of his relationship with bushmen, which built up over time, and especially after he bought his first kill to their notice. He managed to communicate with them sufficiently to suggest that they shared the spoils. This all happened very gradually. The time came however, when he yearned for a real home. One thing in particular persuaded him to come back, a character he named 'Salt Bush Bill'. He had created an original cartoon character.

This is as I remember. Some readers might think that Eric was a trifle boastful. In fact he was the most self-effacing character I had ever met. Every mention came across with genuine surprise. He didn't need nor choose to be anything but himself.

At the end of the cruise Eric asked me to join him and his wife for a farewell drink. I asked him to give me ten minutes. I was doing my rounds of the public rooms to assess the 'atmosphere'. I returned content all was well and joined 'famille Jolliffe' for a final noggin.

The first thing Eric did was to give me an original of his *Bushman* drawings, duly signed and framed. I was touched, as he had dedicated it 'To our favourite Pom'. I still have it.

Eric told me that several years back a bar was opened called the Jolliffe in one of the suburbs of Sydney and he was invited to officially open it. He admitted he was something of a curmudgeon, as he pleaded a previous appointment. Mind you, when the time seemed right, he couldn't resist the temptation to take public transport to the Jolliffe and Salt Bush Bill to see for himself. He arrived, had a good look and was pleased. Its best times were evenings. One young lad about eighteen years old turned to Eric and said in a broad Aussie accent, 'Jolly good isn't it!' Eric nodded to him and then the lad said, 'Do you know, the guy who did this is still alive!' Eric turned to him and with a straight face said 'I, for one, am delighted to hear it!'

* * * *

I never met John Cobbold, but I wish I had. He was a one off, or so I'm told. When I was a Samaritan my mother decided to offer time to 'The Friends of the Samaritans'. John Cobbold was the chairman of the group and mother described him as witty, kindly, caring and unceasingly cheerful. It didn't take long to realise he was a man of exquisite manners. I don't think he ever sacked a football manager he had employed. Even the hapless Jackie Milburn, one of the all-time greats who was a Newcastle hero, could not transfer his playing talents to management and decided to resign. (It should be noted that Jackie Milburn set up a youth policy which is still, in part, his lasting contribution.)

One of John Cobbold's memorable statements when interviewed was, 'When we win a match we open a bottle of champagne. When we lose we open two bottles!'

* * * *

When anyone is talking about the late great Sir Bobby Robson you can guarantee it is with respect, affection and real joy. He had come to Ipswich Town FC as their Manager and had a difficult time with battles, which he soon won. He took up the mantle of Sir Alf Ramsay, who had only left Ipswich Town because he was offered the position of England Manager. In Sir Alf Ramsay's heyday in the early 1960s, he had overseen Ipswich as they won the Second Division (1960-61), followed by the First Division (1961-62). That season they scored 100 goals.

This did not go down well with the football hierarchy. One football pundit, Bill Bothwell, had to publicly apologise. He said *on air* after Ipswich Town suffered a 5-0 drubbing that they could still win the division and that the thought appalled him. That was bad enough, but when he said that the game had been played on a mud bath, he really did make a fool of himself. He was obviously ignorant of the fact that Ipswich Town had the best playing club surface in Great Britain. (How the mighty have fallen.)

My Christmas special was The Boys' Book of Football and volumes always had plenty of space dedicated to the FA Cup Final and the Championship, but in the 1962 Christmas edition, Ipswich Town were never mentioned. (I haven't forgotten about Sir Bobby, but I'm on a roll.) It seems unlikely, but there was obvious reluctance to have Ipswich Town in the European Cup. The laws were such that they (this hierarchy), had no say. In the first round we played Floriana, a cottage team, and won 14-1 on aggregate (10-0 at home). When the score got to 8-0 the crowd screamed to give the other side a goal, but it didn't come to pass. (I was there with my father.)

At last back to Bobby. Our first meeting could not have been more exceptional. Who would have thought it would be in Barbados?

This port of call in the Caribbean was a place where we could not always dock. The lifeboats were put into use to ferry the passengers across to the mainland, where all the coaches were ready for the tours they had booked. When all the passengers were shore side the officers could commandeer a spare boat to take us crew ashore. I can remember diving into the warm waters, then swimming to the beach. I did a double take (Kenneth Williams style); it was Bobby Robson! I tried to be polite. 'Mr Robson', I said, and explained that I was from Ipswich and had been a fanatical supporter since the late 1960s. We shook hands, both feeling astonished, I think. He then introduced me to the players. I felt honoured but, I hope, I responded evenly. Bobby said to me that when I was next in Ipswich he would be pleased to show me round the club.

About three months later I was on leave in Ipswich and with some trepidation I phoned ITFC, unsure whether Bobby would remember me.

'Hello Eddie,' he said. He had remembered my name! 'Could you come on a Tuesday morning, because that will give us over an hour before the weekly directors' meeting.'

He was everything anyone would be proud to know. I was shown the changing rooms, the offices, the gym, the directors' box, the trophy cabinet and how the turnstiles worked to provide accurate numbers. I was in my element (like playing bridge, steam locomotives and the books of W. Somerset Maugham). As we were reaching the conclusion he handed me an envelope. 'I'm sure we'll talk again', he said and we shook hands. I opened the envelope. There were four tickets for the directors' box for the next four home matches. For all football fans as fortunate as myself, it is little wonder that Sir Bobby Robson was a great man for all seasons.

Japan

I was extremely fortunate to visit Japan twice, both times for five days. It was at this time I was still learning 'the craft' with Chris Chapman. We docked at Yokohama and minutes later my telephone rang. At the end of the line was Chris. 'Scott? We've just won the bedside bingo!'

I didn't quite understand his statement, but despite our sexual proclivities being opposite, we did enjoy each other's company. As mentioned, I must have must have been in more gay bars than the 'other choice' but Chris always made sure I was in no way uncomfortable.

I fell in love with Japanese food. I'd always enjoyed oriental specialities; Chris dragged me into a 'choice' we would both enjoy, and I was happy to be dragged. The next day – long before I had to acknowledge my agoraphobia – I found, with great confidence, the nearest station to take the Bullet train. This was in 1973, and we were doing 152 mph. It really was a remarkable experience and also to see Kobe. I easily found my way back to the ship and phoned Chris. 'What did you mean when you said we had won the bedside bingo?'.

You may remember that when I had just arrived on board and found my cabin, I was assailed by the Shop Manager, Bar Manager and Entertainments leading hand. Chris took this one a step further. He told me about the ports of call, which for most passengers were a chance to see a new place. Usually however, a half a dozen would disembark having arrived home or ready to change transport for a different direction. Chris used to get the details of those leaving and the next day the programme would have them as bedside bingo winners!

* * * *

In 1977, the Queen's Silver Jubilee, I had written a celebration 'tableau' for the entertainments staff of *SS Arcadia* to enact. They were keen about the idea and they really did a good job. Our efforts were rewarded with a generous response. It happened that *Arcadia* was docked next to the *Royal Yacht Britannia*. They were built simultaneously by John Brown & Company in 1953.

We had the nerve to 'visit' *Britannia* and were allowed on board, as the Queen was absent. We were met by a senior officer, who was very welcoming and took photos of the tableau we had brought with us. 'I'll make sure Her Majesty receives these,' he said. I don't think the Queen ever saw them. I wasn't offered a knighthood!

I had two relationships during this period of my life, each of which lasted over two years. I met Annette in 1976 when I was back on *Arcadia*. She joined as cabaret (singer/harpist) and proved to be a popular performer. As the others left, she started bouncing on my bed. What a host! 'Can I join you?' (She was twenty, I was thirty.) Thus began a two and a half year relationship which was not monogamous. It was turbulent at times and culminated in an all-paid holiday in Sydney for three weeks. Soon after I 'swallowed the anchor'.

I took my stamp album, less my Penny Black. Annette had a brother two years older than her; he and her father were fanatical philatelists. The stamp collection was my way of saying thank you. There were several that were quite valuable. Their eyes lit up and we hardly saw them for the next forty-eight hours.

Annette had an I.Q of 156, I had an I.Q of 140; some way below Mensa Level (148). I felt the difference, especially when we were driving together. Everything I said was corrected. I only had to open my mouth … 'Oh no it isn't.' The frustrating thing was she was probably right. The second thing was not her fault. I found it impossible to make love when I was in her parents' house. I was probably wrong about that as well.

Titanic memories

Towards the end of 1977, the year when I had recently joined the SS Oriana, a passenger I was chatting to noticed an old man shuffling past. She pointed him out and informed me that she had travelled with him several times and that he was an adult survivor of the Titanic disaster, from Staten Island. We parted company and I noticed him sitting in one of the bars. He had just finished his drink and I asked if I could join him; he agreed. 'Scotch?' I asked. He nodded and said thank you. I asked him his name, which was Reuben, and said to him 'I believe you were on the Titanic?' He nodded. I asked if he would tell me about it, and he said he would do his best; after all he was eighty-seven. I decided to take notes of all he said, and hoped I might make, if acceptable, an opportunity for a daytime activity which would be unique. This was his story:

'I was about twenty-one and living in Belfast. My parents had emigrated to New York, Staten I think. They wanted me to join them. I don't remember exactly why I agreed. I don't think I had a good job, so I booked steerage class. I think we sailed in the April. Anyway, I did think I had made the right decision. A few days later in the night I heard a noise, unusually long, and my instincts told me it wasn't normal. As I remember, I sensed it might be right to get myself at the front of the boat [sic].'

He stopped for a while and had a good peg of the whisky. I was happy to wait. He came to life when he was talking of his escape from steerage class.

'I don't know if I was the only one, I shouldn't think so. But for me, it was some instinct for my own survival. I had to keep moving upwards.

'I was on my way up when I heard a deafening hammering. I didn't at that time understand what was causing it. I have since realised it was probably the leading hands battening down the steerage passengers, leaving lifeboat room for 1st and 2nd class passengers only.'

(It is said of *Titanic* that there were nineteen separate things which, if they were to come together, would cause her to sink. And all nineteen did indeed come together.)

NOTE: As I was putting this book to bed a fallacy about the *Titanic* which had been promulgated for a century was exposed. There have been several TV programmes dealing with different aspects of the *Titanic* disaster during this last autumn. Only the penultimate episode included an apologist for steerage passengers. The reporter was likely privy to the episode. This I watched. It has been decided that the two-man submersible was used purely to ascertain details of the steerage class doors. Two miles down on the ocean floor they found what they had been instructed to look for. The filming proved that *every* remaining door was locked. This totally vindicated Reuben's descriptive version during our production in 1977. It proved that everything he had remembered was honest and true. He had fought to get up on deck when he also heard and remembered the battening down. Perhaps he was the only steerage class passenger to survive the *Titanic*.

I bought Reuben a third whisky, which he accepted with alacrity. I noticed by now that he was choosing to talk, and he remembered much. He said his next adventure was moving forward, as he had to cope with the Master at Arms, who was bearing down on him.

'I was young, twenty-one and felt able to cope with him. It was a tough battle, but I nearly heaved him into the ice. I ran and he couldn't keep up with me.'

One thing that amazes me is that White Star only had enough lifeboats on the *Titanic* for about two thirds of their passengers. This would have been of no concern to them. It was the Board of Trade which decided such things. If anybody in authority had some understanding, they should have realised that if they drove into an iceberg there would be a situation where the watertight doors would have been worthwhile. And there need not have been loss of life. Even the plate quality was suspect in freezing conditions.

I asked Reuben if he remembered if the band actually played *Nearer My God to Thee* on the deck.

'I honestly don't know, I was on the other side of the ship

and the noise was so loud that I can't be sure. They might have done. I was thinking more of the lifejacket I didn't have. I also thought about what was happening with the lifeboats. They seemed as if they were being lowered, some less than half full. I even saw a man dressed as a woman so he could get into a lifeboat with the children!'

Reuben had been strong enough to swim, without a life jacket, through the ice-strewn freezing water to the first lifeboat that was 'half empty'. In fact there were eleven or twelve passengers aboard, and they all made sure he was pulled to safety into the boat.

I remember asking Reuben if the band played 'Nearer My God To Thee', as the ship went down. He said that they might done, but that he couldn't confirm it.

I asked him if he could manage one more whisky. He gave me a wicked grin and said, 'Make it a double!' I wish I could write in Bronx, as Reuben's accent added to the poignancy of the occasion.

I also asked him about the possibility of a fire on board when *Titanic* sailed on April 10th. He thought it unlikely and said if the ship had one it would have been well under control, as if it wasn't the ship would have sunk before it saw the iceberg.

Fatal for *Titanic* were the bog-standard iron rivets, of which there were nearly two million. The money saved on the rivets was used for the adornment of the main ballroom. I'm given to believe that order came directly from Bruce Ismay, the owner. When Titanic was sliced down the starboard side by the iceberg, thousands of these second-rate rivets literally popped out. Had they been class 1 rivets, their loss would have been much less, and the collision might not have breached the side of the hull, whatever the quality (or lack of it) of the steel plates.

The reason the ship carried on through the ice field at 23 knots was that the directors of the White Star Line wanted to win the 'Blue Riband', or whatever it was called in 1912, for the fastest crossing. What wonderful publicity to aid an ailing organisation!

Reuben went down with the ship and dragged himself through the icy water to a lifeboat. He said there were no more than six people in it – what a shambles! I did visit the cemetery in Halifax, Nova Scotia years ago, and I can't really describe how I felt; it was such a waste.

SS *Carpathia*, captained by Captain Arthur Rostron, was 58 miles away when she heard the SOS messages. Captain Rostron made sure they made it to the wreck as quickly as possible, taking into account the safety of his own ship. He made it to *Titanic* in just over four hours, having already ordered his crew to make provision of blankets, and of medical care for survivors. The galley had been instructed to provide hot food. All non-essential power was shut down as Rostron pushed his ship to her limits. He was highly praised from all quarters, as were his crew, and was later knighted. He was believed to have saved nearly 500 souls, even though Titanic had sunk three hours before. They included Reuben.

The *Carpathia* was not the nearest ship to the *Titanic* when she went down. Captain Stanley Lord in his ship the *Californian* was only about an hour and a half away. Unlike Captain Smith, Lord had halted his ship because of the ice. He had already instructed his wireless operators to alert other ships in the area to the ice, but the *Titanic*'s duty wireless operator told the operator on the *Californian* to 'shut up'; they ignored his warning.

Later that night, the *Californian* spotted the flares from *Titanic*. But when Captain Lord was awoken, he had already completed a long shift, and had gone to bed. He thought the flares were company rockets, signals between ships of the same line. His wireless operator, following the poor conduct of the *Titanic* operator, had 'shut down for the night', and could not receive the SOS messages. It was only later in the morning, when the office re-opened, that the signals were picked up. By the time the *Californian* reached the scene *Titanic* had sunk, and all that was left were floating bodies and wreckage.

This was all established later at the inquest. Captain Lord was not censored. He was no hero, nor was he a 'villain'. I am inclined to side with the judiciary.

I am an amateur with regard to the *Titanic*, unlike the professionals on the Channel 4 programme. It may be unpalatable, even pompous of this amateur to doubt the veracity of the experts with regard to their belief that the fire on board was the main cause of the sinking.

* * * *

I sensed that Reuben was ready for a rest. I stood him up and returned him to his cabin, but not without telling him that two hostesses would escort him to the public room at 9:45 am.

'Two hostesses?'

'Yes Reuben, don't oversleep.'

I noted his cabin number and went to the print shop to make sure the interview would be in tomorrow's daily programme.

The public room held 400 people; 600 who had wedged themselves in. I was concerned Reuben might be overwhelmed by the occasion, so I used my notes and let him join in at convenient moments. The atmosphere in the room was something I had never experienced and at the end the applause was louder than at all my shows put together.

That evening the Captain had a private cocktail party in his cabin. This comprised of Conference Officers, the guests who sat at his table and about another ten passengers of his choice. A lady beat me to the introductions and said how much she enjoyed my interview with Reuben. She then said, 'It touched a chord because my grandfather was Captain Rostron, the Master of the *Carpathia*, and his ship saved 500 lives'. You couldn't make it up.

CHAPTER 6

BrIDGe, anD oTHer DIversIons

The homeward journey on the *SS Oriana* was destined to be my last. It was my fourth 'trouble shooting' exchange, and I was honoured to be trusted to pick up the pieces. P&O had been incredibly good to me and they had offered a further contract. It was by far the most difficult decision I have ever had to make.

When in reverie, should I, shouldn't I? I look to my three daughters and a marriage that lasted twenty-three years, and say to myself, what could have been? I doubt if I would have married; I might have been wealthy, but how does that compare for a lonely retirement?

There was some talk of me working in head office, but the gentleman I would have worked with died suddenly at fifty-four. There was really no other option. I still have no regrets.

The first thing I did when we docked in Southampton was to follow up a recommendation given to me by one of the passengers. He knew I was a very keen bridge player and gave me his card. He said if I approached the manager of the Eccentric Club in St. James', he might well be interested in making you a member.

'The fact that you play bridge and your involvement in the entertainment business would give you a real opportunity. There are several members who were entertainers. The food is very good, there is a very large bar, the bedrooms are very comfortable (if you want to stay overnight or even longer, you just have to book at reception).'

This seemed ideal for me at that time. I phoned home to let the folks know I was going to stay in London for a few days and promised to keep in touch.

I caught the underground to St. James' and discovered that the Eccentric Club was everything my kind passenger had promised. I went to the reception with his card and met the manager, who wore half-moon glasses. I just did my best to appear personable. He told me the bar was open and handed me a form to fill in. He then put out his hand and I shook it. 'I'll be here until 17:00 hours.'

I went into the bar and ordered a pint of bitter, then looked around for somewhere to sit. A chap invited me over to where he was sitting and there was an empty chair. He introduced himself to me with an outstretched hand: 'Dennis Main Wilson.' 'Eddie Scott,' I said. Dennis produced nearly all Tony Hancock's radio shows. His glass was nearly empty, so I offered him a drink. He had been on bitter but asked for a 'wee dram'. The drinks were so inexpensive, I thought I must get him a double. I asked him if he wanted anything with it.

He said, 'Just water please, half and half.' He thanked me and we talked of Hancock.

It got to about half past four and I excused myself, saying I had to fill in a membership form. We shook hands again, mutually agreeing that we would enjoy a further get together in due course. I took my form to the manager who read it through. He asked me a few questions and with hand outstretched welcomed me to the Eccentric.

* * * *

At my first passenger dining table on *SS Iberia*, I found a variety of personalities. The gentleman on my left was delightful and had been Headmaster at Repton, that esteemed public school in the north of England. There was also a lovely lady travelling alone who was in love with gin. Every night, at least twenty minutes late, she swayed towards the table with an enormous tumbler of it. Slopping it all over the place, until a fellow table member relieved her of it and placed it to her right to protect her from knocking it over.

She suddenly regaled us thus: 'I don't drink much, two at the most. Three I'm under the table, four I'm under the host!' She was about seventy. Following a further sashay to the table, she informed us, 'I'd completely forgotten his name; it came to me when I was taking my knickers off!'

I was very fortunate in friendships forged in Sydney, Australia, to the extent that I spent nearly two years there, mostly on leave, with people whose company I enjoyed. On one of my leaves I was able to take advantage of international cricket, my favourite sport (as mentioned earlier). I thoroughly enjoyed the atmosphere of the Sydney Cricket Ground, watching both Test cricket and a fifty over day match, which was in its infancy.

I was well aware that England were up against it. This was an extremely strong Australian side. They won the 50-over game comfortably. Geoffrey Boycott wasn't the only one who found it difficult to adjust. We were also struggling in the Test Match until Derek Underwood played a good hand for 43. Ian Botham came in and was quickly out for 0. It was the first and last time I saw him bat! Derek Pringle scored over 20 when he was adjudged caught.

All this time England's David Gower had kept his end up and was 80 not out. In came Bob Willis, who was the last man in. He wasn't the best batsman in the world, but he could hang about, and he did so until Gower was 98 not out. Willis was caught at slip. He fell on his knees and didn't move. Gower had put his bat under his arm and arrived at the pavilion gates before Willis had got to his feet.

What a difference in outlook and personality. They played in many tests seemingly together in total harmony.

On my next cruise before we left Hong Kong, the entertainments staff did the usual things; welcoming people on board, doing our best to be helpful and finding directions for 'lost souls'.

At 8pm that first evening, I gave the passengers an introduction to the cruise staff. At the end I always remembered to assure them that they would be welcome to join in as many activities as they liked. For the people who didn't choose the programmed events, none of us would try to get them involved. We were not a holiday camp!

I completed my 'chat' and to polite applause I left the stage. I then introduced myself and chatted generally on a one to one (or two) basis. On this evening I met a gentleman who I assumed was travelling alone. We shook hands and he said he was sure he would be one of the latter ones. He said (with a twinkling eye), 'Shan't see you until we disembark.'

I didn't think too much about it or mention his' needs' to the staff on board. They knew well enough that you didn't corral passengers.

In early '78 I met Chrissy. I had seen her briefly in 1969, on that night when Clive and Myrtle (now Caroline) invited me that evening when I played my first hand of bridge. She was twelve. I met her and Caroline when they were in Los Angeles (they lived in Fresno), having emigrated to California. We were together for over two years. I naively didn't realise for a long time that she was a drug addict. I was sad when the relationship came to an end, but it may well have been for the best for both of us.

* * * *

It was whilst I was Cruise Director on SS *Canberra* that I visited Madeira for the first time. It really is special. Its colours, aromas, temperatures, Reid's Palace, restaurants of wonder and even sledge riding.

My team recommended a particular eatery. They had been before; I hadn't, so it was easy to fall in with their ideas. (I certainly did not play politics ashore.) Vegans look away; vegetarians might remember that no one criticises their choices. It was roast suckling pig. I had never tasted anything so exquisite. I'm not sure though that I would choose that now.

The next five visits were a washout. It was always touch and go if we could dock. We had a second chance, using the

lifeboats, but that depended on calm waters. The Captain
on one of these aborted efforts could see that no passengers
could have survived, if they had been allowed to attempt
the impossible. There's always one! While 1199 passengers,
however disappointed, appreciated the Captain's efforts before
he reluctantly had to abort, there was always one moaner who
thinks he should have found another way.

Eventually, two or three years ago, I was acting as Bridge
Director. I was alone and much work was demanded. The day
the ship was going through the Panama Canal (a wonderful
visual experience), I was still asked to run the bridge. There
was one passenger in the morning and one in the afternoon!
There were usually 72 for bridge. I retired soon after that and
decided I would like a cruise with no responsibilities.

We were due to dock in Madeira. I booked Reid's Palace
for afternoon tea. The weather was gorgeous, the seas calm
and Reid's overlooking the bay was sumptuous.

* * * *

In early 1976 I was Cruise Director on SS *Arcadia* when the
Captain had one of those situations when he was damned if
he did and damned if he didn't. Even after all efforts to avoid
it, the ship was suddenly trapped in the middle of the Atlantic
in a hurricane, force 12.

The first thing for the Captain to do in this situation is 'hove
to'. This involves placing the ship in the face of the winds. I
would have thought it should have been the other way. They
decided I would not be left to scupper the whole fleet! The
next crucial thing the Captain had to do, quickly, was to check
his manifest. This showed him areas of weakness in the ship

in the worst possible weather conditions. There was one: B Deck midships. The cabin was the temporary 'holiday home' of a Mr and Mrs Noble. It was the Captain who now had the further responsibility of evacuating the Nobles. I happened to be on B Deck when suddenly there was a bang like I had never known before. The Nobles did not have a porthole. Instead on their portside they now had two enormous oblong windows. I had to see the damage. If the Nobles had still been in their cabin, they would have been cut to pieces!

We were hove to for five hours. I looked out at the area of carnage and saw that a sixty-foot wave had moved the inch-thick steel to an angle of 45%. When the Captain was sure the hurricane had subdued, he reset the course. The dear old *Arcadia* caught up three and a half hours and the Nobles survived for future cruises. And for the Captain? All in a day's work.

* * * *

I was at a lunchtime party when a gentleman to whom I had been teaching bridge introduced me to his wife. We chatted for a while, then he said she was looking for a public speaker. She told me her organisation was similar to the Women's Institute and had large numbers of enthusiastic members, people who realised they had been fortunate in life and felt they could give something back.

I told her I had spent much of my working life as a front man and would be pleased to offer my services 'gratis'. She protested. I insisted!

At this stage of my life I still had my joke books, a fortunate life to admit to and reasonable confidence. I did three talks, all different – and all ended in abject failure. After all, I had over the years been a useful comedian/impressionist, yet whenever I tried a 'funny' it was like the South Liverpool FC gig all over again. I make no excuses. It seemed after dinner speaking was not for me, and apparently not for them. I am grateful for my 'gratis' arrangement. I don't think I could have lived with the guilt if I had charged for my 'work'.

Bridge, the great of all card games

I left out two important features of daytime on board. First, I will introduce you to my favourite Bridge director, Nico Gardener. He was of Russian extraction. A Grand Master, he had won every honour, not to mention aspiring to be World Champion in 1960.

Bridge is the greatest of all card games. It commands a large room on every ship I have ever sailed on. I should say that it isn't everyone's cup of tea, but is not as difficult as some folks think. If you don't like card games there are many others you might shine in; Scrabble comes to mind.

On this world voyage, Nico was doing the complete trip. His typical day consisted of a Beginner's Course lecture from 10am to 11am and an Improver's from 11am to 12pm. After lunch at 2pm he organised 'duplicate bridge'. This simply means that every couple will eventually have played all the same cards with different opponents. If that seems complicated, it took me nearly twenty minutes to write it.

After dinner Nico would go to his room for the third session, where he organised the group into fours (usually 24 or 28), so they could play social bridge. Nico, about once a week, came to my room just for a chat and to keep up to date about how things were going. This was usually at 12:10pm, when he had finished his second lecture.

One day mid voyage, he came in with the story of the morning. A man playing with his wife had let forth a tirade of abuse at her until the tears flooded. One of the lady's opponents said quietly and kindly, 'You shouldn't let him talk to you like that.'

The tears subsided. 'You mind your business! If my husband wants to talk to me like that, he bloody well can!'

Finally, I must not forget our dance couple. I thought they were excellent, and this goes with many cruises in the past which would always find a high standard. It was invariably a married couple who had a good CV. They always seemed to be really enjoying what they were doing. I watched them on many occasions and praised their patience.

Many adults love to dance, be it Old Time, Modern, Latin American or others. Some pick up on the teaching quickly, others take longer. The tutors never seemed to show frustration. Their main aim is to get the individuals as far as they are capable. When they've finished teaching a particular dance, they don't make themselves small. They will have already worked out those who do not have a partner and have come alone to the class. These people will then be asked to dance with one or other of their tutors and are made to feel like pools winners. It really does lift them as they might not have expected.

In my earlier days as Entertainment Officer we were docked in Southampton, with still three hours or so before we sailed. It must have been late 1972. Ronnie Owen, my mentor, found out I was on board and decided to look in. Simultaneously, one Len Rooker, who was the pianist on the RMS *Pendennis*

Castle, still had two days of leave before sailing. They both found me. In fact, they were, timewise, exact and had been chatting as they aimed for me.

I was thrilled to see them both. Ronnie looked in very good form. I offered him a Coke, saying this was the cheapest. I sidestepped as he made for me and nearly joined the bed! They settled for large whiskies, using the excuse that no man should pour drinks and not have one himself.

There was so much to talk about. I had officially introduced Len to Ronnie; I needn't have. They had so much in common, me in part. Ronnie was in great form, but Len was noticeably not quite the man I had known six years before. I tried to bring him into the conversation, but suddenly he would say things that were totally incongruous. Ron and I tried to ignore it.

The loudspeaker started to encourage those not sailing to remove themselves and Ron offered to escort Len off. I shook hands with Len and wished him good luck. I noticed that he had spittle on his cheeks. I didn't think much of it as I had another problem to cope with. Apparently, Len kept getting lost and Ron only just had time to leave him in the care of a leading hand. The gangways were hoisted, with Ron still on board. He got through to the Captain and apologised profusely. He was requested to attend the bridge and instructed to go down with the pilot boat and got back to Sydney. I felt sorry for him, he'd done his best.

* * * *

One of my happier times, despite suffering clinical depression from time to time (which responded to medication), was in the early part of '73. I was Entertainments Officer on the SS

Arcadia. At the time the ship was due to sail on a sixty-day cruise from Australia.

I met Marie early on in the cruise, in fact just after she embarked at Melbourne. She was twenty, and for me it was love at first sight. We spent as much time together as possible. She had a boyfriend in Melbourne to whom she was engaged, but she had insisted on taking this trip to see as much of the world as possible before settling down.

My most wonderful experience with her was when we booked a junk (motorised) from Hong Kong harbour to Aberdeen. Aberdeen was the home of many junks where people, including Buddhists, lived their lives from day to day. You could feel the karma, despite not being a part of it. After twenty minutes or so it was time to drag ourselves from this extraordinary magnet.

We still hadn't finished our wonderful trip. As part of the excursion we were booked into a floating Chinese restaurant. (Despite being the only ones on this particular trip, the drinks were free, and I at least took full advantage!) We were given a pair of plastic chopsticks as a token of their best wishes.

The only thing that didn't quite work for us was Marie and her chopsticks. I'm not very good with them myself, but I could muddle through. Marie had us both in stitches, as after ten minutes she still hadn't managed to get hold of anything. I called the waiter and asked if the lady could have a plastic knife and fork. They duly provided. What a wonderful, unforgettable evening.

* * * *

The final chapters of my 'ramblings' include one of the most memorable. We were sailing on *Arcadia*, because an unusual cruise had been considered viable. It was for six weeks, the two in the middle being reserved for the ship to have a much-needed and expensive overhaul. (The fact was that another eighteen months would take her to twenty-five years of service; a long life for a cruise ship built in the fifties.) It was prudent to nurture her and avoid a full refit, which would not have been financially viable.

Passengers had been given plenty of options regarding this 'rogue period'. P&O had really done their homework, and attractive alternatives included luxury hotel stays, shore excursions, casinos, cabaret, specialist native dancers and of course golf. Their choices were manifold. But what to do with the entertainments department?

We all worked hard during the three days of organising the passengers and felt we had put in a good shift. There was a suggestion of banter, especially from the deck department and the engineers; it was good hearted.

I had done my own homework for the break and decided to travel on the Indian Pacific Railway from Sydney to Perth. This journey was approximately 2,700 miles! I had done some packing in advance, so embarkation was without stress. My steward led me to my cabinette and pointed out the bell which would summon him. He was both friendly and respectful. A brief ring of a different bell heralded important news; the bar was open. Evening dress had been advertised as optional, so I thought I would give it a chance.

The bar took up one carriage, as did the restaurant. The atmosphere was 'family friendly', despite the lack of children. It was time to mingle.

As I had a brief period whilst waiting to order, I looked around me and kept seeing familiar faces. Before I could ponder a new a couple came towards me, introducing themselves as Joy and Alan. 'It's Eddie Scott from Arcadia isn't it?' I smiled warmly and we shook hands. It transpired that twenty-four other passengers were choosing this journey as their special excursion.

We were soon herded towards the next carriage, which was our restaurant. It was superbly laid out and I doubt any traveller would have it in their minds to count the calories. Another couple approached me at the time coffee was being served to 'refillers'. The gentleman, with a total lack of presumption, asked me if between us we could 'provide an informal sing-along like your pub night on the Arcadia?'. He was almost apologetic when he said he could play the piano a little if no one else could. I grabbed him, saying 'Yes'. Experience has shown me that such humility will always pay dividends. We had a lovely evening, sharing with the resident pianist – a perfect balance.

The next evening, everything just fell into place. One of the most interesting travellers, outside our group, was unable to fly. He was a renowned toy inventor, established throughout Southern Australia. He made good value of the 'iron road'. He called me over to his table and told me that the Locomotive Manager was waiting for me to approach him. A knowing wink was enough to encourage me.

I knocked on the Locomotive Manager's door and I was called in. He said to me, 'We have a first-class cabinette not in use and I watched you last night and the way you and our resident pianist knitted together. You achieved a very good evening's entertainment. Now about this first-class cabinette, would you like me to instruct your steward to move you?' I thanked him profusely and he told he would hold it for me for the trip back.

This surprised me. How did he know I was taking the journey back? It transpired he'd had a longer chat with my toy inventor friend; I'd told *him*.

I was ready to leave when the manager said, 'Are you up for it tonight?' I nodded. 'Do you perform Opera?' His expression was neutral. 'Wagner or maybe Verdi or Borodin?'

He got the desired effect. He kept a straight face, I dissolved.

* * * *

One thing I haven't talked about yet were the scenic views. There weren't any! Our journey took us through a desert void. And yet, this was its very fascination. This area of Australia is known as Nullarbor, which translates as 'no trees'. Strange as it may seem, every one hundred and fifty miles or so was a group of six dwellings on both sides of the track. They were basic but quite large. I discovered they were offered to criminals as a choice between working on railroad maintenance or completing their sentence inside the penitentiary. They had to work eight hours a day, six days a week. Provisions were dropped off every week by a passenger train like ours. A family could choose between togetherness or separation (wife/ partner, not children for many obvious reasons). Remission could be earned if the railway inspectors gave a favourable report. I gained most of this information from my inventor friend. There wasn't much of that enormous distance he didn't know about.

We did have stop-offs along the way, though I can't remember many after so long. But I do have fond memories of Adelaide at night and most of all – Broken Hill. I even persuaded a fellow passenger to take a photograph of me with my hands on the sign. (Don't we do some ridiculous things at times!) Once the excitement of seeing six houses in a row had passed, we settled back into the desert for the next one hundred and fifty miles.

After dinner that night I told our pianist about the Train Manager's request for opera. His response was the same as mine, but he did say he could play something from Borodin's *Prince Igor*. I had it in a pack of four vinyl records and said I could 'operate' (ouch) a few verses, 'Let's catch him on his rounds'. We duly did this; he took it in good heart.

And so we continued until journey's end, and I enjoyed every moment immensely. I had always enjoyed rail travel and this was as good as it gets. The Indian Pacific locomotive glided majestically into Perth and one by one the passengers disembarked, leaving their best wishes, handshakes and 'see you back on the ship Eddie'. I wished my inventor friend all the best and then shook hands with the Train Manager. He said it had been lively having me on board. I thanked him for his kind gesture and told him I'd see him in the evening for the journey back. 'Saints preserve us, will no one free me from this turbulent compere!' he said.

I was last to alight. I made it to the exit, hailed a tax and asked to be taken to the address I gave him. This was not prearranged; there was no certainty that Mike would be in. On arrival I asked the taxi driver to wait, in case I needed to make other plans. I did, and it so happened I needed a haircut, so I asked him to take me to the best barber in town. Following the snip job I spent an enjoyable afternoon walking around the parts of Perth I had time for. What a lovely city, so fresh and clean. The residents should have been proud of themselves.

I returned to the railway station in good time and joined

the train. Once I was settled back into my spacious cabinette, I wended my way to the piano bar and ordered a heart starter. Several other passengers had the same idea, and looking around I thought there were some familiar faces. 'Hello Eddie' rang in my ears and I realised this group included those who had flown directly to Perth after disembarkation; some to visit family and friends for a couple of days, others to join a variety of shore excursions, sightseeing etc. For them it was back to Sydney on the Indian Pacific.

I had my first class cabinette. I spoke to the resident pianist to be sure we were not intruding, and he assured me we were not. Again we had a sing-along thanks to a different passenger who tickled the ivories. I enjoyed the return journey just as much as the outward. The atmosphere was jolly and friendly. We hardly noticed those houses for convicts.

Soon we were back in Sydney, disembarked from the Indian Pacific and reimbarked on a fresh-looking *Arcadia*. We were soon re-established at sea with a busy fortnight in front of us.

I have been asked by several people about the distinction between a voyage and a cruise. It became apparent in the early '70s that there were other people wanting to go afloat apart from retired bankers, generals, colonels, insurance magnates, owners of movie houses, bishops and above, lords, ladies and gentlemen.

In the 1920s, '30s, '40s and '50s , even successful businessmen had to work hard to go voyaging. There wasn't a plethora of inherited wealth. From the mid-sixties this was turned upside down. By the time I joined P&O in the early '70s, voyaging was of the past and no longer financially viable. There were many modern magnates who would look forward to a two-week cruise, maybe two in a year. The standard of entertainment for the majority was just as important as the quality of the food – a complete volte-face compared with little more than a decade past.

The world voyage still keeps its name. About two or three of the largest shipping companies leave port around the second week in January and return home after about 100 days.

The Beautiful Game

As mentioned previously, I was a keen Ipswich Town FC supporter in the glory years of 1960 to 1982. Following them was a wonderful experience, as trophy after trophy found their way into the esteemed cabinet in the Director's hideaway. In 1960-61 they were 2nd Division Champions, 1961-62 1st Division Champions. Many will remember with pride how 'insignificant Ipswich' felt when their beloved manager Alf Ramsey was appointed Manager of England. Who of us over sixty will ever forget England becoming football World Cup Champions?

After a few quieter years when Ipswich (relegated after three seasons in the 1st Division) trod water, Bobby Robson came to Ipswich and after a few fractious weeks, established himself as a worthy successor to Sir Alf Ramsey. He would in his time emulate the great man by his outstanding contribution to Ipswich and becoming Manager of England.

In Robson's day Ipswich had a great side, despite the lack of money. He felt the team needed one more facet. In an astute move he approached a strong Dutch side, FC Twente, and found two players who were out of contract. He interviewed them (he had already seen them play) and considered that they both had great skills. Their names were Arnold Muhren and Frans Thyssen. They completed the jigsaw and it was all systems go.

During those days of the mid '70s, Ipswich Town team were regularly in the top five. They did everything (including reaching the second spot) but actually win the Championship. I think Bobby Robson certainly felt with more money to spend they would have been able to cover injury problems. The substitutes bench was never quite so endowed as the first eleven.

This brings us to 1978 and my last trouble shoot on SS *Oriana*. The Cruise Director, Billy Maine, had had problems and was booked to return to England in the next day or two. I was flown to Hawaii to take over for the last six weeks of the *Oriana*'s cruising season.

The day before, Billy had spent the whole morning overseeing an aerial photograph of himself in front of the entire entertainments staff of fifty-five. It was quite spectacular, and I rather wished it could have been me in the front.

The FA Cup in 1978, which had first been played over 100 years before, was in full flow and as the minnows fell by the wayside, the usual top names homed in on the semi-finals. This small group, for the first time in its history, included Ipswich Town. They were destined to win the semi, which put them in the final against Arsenal.

I was marooned in the erstwhile Crown Colony of Nassau. I tried to work out times of flights from Nassau so I could return immediately after the match, but it was nearly two hours out. The Captain did not take kindly to recalcitrant Entertainment Directors holding up the ship!

So instead it was the World Service Radio at noon (we were three hours ahead of GMT). My deputy and number three were football fanatics, one a Leeds supporter, the other Liverpool. But on this day, they were staunchly behind Ipswich. It was a great clean match and became known as the friendly final.

What a heart stopper! During a short period in the first half, Johnnie Wark smashed the ball against the post twice and Paul Mariner hit the bar. I thought Town would never score. They left it late, whilst denying Arsenal many chances. Then in the 78th minute a ball, deep into the Arsenal penalty area was partially cleared. It landed at the feet of Roger Osbourne and he steered it into the net. The three of us cheered louder than Wembley!

I poured us a drink and reminisced. I really don't mean it, but at times I can be negative. All I could think of throughout the match were those posts and crossbar. I felt we were destined not to score. My colleagues buoyed me up. A funny way to celebrate Ipswich Town, but equally memorable.

On a sad note, Roger Osbourne was a country boy and a fine player who was a regular first team player. The effect of scoring that goal led, within seconds, to a collapse. He was brought round with smelling salts and was immediately substituted. He only played 45 minutes more for Ipswich, coming on at half-time because of an injury to another player and ending his career as a part-time professional.

I had arranged for that evening a cabin party of officers and passengers. It was either going to be a celebration or a wake. I've said before how supportive our stewards and leading hands were. They just needed to feel a part of the team, and were only ever difficult if they were treated badly. Each man should have respect.

I was never really turned on to decorating. I used to see our leading hands Ted and Mack for the theme nights and briefly but regularly, I would check that they were all right and had everything they required. It was a large part of their working day. They knew they only had to ask.

Ted, like surgeon Ross Wheatly (Alice's House), had a short but perfect contribution to pub night. He could play the spoons very well. Like Ross, Ted was always appreciated. He would first fill his mouth with peanuts, somehow holding them there. He would then get to work playing the spoons; I can't remember how many different surfaces he hit. Finally, he played the spoons really hard on his teeth whilst firing the peanuts from his mouth. The effect brought a roar from the audience. They really did look like his teeth!

Ted and Mack did not forget as I forgot. In my absence after the Cup Final they came to my cabin and festooned it in blue and white (Ipswich Town colours). They had started it in the aisle which led to my cabin. This was not any old offering, it was stunning. I went up to their cubby hole and told them so, and as an afterthought invited them to the party. It was a great success with 'Barman John' and my steward dispensing drinks adroitly. I wasn't at the match, but my goodness I don't half have wonderful memories of the day.

Towards the end of the party I saw my Goanese steward outside the door. He was crying, as he'd heard I was leaving. I wasn't alone in this as many officers had had the same experience.

Sailing into danger

In the eight weeks before my journey's end on SS *Oriana* in Southampton, we had two frights. Many sailors would see out their careers having never had these experiences.

My deputy and I were doing the count from a casino night which had finished half an hour before. We had just completed the tables, which as usual were manned by crew members. All were senior crew and knew what was required. Not for the first time, all the gambling tables had secured a profit (albeit small). I don't remember in my seven years at sea a single complaint from passengers regarding doubtful payouts.

We were suddenly aware of the ship's horn. I counted seven short blasts, which was followed by one long blast. Andrew (deputy) said, 'It's probably a practice.'

'They don't practise emergencies at nearly midnight'. I said. 'Get your lifejacket, I've got mine, I'm off!'

He followed me and we encountered masses of passengers charging to their emergency stations. We were there to direct, help with lifejackets and reassure. After about twenty minutes the Captain came on the blower to say, 'Emergency over; chip fat fryer fire extinguished (It was hard enough to write, let alone say) in twelve minutes. Thank you for all your forbearance. You may all return to your cabins. On behalf of all the crew, sleep well and see you tomorrow.'

It was a close thing. Had the fire not been extinguished after twenty minutes, the ship would have been lost.

Three weeks later in mid-ocean I had a summons from Captain P Jackson. He was there days into his first tenure at the 'top'. His voice was so serious I thought I might have committed some heinous crime for which I was to be discharged, or that one of my parents had died. As I entered the lift, the presence of most of the other conference officers reassured me. The new Captain's demeanour had rather put them on the back foot. We were soon to appreciate the gravity of the situation. The Captain informed us that the Home

Office had ostensibly received a death threat from the IRA. It had been graded by the experts as a 50% chance that there was a bomb on board. If so it would be detonated at 18:00hrs. No wonder the Captain had sounded serious.

We were all told what was expected of our departments. Entertainments were to search every locker in every public room; a prodigious labour! It was now noon and the emergency programme was to begin at 12:30pm with the warning calls.

The passengers were not called to stations at this time but to the public rooms (with their lifejackets). I had thirty of the entertainment staff on the lockers – apart from the bands – and I told them that their best support would be playing for the passengers. There were three bands and two pianists, which largely covered the public rooms required. I called the band leaders over and said to them, 'If we survive this, I can promise you extra overtime!'

I remember well how stoical the passengers were during such life-threatening circumstances. We even had three Hercules bombers flying just above us, sent by Prime Minister Callaghan. I never found out why.

As the ship's clock moved to 17:55 there was a stir and not surprisingly an atmosphere of fear. The ship's bell rang out 18:00 and then 18:01 and 18:02. There was a wave of relief. Captain Jackson came on the blower to thank the passengers for their exceptional fortitude in such circumstances and told them to remain where they were until 18:10hrs before returning to their cabins. 'I trust we will all have a thoroughly enjoyable evening,' he remarked.

The moment I walked back into my cabin the telephone rang. It was our Captain.

'Eddie a big thank you to all your team, bring yourself up for a drink at 7pm.'

'Thank you sir, though I think the plaudits are yours.'

'Are you after my job?'

'No sir, I'd hit an iceberg in the Pacific!'

On behalf of us all, the Purser was deputed to speak. He was humorously loquacious, but the deep respect was never far away. He spoke for us all. Three cheers hit the deck head!

In conclusion, when it was time to say farewell to cruising, there were so many remarkable memories. Most I have already shared with you. I don't remember how many times I crossed the International Dateline, but rest assured I was fodder for officers, crew, leading hands and passengers. I was spirited to the pool by a chosen 'press gang' who unceremoniously tossed me in the pool (clothes and all). The smile was still there; it had to be.

An adjusted 'Mussel Shoot' caused me to be stripped in the ballroom. Having organised this event I was wearing red shorts and a yellow T-shirt.

My final cruising memory is not about me (hooray, you say). As officers at sea we were expected to attend the call to our emergency stations once a week. A newcomer, third officer, was parading up and down like some royal potentate when he fixed his eyes on the Johnnie Graham Trio: 'Get back to your quarters and get your headgear, quick march!' he shouted. All three saluted to him and moved off Wilson, Keppel and Betty style (sand dancing). They returned, all wearing minute elasticated party hats. It had to be seen to be really appreciated but just imagine, Joe (bass player) 6'2' with a Robin Hood hat, Harry Graham 5'7' sporting a policeman's hat and Martin (drums) 6'3' as a nurse. Our third officer turned scarlet and struck dumb. Somehow the band managed to keep straight faces! The rest of us couldn't.

The days went by and all too soon we were back in Southampton, I took the train to Liverpool Street and from there a train to Ipswich. I didn't look back.

CHAPTER 7

walk-on work

People often ask if I would have liked to have been an actor. The answer is always the same: negative. For one, I would never be good enough. The standard required is so high I'd be reaching out forever for the grapes of Tantalus.

On one occasion I was asked if I would do a Scottish training film with regard to the fire services carrying dangerous chemicals. There was the Senior Fireman, me (very junior) and a chap who was driving a unit police car. We were to be paid £100 each. It so happened that the Senior Fireman had not even bothered to learn his lines. The driver of the police car managed on his first take to crash the car into the fire engine! It took nineteen takes (number sixteen was my fault; I missed a cue).

This started as an aerial shot coming back to earth behind us, so there was not much room for manoeuvre. To cap things off my fellow fireman, at the eventual end, went and shook hands with the Director and said he looked forward to the next time they 'worked together'. I wonder why he never throttled him. The upshot was I ended up the only one who pocketed £100. (This sounds a bit defensive. I only had five or six lines but I'd worked on them and the Scottish accent the whole week before. I got away with it, that's all.)

In my first season at Holimarine Holidays I was approached by a Norfolk agency. They knew I was an Equity member (good luck again) and enquired if I would be interested in television walk-on work. I was delighted to affirm and told the agent I was booked for a season at Holimarine, but had a day off which could, if necessary, be adjusted. I was asked if I could make myself available on the coming Thursday. My luck was holding; it was my day off. The agency directed me to the Swan Hotel in Southwold to book in at 8am. Having always been a stickler for time I arrived at 7:50am and was 'ticked in' and fussed over. Although I didn't meet Wendy Craig (it was a programme called *Nanny* which she starred in before *Butterflies*, set in the 1930s) I met others. Patrick Troughton (Dr Who and many other starring parts) noticed me listening intently to my small radio. He came over to me and asked if I was listening to the Test Match. I was able to give him up to date scores during the day when I wasn't in the bar!

I was called to go to room 108, which had been appropriated by the hairdressers and makeup teams. My hair was rather long and the shot I was going to star in was based in the 1930s, an era of 'short back and sides'. Make-up decided I needed a slight 'browning' for the scene in the sun.

This was great fun; I loved the attention and it was a bit of a let-down when they finished with me (The actor John

Shrapnel was in makeup while I was being moulded.) He was very chatty and circumstances were such that I happened to be on location with him several more times. It was always the same routine – 'Oh Eddie not you again!' said with a smile.

I arrived back at the muster point to see lunch being set up. What a sumptuous feast was laid out before us. The salmon must have won top prizes for the person who not only hooked it but managed to land it.

I was woken from my recovery by one of the locations assistant managers. She was kindly and said, 'This is your first experience isn't it?' I nodded, and she told me that when lunch was called, the principal actors were allowed to start at the front, because they were likely to be on call first. She looked at my locks and said, 'Samson you will never be! The bar is open and Southwold Bitter will give you strength.' She smiled and told me to come back in three quarters of an hour. This would give time to enjoy the BBC provender, and my appearance would be at about 4pm. I thanked her and resisted the temptation to salute.

I walked into the bar and ordered a pint of Southwold Bitter. There were three gentlemen in the bar, and I wished them a good afternoon. They had, it seemed, taken for granted that I was a part of 'Thespians United'. There was something about them which convinced me I was not in the company of any 'hoi polloi'. I was so convinced that I was about to say so when an order to the bar steward heralded another pint coming my way. They were really enjoying this. Enough was enough. I blurted out, 'I don't know in which discipline but I'll bet between you you are something very important'. When you work with people you begin to recognise the types who, when they unnecessarily make an inaccurate statement, will be unaware of the unlocked door they have reproduced.

I deserved to have the pint they had kindly provided poured over my head. But their reactions were fascinating. They didn't even join readily with the verbals.

'You're right' one of them said. 'Spill the beans, where did you find this philosophy?' I told them I'd been a foot soldier in the Samaritans. They came clean. One was John Lill, considered the greatest exponent of Beethoven's piano opi in the world.

Just before I left for a slice of salmon, I shook hands with the trio and told them I was honoured to have met them. John asked for my address, saying he would like to send me a copy of his latest recording. I promised to send a copy of my first book of poetry – 1978. We stayed in contact for at least two years.

I returned for lunch, which was sumptuous. Much of that delightful salmon had been consumed, but there was still plenty left. Nobody had been greedy.

At the end of the 80s the 'closed shop' wasn't the flavour of the month. Extras/walk-ons no longer had to be members of Equity. There was a milkman, a sandwich seller, a homeopath, a hospital worker and a cobbler. If that isn't exact, it's not far off. The food was sometimes being scoffed before it had been laid out...) But I digress. I was released at 5pm. The lady was very sweet and said they all looked forward to seeing me on location again soon.

All that was left was to bring the family round for the evening on the night my episode was to be aired. We watched the whole programme from start to finish....

There was no Eddie.

You will have heard the phrase 'the cutting room floor'. That's where I'd ended up.

I was not persuaded not to try again and the next call from the agent sent me to Weybourne Station in North Norfolk. The programme was *The Burston Rebellion*. It was set towards the end of 1914 and was about a school which had rebelled against its governors. The standoff lasted for over 25 years. John Shrapnel was on location but not, I'm sure to his enormous relief, at the station. He had the principal role of Head of Governors. It was harrowing, but he was superb.

I was cast as a porter on the station platform and was given the appropriate uniform. It was after the first rehearsal that the Director said to me that he would like a link with the first take. He asked me to say, 'Have you heard the news sir?' And after being ignored by the principal, Bernard Hill, to just say 'I only asked'. I was delighted. It wasn't cut and seemed okay.

The Director then asked me to join the train which was coming into Weybourne Station and shout 'Diss Station!' (the rebellion was there), which was difficult because the two words sound like one. I did as bid and the Director nodded. That was enough.

I returned home in my small car, pleased with the way the day had gone. And watched, in due course, my efforts when the programme was transmitted.

As previously mentioned, I had been under deep mental depression, which was exacerbated with my doctor's diagnosis of ME. I had experienced the worst, and honestly the most negative season since I had been a Butlin Redcoat; and that was okay at least. The only positive that came out of Gunton Hall was the money, which helped me cope with a massive tax bill.

At my lowest ebb I had a call from the Norfolk agency,

asking if I could do four days in North Nottingham with more days likely. I jumped at the opportunity. It was just after my first daughter's entrance into this doubtful world. I held her when she was less than two minutes old. I would swear she looked me straight in the eye and said something like 'oh well'. I fell in love with her there and then.

The extra/walk-on work took all the pressure away and eased my mind. I arrived at Ollerton in the midst of the miners' strike. The weather was appalling and to describe it as dank would be kindly. The star was Dyan Cannon, ex-wife of Cary Grant. She had her own personal caravan, which was the size of a penthouse. She spent hour after hour making herself unpopular yet giving the impression she didn't have the brains of a rocking horse! The final 'finished article' was a disaster. (This may sound heartless, but it was cathartic. I needed that more than she did.)

On location I learned a great deal of the 'disciplines' I had never been good enough to be a part of. I was lucky enough to be offered some linking – that was challenging enough!

Whilst on location in Nottinghamshire, I met three people who were from London. They told me that the more agents you had, the more work you got. This was full-time employment for many of us. The agents didn't mind, as the more they had on their books the better. Telephone numbers and addresses tumbled in my direction, and as soon as I returned home I made contact.

One of the earliest was *Only Fools and Horses*. The scene was set in a Catholic Church. It has a statue of the Virgin Mary, who suddenly starts having tears seemingly issuing from her eyes. Del Boy thinks he could become a 'miyionaire', selling phials of the tears to the public. There were eight of us on location – principles, David Jason and Nicholas Lyndhurst and six of us walk-ons, booked as 'walk-on 3'. 'Walk-on 3' was next, in the pay structure, to a booked actor. When I started, basic pay was £36. An example being in a pub scene – necessary background, extra. If the Director asked you to walk to a table in front of the principles' entrance, this was 'walk-on 1'. Moving out of the bar and acknowledging the principles was 'walk-on 2'. Any linking dialogue requested by the Director was 'walk-on 3'. I trust this gives the reader an idea of how the pay structure worked. We were booked as 'walk-on 3', but when directions were so complex, dialogue didn't come into the picture.

Returning to this location, nothing happened before lunch, which was enjoyed al fresco. When called we moved into the church and awaited developments. The Assistant Floor Manager chose five, and when he came to me he said he would probably use me later. I just said to him 'I'll stay where I am and take what comes'.

It was an unusual requirement, but the job was to give the impression that we were a film crew filming the Virgin Mary. It had a mobile track that moved both ways. This enabled us to film the queues of people waiting patiently to see the vision and to receive their phial of the holy tears. The actual Floor Manager had to explain to us (I had decided to take the instructions as well), how we must make it realistic, as *we* would be filmed by the camera team, filming the tableau. I returned to my chair at the back of the church and lost myself in a good book.

There came a call for a short break for tea; the Assistant Manager caught my eye and said to me that I would not be used, and I was given the option to be released or stay until the end. As the six of us had been bused to the location from Central London, I decided to wait.

I can't remember the exact plot of the episode, but it was something along the lines of Del Boy and his cronies, during the previous week, having stripped the lead off the church roof, leaving a gap above the Virgin Mary. A heavy downpour had created a gradual drip of water which landed on her eyes and cheeks.

One thing I have already mentioned was that as an extra, you had to remember that a) you turn up on time and b) unless directed, don't act! For the extra, the first is of paramount importance. As soon as you are booked in you will be paid whatever. If you are not used or your scene is cut, you still automatically get paid. My first day on *Nanny* at Southwold was a good example; within ten days my cheque for £36 arrived with my bills.

As for *Only Fools and Horses*, the initial fee was £92, but we were paid repeat fees for twenty-five years. Over that time the fee increased to about £120, and the programme was repeated at least eight times!

I arrived on time; I was ready and willing. I sat at the back of the church in view and read my book. For that I was to earn just shy of £1000.

Around about this time I was given a booking from my Norfolk agency. It was a PD James mystery with one of her fictional heroes, Adam Dalgleish. I was told I would be driving fast in a late '80s official police car, a 2-litre automatic.

I arrived on location on time and booked in. At this time Suffolk/Norfolk were flavour of the month, especially for television. There were many unspoilt areas, and I understood we were always welcome. At least we were treated, wherever we happened to be, with respect. We extras can take a modicum of the credit. We were mostly members of the Variety Artistes'

Federation – which had joined up in 1966 with Equity, certainly before my time (1977). This was an honour and we all made sure we disported ourselves to the high standards which had been already achieved.

The Crew Site Manager approached me and asked with a twinkle in his eye how fast I could drive it. I told him I had driven an automatic once and would be grateful to have a rehearsal. He sent me to the dressers, who had my shapes and sizes all organised, and I donned my appropriate police clobber. I returned to the guy who was responsible for the 'goods and chattels'. He volunteered to drive us out into the country where I could take over...

As far as the following is concerned, I have never blamed it on being a technophobe. But I wonder? I exchanged places with 'Mr Chattel' and fiddled for a moment or two with the controls until I felt ready to switch on. This I did, but like railway barriers, computers, Russian undergrounds and doctors' surgeries, the car engine ignored me. I waited and tried again (I didn't want to drown it). Once again I waited and tried again. It had worked; it didn't now. My saviour said, 'It was working, otherwise we could not have got here.' He took my place and spent a quarter of an hour trying to get her started. He told me to hide in the car while he went in search of a house which we had noted outward bound and it felt like Russia all over again. I could, if seen, be arrested for impersonating a policeman! I got into the back seat. I did, believe it or not, manage to open a window! It was a hot day.

A short while later my guardian returned and looked extremely sheepish. He shared with me the fact that the Director was absolutely livid. But I was the one still in uniform! Arrangements were made to collect the worthless exhibit, but there was no taxi to protect me. I had to make the two miles back on foot. I had no sympathy from the Director. If he hadn't blamed me as much as his employee, the latter could well have been given his cards!

The upshot was such that the Deputy Director was asked to enquire if the local police force could provide, on loan, a high-powered police car if possible.

They came up with a Morris 1000, which did have the insignia of its responsibility. There were odd little police signs all over it, the same style as an ice-cream van!

I did my best to give an indication of my purpose, but she was hard work. (My mother had one of these 'footpads' for over thirty years. She drove for seventy years, starting with the first years driving test in 1938. In 2008, at eighty-eight years of age, she retired with an eye problem. She is now ninety-eight.)

I watched the PD James programme. The replacement car really looked like mum was driving it!

At this point I thought you'd be interested to see a list of some of those I worked with over the walk-on years.

Bruce Forsyth. I met Bruce at the time when he had just had a son, after five daughters. We'd passed the time of day during the period before our scene, discussing sons – I had three daughters and seemingly could not make the extra pieces. The director put me in the wrong place, and along came Bruce. 'I'm the star of the show, not you!' he said. He picked me up and moved me to the other side, opposite to where the director had placed me. I must have looked forlorn because Bruce said, 'Don't worry son, it's typical of this director!'

David Warner – Actually it was a long shot. He had starred in the programme *Hold the Back Page*. He was very likeable.

Ronald Lacey had starred in *Porridge, Sherlock Holmes* and many others. This was my most testing experience of all. I was to drive a taxi in busy London (no closed roads) at 25mph, whilst staying exactly level with the camera car, and I had to deliver lines to Ronald over my shoulder. The director and crew were very supportive. The director said, 'We don't expect it in one take, just do your best'. It seemed they were happy, but I still expected a re-take. The cameraman checked, and it was fine. 'From now on we'll call you 'One Take Eddie'.'

Bernard Hill – this was my first experience of having lines. The programme was *The Burston Rebellion* and the filming was at Weybourne Station in Norfolk. It went okay as far as the Director was concerned, but I was a trifle miffed when Mr Hill completely ignored me. I was ignorant regarding the scene. He faced a billboard, regarding the outbreak of War 1914.

Stephen Fry. What a sheer delight this man is. I was called with no notice and asked if I could be a cameraman at a wedding, which was ready to shoot. Stephen was the best man and he nurtured me through the scene and then thanked *me*!

Nigel Hawthorne. Yet again, what a lovely man. I was booked as an extra yet given a linking line. He had one of those brilliant speeches which seemed to last forever. We extras had a 'curtain round' area and at that moment I was alone. He came in and said, 'Ah Eddie, could you watch the next bit and tell me after what you thought?'

'It will be a pleasure, Mr Hawthorne.'

'Oh, Nigel, please!'

I was amazed that he knew my name. I suppose the director mentioned it when I did my miniscule contribution. But even great actors are not likely to remember. I watched assiduously and just found one very small piece of timing. He came in directly and asked me what I thought. I felt it only fair that I should tell him what he had asked for. He thought for a few moments and then turned with that engaging smile and said he was certain I was right, 'I'll have another take'. He was not only perfect, it was as if he'd grown totally into the part. He put his head round the curtain; I gave him a thumbs up. He said thank you and was gone.

Davy Kaye was a 'one-man band' act who few readers would remember. I remember him particularly for a cameo performance in *Those Magnificent Men in Their Flying Machines*.

Freddie 'Parrot Face' Davis will be remembered by many. He topped the bill on the *Oriana*. As his act came to a crescendo most of the audience started taking photos of him. He bowed several times and left the stage. Then he picked up his own camera and for a curtain call he took photos of the audience!

Veronica McSweeney was a classical pianist. We were very close during several cruises.

Patricia Cahill was a soprano who appeared on many television shows.

Robert Harbin was a top-class magician. He was also a gentleman, unassuming, humble and we all enjoyed his wicked sense of humour. I shall always remember his wooden dog on wheels. He had asked a member of the audience to take a card from a very big pack; this done, he said, 'Rover will pull that card from the pack.' However, he informed the audience that he must not make it easy for Rover. From inside his pocket he pulled out a scarf and proceeded to tie it around the dog's eyes! (Rover was still able to pick the right card.)

Robert came on board with the dread of cancer having been lifted by his surgeon and was in remission, but it was not to last. He'd been on board carrying on doing his shows until we reached Hong Kong. Here he went ashore and was seen by a specialist which the ship's surgeon had organised. The news was dreadful; the cancer had spread throughout his body. He was given just three weeks to live.

All efforts were organised on board to enable Robert and his wife to disembark and return home by a private flight. He even knew what day he would pass away. Like any great magician, he was right. It was the first and last time that amongst all cabaret reports, there was one to the late Robert Harbin. I owed him that.

CHAPTER 8

Ancient Lights and new Temptations

During my time with P&O the majority of passengers were senior citizens. They dressed to the nines, especially for the Captain's cocktail party. Couples aged 70-plus seemed to rejoice in each other. His lady would have been young and attractive when they married and was still beautiful. Couple after couple were at their happiest, as if the pair alone 'shared a paddock'.

I remember an elderly lady passenger in a panic. She had temporarily misplaced her husband. You might have thought her attitude would be, 'He's a silly old darling, always on some sort of adventure. He knows where I am. I'll just stay here and enjoy my book'. But this particular lady was in a panic: 'What can I do? He's very forgetful. I just don't know. Oh dear, I hope he is all right. Is there anything you could do?'

With hindsight, it could well have been the personality of each lady. In fact both reactions appear kindly.

* * * *

So came the last day of July 1978. I walked down the ship's gangway for the last time, leaving P&O, and the most stimulating position I had fulfilled. It was the hardest decision I had ever had to make. I was now 'not employed' and would spend the next few months between Ipswich, staying short term with mother, the Eccentric Club in St. James and as top priority, looking for my own home.

In Ipswich I was able to keep in touch with friends. The pub group '65' was still metaphorically hell raising. I attended a weekly bridge game in the house of an accommodating bridge couple who charged nominal 'table money' which hardly covered the cost of tea and biscuits.

It was at this time I forged a bridge partnership with one Fred Cowles. We played together for over five years and were known as 'Ed & Fred' from Peterborough to Aldeburgh and Frinton to Southwold! (Not because of any special bridge prowess; it just caught on.) We managed to win two or three competitions and not infrequently we finished in the 'frame'. We played for Suffolk very sporadically, but hardly distinguished ourselves.

We played in the East of England annual shindig at Clacton Town Hall (fifteen years on from Butlins) and made the final each time. In all five finals we finished below halfway, but we didn't get despondent.

In our last year we played in what was called 'Swiss pairs'. This was the final competition after the long weekend. If you lost you went down the hall and would play against the other losers. If you won you would play winners, a great equaliser. (Before I move on, I apologise to readers who have had no contact with bridge. It won't be mentioned again. Although whist and solo have similarities.)

There were about sixty tables of four (two pairs of ours and two pairs of theirs). We had done well, as our partnership pair. We ended at table one for the final round (our other pair at table three). We knew from scoring up to date that we were never going to win, but we might just come second.

We bid a slam, a challenge to make twelve out of thirteen tricks. Our partners – the message came through – were *not* defending a slam. This meant that all things being equal we would come second. Fred brushed his little finger on the wrong card. This made it played. It cost us 1,600 points...

We ended eighth. Fred was devastated. I had to swallow hard. After all, it could just as easily have been me. So near and yet so far; we continued to play quite happily until family commitments pulled him to Gorleston, fifty miles north. As a partner, and as a person, I miss him.

* * * *

I'd been staying with my mother for a week or so when she showed me an advertisement for a Tudor property in the village of Bramford, three miles from Ipswich. I thanked mum and added that this might be perfect for me. It comprised a first-floor divide, front and back access, three bedrooms, kitchen, bathroom and large lounge, price £15,000. I contacted the estate agent involved and being 'not employed' I was available at most times. We arranged to meet at the property at 10am the next day.

When I arrived I fell for the outside view. I had always enjoyed history and ancient architecture was a large part of this; oak beams, mullioned windows, even the Roman numerals burnt into the beams. (The house would have had its skeleton erected not on site but in the grounds of the builders. The Roman numerals were burnt into the beams as a guide to those who erected it on site.)

We (agent and potential purchaser) entered the property and found a view of what seemed a 1930s building which had had nothing done to it since. It wasn't even Art Deco! The beams (black on the outside) were whitewashed on the inside, and as for the wallpaper – yuk. However it was one of those rare moments when this 'bear with little brain' saw through the mire, and could somehow imagine a Tudor residence.

I offered £13,500 on the spot. The vendor was a wily old character and refused my offer. I kept my own counsel. I thanked the vendor and left with the estate agent. I said I would stay in touch.

That evening was the bridge session when I was first introduced to Fred.

Throughout the day I became more and more sure I was playing dangerously. The longer I held out, the more likely someone else would accept the asking price. After all I could at the time afford an extra £1,500. Why cut my nose...

During the bridge interval I asked our hostess if I could use her 'phone for a brief local call. She acquiesced. I made it through to 'Mr Wily' and re-introduced myself. I offered him the full £15,000, which (what a relief) he was happy enough to accept. The usual process resulted in finalisation. What luck again. I could easily have lost it.

The house – the address at the time was 4 Church Green, Bramford, Suffolk – was built in 1499 during the reign of Henry VII. Henry VIII, our most redoubtable king to come, was eight years old. The property was Grade II listed. This was a talking point, less than it proved to be a restriction. Years later I found myself in the grip of planners who thoroughly enjoyed being officious.

I had a typical night out with the lads, and by that stage, after fourteen years of carousing we were drinking more than two pints. It was by now two and a half pints; really! It was enough for a jolly good evening. But it changed nothing.

We were, not surprisingly, chatting on and off about the Tudor property when Jack (one of the original duo) just happened to mention the law of Ancient Lights. He thought it was still on statute. For readers who are hearing of it for the first time (as I was), it refers to new buildings not being allowed to secure a build which might obscure the windows of the older properties. I said, 'thanks Jack, you've given the old place a new name'. And Ancient Lights it was, for twenty-seven years.

****

At this time just, before I met Judith, I was attracted to a lady who was part of the weekly bridge sessions. She was half-Indian and more than ten years older than me. The relationship was a sheer delight in all ways, particularly socially. She had an 'open marriage' and at this time her husband was a Senior Engineer in the United Arab Emirates. They were not short of a few bob. We were together for over a year, and it was a mutually enjoyable time. She had four sons, and her name was Rashida.

We attended the Foyles literary luncheon for the launch of David Attenborough's *Life on Earth*, a copy of which the great man duly signed. Sir Peter Scott, then towards the end of his life, was at the top table.

Rashida's mother (the English half of the marriage) was living with a new partner in North London, which we visited. She had initially married into a sect where the Sahib only had to say, 'Memsahib, I divorce you, I divorce you, I divorce you'. That's all. She lost nearly all she had that belonged to her. Her new partner was strait-laced, and Rashida and I were allotted separate bedrooms. That was before 'mem' put something soporific in his cocoa. I hadn't even made it into bed when in came Rashida! She beckoned me out and gesticulated towards one of several closed doors on the landing. I followed and entered the suggested bedroom...

* * * *

In 1978 I published my first book of poetry, entitled *Freezing in the Heat*. I sold quite a lot of copies. In my last year with P&O I sold about eighty. Looking back, there were a few fair efforts, but I was not ruthless enough when it came to the disciplines required. If I had two lines that both needed twelve syllables, I'd settle for one with eleven. When it occasionally comes to mind, I go hot and cold! If after much effort you cannot bring it together, it's time to screw it up and start again.

In October 1978 I returned for just over a week to the Eccentric Club, where I played bridge, went to a couple of

West End shows, and finalised my financial arrangements. Most of which turned out very well. The Eccentric was comfortable and relaxed. I thoroughly enjoyed the bridge, not least because I had the most incredible run of good cards and luck. I was privileged, one afternoon, to have the Chairman of the Eccentric as my partner. He was as lucky as I was with good cards, and he made the most of it. He was a very good player.

I know I promised to avoid bridge, but this is both brief and can be explained clearly to non-players. The highest you can bid is 7NT. This contracts to make all thirteen tricks, without a trump suit. In the clubroom we played for 25p per 100 points. Our score was 2,200. 25 x 22 (hundred) = £5.50 each, on one hand, and that was forty years ago! Today it would be about £20 each, and that was just one hand (out of 24). But I had good cause to have a long think… These people I was playing against had more money in their back pockets than I had in the bank. I really couldn't afford to play in their company. The decision was rather taken for me. Suddenly it was announced that the bridge room was closing for bridge and being reopened as a coffee/snack bar. I felt sorry for the other bridge players and hoped my winnings weren't the reason!

About halfway through that stay David Cahill, other half of Patricia, the lovely singer, arrived at 11am as arranged and I duly signed him in. He followed me into the bar, which was on the point of opening, and we found a comfortable spot in a corner enabling us to do business. As aforementioned I didn't need persuading that all my pennies in one building society was sound investment. He opened up his portfolio and started sorting his papers. I went up to the bar and signed for a gin and tonic and a pint of bitter, the latter mine.

David was a good communicator and he made it absolutely clear what he was suggesting for me. There were two separate 'build up' polices, feeding into offshore banks in Jersey and Ireland. A silver bank would take £4,000 and had never made a loss. David suggested I left a nominal sum in my building society account, for day to day needs, and penultimately, he suggested one small gamble. This was to invest £1,000 in the commodities market. He was fair with regard to this and said to me that I might win a lot or lose the lot.

It was time to visit the bar for refills, which I accomplished. I said to David I'd take the gamble on the commodities. (This was fifteen years after I had said I wouldn't risk spending for the sake of it.)

Finally he suggested something which he thought was the most important of all. It was a PHI (Permanent Health Insurance) policy. He explained to me the necessity of such protection. Health wise you never know Eddie (I did). He continued to say that this particular organisation was, unlike many others, anxious to get things right and was not looking for loopholes. I embraced his recommendation. I was happy with his professional aptitude and gently guided him to the restaurant for luncheon.

David Cahill had done a very good job for me. Just two things went wrong, one of which I had been warned about, the other could not have been anticipated. The commodities decided it was downhill time. I only salvaged £200. It wasn't David's decision. The other thing was that out of the blue, there were discovered to be certain 'anomalies' regarding the silver bank. It took nearly five years to sort out, but we (investors) retained 90% of our portfolio.

In the long term, as I will expand upon, the PHI proved to be a life saver.

****

Towards the end of 1978, all the legal aspects of my purchase of 'Ancient Lights' were completed and without much delay came completion. I picked up John Cooper (he of the initial drinking buddies). His father was a cabinet maker, and John had inherited his father's gifts. By the age of ten he could strip a car engine and put it back together. He was good at carpentry, plumbing, electrics up to a point (sensibly, if he had any doubts, he would leave it to the professionals), plastering, rendering and painting.

At this time he was working in the Drawing Office at Eastern Counties Farmers, but he seemed interested in seeing my new project and wanted to hear of my plans. I could see in my mind's eye exactly how I wanted it to be. This wasn't much help when I could do nothing to produce it. I have always been entirely impractical. John had a good idea. A young chap by the name of Tony Tweed had done his apprenticeship with John's father. He had three or four chaps working with him – when he *had* work. I was told he would relish this. He came to see the place, learnt of my plans and started at the beginning of 1979.

Three weeks before this, I had received an unexpected call from Graeme Heape, who had been a senior officer in the Pursers Department. In fact, his title was Deputy Purser, Catering. I had sailed with him several times. He was very personable.

'Where on earth are you phoning from?' I asked.

'Thorpness, near Aldeburgh. I'm General Manager of the Country Club here.'

'I thought you worked for P&O?'

'Another story, dear boy. Why not come over? We could celebrate the passing of the fifty shilling tailor. And I've got ideas for next summer.'

We arranged a date for the middle of December, and I duly drove towards the coast. Yet another adventure, I thought. When I arrived, Graeme was at the main door of the clubroom/bar. We shook hands warmly. It was good to see him. He was just not able to control his excesses – drink, money, women (always living on the edge), and men! I never knew the exact reason for his sudden dismissal from P&O. But it would certainly have been one of these excesses. Anyway, he had fallen on his feet and I was glad of it.

That evening he was on tequila. There was plenty of salt, for effect. I stuck to draught Guinness. I was driving. He had one local lad (just old enough to help in the bar). It was quite quiet, but there were, most nights, locals who looked in for a bevy, and worth (just) keeping open. He ordered drinks and asked the lad to repeat his order every fifteen minutes.

'Right', he said, as he sniffed the salt. 'I know how you work and the success you enjoyed. I was very surprised when you left.' I decided to bow.

'One of these days I'll tell you why I made that decision, I felt I had good reasons.' He nodded thoughtfully, and then continued. 'I am paid so much a year and I would pay you £4,000 for five months, 1st May to 30th September. Percentage wise you'll be ahead of me. I know I can trust you however, because of your versatility. If I can ask you to take over a 'project' I'll know you can and will do it for me.' (I'm far from comfortable with praise and sometimes doubt its veracity. However, this was the conversation.)

Graeme's next tequila arrived. He was soon into his ritual. I had a generous half of Guinness top up, taking into account the drive home. We talked of this and that, as tequilas came and went. I said that I was very interested as it would give 'project house' four months. This should be enough. I said to Graeme I would confirm in a couple of days, and it was probably going to be yes. I shook hands with him and thanked him for his offer. As I was leaving, his next tequila arrived...

I duly confirmed with thanks. By then I'd been 'not employed' for nearly six months. This couldn't go on forever. After all, my father never provided me with an allowance!

Tony Tweed & Co made a start on the property before Christmas '78 and continued after. His only condition was to ask for renumeration as certain projects were completed, to be able to pay his employees. It was a fledgling business, and I was pleased with their progress. I took time out so I could be with Rashida.

Now my future home would be Bramford, I explored the environs. Within a short walking distance were three hostelries; the Bramford Cock, the British Legion and the Angel Inn, all on the same side of the road. When you passed the Angel the next stop was outside Bramford, where you would soon arrive in a village named Claydon.

I enjoyed the Cock, which in my early days was packed at weekends with gents playing cards or dominoes. The landlord was welcoming, the atmosphere special. Although I patronised the Angel from time to time, most of my drinking hours were spent at the British Legion and would be for many years to come.

As for 'Ancient Lights', the result of the work accomplished was beyond my dreams. In the main bedroom I had acquired a four-poster bed. A wall between this and a smaller bedroom was opened up. Doors were designed Tudor-style, as was all the furniture, which I chose to purchase with a distressed finish. I was thrilled with the final result. It really felt like home.

I was pleased that Thorpeness and pennies to come were on the horizon. I'd had my period of being 'not employed'. The home had cost a reasonable amount. I now needed to work to justify my keep.

I spent my days off with Rashida until the August, when she told me her husband had decided to retire and was returning to England at the end of the month. We spent my next weekday off as a somewhat tearful farewell. But it ended in the right spirit. No one was hurt.

I arrived at Thorpeness during the early part of May '79 and presented myself, having been called to Graeme's office. We greeted each other as we always had and he said, 'I've already got a possible problem. The locals have been established for years and they are prepared to do as they have in the past. Gardening, setting up before a competition, establishing the microphones when required, helping behind the bar and if necessary washing up. But when I suggested running the swimming pool, silence erupted! If you would take responsibility for that, we'll run the evenings entertainments between us.' (Graeme was quite capable of the latter. His mother was a BBC pianist and performed for many radio programmes, especially *Much Binding in the Marsh*, Kenneth Horne presenting. Again I apologise to anyone relatively young.)

I happily agreed to take responsibility for the swimming pool. Graeme left me to organise prices. I suggested a membership card or the choice of paying each time you swim.

The day before the pool opened, Graeme showed me the locker which held the disinfectant I had to use every day. I felt I could cope with the responsibility, despite not being a strong swimmer myself. I had in fact (as previously mentioned) taught a small group of children to swim at one of the Entertainment Centres I had worked in for a summer season prior to P&O. I cannot dive; if people wanted to have a really good laugh, they came to the pool where the attendant tried to teach me. I just could not co-ordinate the basics. And yet I could teach other children, until they would be seen as competent. I suppose I knew the order of movement, but just could not realise it for myself.

During the evening we had a quiz twice a week. I ran a couple of singalongs (pre-karaoke) and provided variety, with effort at comedy. At least I avoided a South Liverpool FC debacle. We also had a dance once a week, when I usually did the cabaret.

Thorpeness Country Club was an unusual establishment. Its heyday would have been the 1920s – 1930s when the wealthy took six weeks off in the summer and returned each year to one of the chalet houses which most had bought. I don't know exactly how the 'system' worked, but it appeared not much money changed hands. From day one, week one, until day six at the sixth week the sound that permeated the hallowed portals was, 'Do *we* have to pay?' It resonated in the bars, on the boating lake, the local shop, the ice creams there in and the swimming pool. In fact I remember several of their ilk would shin a tree and climb over a wall to get into the swimming pool rather than pay the 50p it cost everyone else.

The season drifted by with ease and towards the end of August a mother and daughter came to stay. During their week, I played bridge with mother and noticed daughter Judith in the swimming pool. I was actually with a different young lady that week. I do remember that they won both the quizzes. I joined them for a while and discovered that Judith had just completed her first year at St. Hughes College, Oxford, reading history. It also transpired that it was their first holiday together since Judith had lost her father following a car crash. He had passed away on July 30th, the very day I left P&O. She had obviously been very close to him. On the Saturday of their departure her mother said to Judith that she should say thank you to me for helping to make it an enjoyable holiday. We chatted for at least half an hour. It was very stimulating. I asked if I could see her again, and she gave me her telephone number.

Concluding my time at Thorpeness, everyone involved, (except the locals), moved on. It had been an enjoyable episode. Sue Haywood stayed a good friend of the family (she and her husband John broke up), and Sue in due course remarried. We were invited to the wedding of Jo, her younger daughter. It was a lovely occasion, but again the marriage didn't last. That was bad enough, but Mary, the eldest daughter, suddenly packed and left with the parting shot 'I don't ever want to speak to you or see you again in my life'. And she was gone. They never did (even by 2019) see or hear from her again.

I had a suspicion from the time that Mary was about twelve that she might be gay, and maybe she couldn't cope with that situation. I can only say I must have been extremely lucky in my own family life.

I end my Thorpeness reminiscences with an unusual experience. Mid-season, a family arrived with whom I became close, for an unexpected reason. The family comprised husband and wife, Bob and Veda, and two daughters aged sixteen and eight. From the start of their holiday, the eight-year-old, Nadine, born 1971, seemed to be wherever I was. It was uncanny. When I arrived on time to open the swimming pool, she was already there. During my times away from the pool, she was wherever I was. This was my first experience of trying to cope with the 'in your face' syndrome from a child. I didn't try to discourage her, but as soon as possible I did say to her parents that I had a problem. When I told them all I had to explain, they seemed much more comfortable than I was!

From then on, I felt less inclined to be uptight. I was invited to their double chalet, where they exuded a totally relaxed atmosphere. When they departed at the end of the week, they talked of Nadine and said that she would very likely write to me. 'Do keep in touch. We'd love you to come and visit for a weekend.'

They lived in Postwick, close to the city of Norwich, and had a lovely house in a leafy hamlet. I was living alone at the time, and I enjoyed the change. I grew to love Nadine as if she was my own daughter.

A relatively short time later, Bob, left the household. I know very little about it. Even if it was due to wife-swapping, like the late Clive & Caroline. But in due course Mum Veda got married again – to Bob's boss in Switzerland! And I thought I had a varied life.

I did have a memorable finale at Thorpeness. During the season, I had volunteered lunchtime swimming lessons for children and adults. I had already taught a young lad to swim at one of the summer seasons I enjoyed before P&O. They were very well supported; about fourteen children and eight adults. Graeme had very kindly printed up certificates, so all was 'set fair'. The youngest was four, the eldest sixty-four.

I asked for a microphone, to add a little to the spectacle. I started with a roll-call, and wished all the contestants good fortune. The pool was about 20 metres long and 10 metres wide. All involved were expected to swim 20 metres.

I decided to start with the children. (I should say that when we began the challenge, the swimming pool was packed.) Children were supported by parents and families. The adults had family and friends who hoped, but never thought, they would make it.

I called their names, having decided to start with the youngest. She dived into the water (they all had the choice of diving or starting in the water, touching the end). I can see her now, forty years on. I believed she would become a great swimmer. She succeeded without fuss, and received enormous applause. Each child swam, one by one, and all achieved their length. The last lad had been my most demanding student. When he started he was petrified of the water, in or out. He had tried so hard, and started well. But just after he had completed fifteen metres, he began to fade. A spectator by the side of the pool instinctively reached his hand to the boy's stomach, and gently lifted him upwards. The boy reached the edge. I think we heard the greatest applause of the whole evening. After all, it wasn't the world championship!

When it came to the adults, they all succeeded too. The lady who was sixty-four, and rued a dreadful experience as a child, completed her swim. She lifted her head and burst into tears. She had achieved something that had eluded her for over fifty years.

I thanked everyone for their enthusiasm and said that five lads had wanted to learn how to dive. I felt that I could teach them, despite the fact that, (as mentioned before) I could not dive myself!

As the evening in the pool closed, a gentleman approached me; I had noticed him throughout the evening and had assumed he was somebody's supporter. He was in fact, a representative of the ASA (Amateur Swimming Association) for Teachers.

He shook my hand, and said it was a good evening. 'I've added the diving into your certificate,' he said. From nothing, I felt a mile high!

* * * *

The first thing I did when I returned home was to contact Judith in Oxford. (She was, as mentioned, at St Hugh's, reading History.) She invited me down, and we met at the Oxford Union. This was a different intellectual level, one which I had never experienced, and I have to say I enjoyed the stimulus and appreciated the 'cut and thrust' of the esoteric.

We went back to her rooms in St Hugh's and quite unexpectedly, we ended the evening making love. Yes, I was a lot older than she was, but at least she was twenty, it was not as if she was thirteen or fourteen. She cried her eyes out, but not resentfully, and we enjoyed closeness for the rest of the weekend. When I left, she asked me if I loved her. I said 'Honestly, you are the closest I have ever been'.

Aged 2 – was that you Dad?

Hands off my money, Mum

Signs of early athletic prowess

Before the bullying   Early concentration

With sister Cathy

Era of the body wave hair

Promoted to Entertainment's Director

Knobbly knees at Butlin's, Clacton

With Alexandra Bastedo – do I propose now?

With dear Captain Joe

Mum and Cathy

The folks with Grandma

As Father Christmas - 'I'll see what I can do'

'Lurch' on the Mussel Shoot - without muscles

Cheers Dad!

Formerly yours

More tea vicar?

Lurch at Caister

Eddie with his loyal team

In front of Iberia – Eddie's first experience at sea

The old Arcadia – Eddie's favourite

Wild West Night

Topping the bill - after
Opportunity Knocks

Closing Sunday Showtime

Eddie, Jude and the girls

Fun with the folks

Ready for another ice-cream

Roman Night – 'Twiggus Caesar'

The Commodore's Conference team – 1975 world voyage

The man with the moustache –
Old Time Music Hall

Oriental Night

Cocktails with Kenneth Williams

Our Queen's Silver Jubilee pageant, 1977

World Voyage,1975, main team

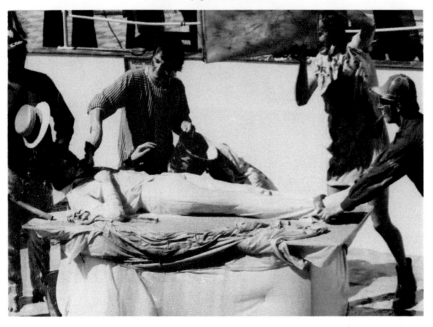

Crossing the Equator 'ceremony'. Eddie ends up in the pool!

Chairman of the Music Hall

South Pacific

Roaring Twenties

Oklahoma!

Oceans of Champagne - Glacier Bay Alaska

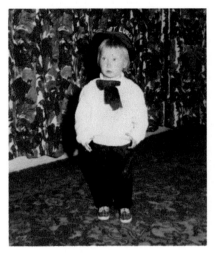

Lurch's little stand in

Annette, harpist and girlfriend

Sir JOHN BETJEMAN A

29, RADNOR WALK,
LONDON, SW3 4BP

6th December, 1976.

Dear Mr Scott,
    It was kind of you to send me FREEZING IN THE HEAT. I won't
just glance at it, I'll have a read.
    Many thanks,
                    Yours sincerely,

Kind words from the Poet Laureate

Three young ladies off to school

Eddie with his older girls

Dad with Vicky

Baby Kate

Happy families

The author

CHAPTER 9

Back on Set

I was fortunate in that there were several popular television series at this time which had very good shelf lives. *Hi-De-Hi, Allo Allo, Lovejoy, Miss Marple* (especially with Joan Hickson in the title role), and *The Bill* were all good examples of these. They all gave us extra ongoing employment. Some of us who were London based made the best part of a living out of *The Bill*, which was based in SW19, with an enormous area of studios and a large restaurant. There were many programmes which were filmed on location, then returned to the studios for inside filming.

The first time I was called for a day, Moira Stewart, the most attractive news reader, was dining, as were the principal cast of *Last Of The Summer Wine*, Clegg, Compo and Seymour (played by Michael Aldridge) and the team of *Blankety Blank*, I think all busy in their own disciplines.

I loved being on the *Allo Allo* location, which was based in Thetford, Norfolk. It was often an early start for us, but the day spent (over a two or three-year period) was always a delight. The director, David Croft, could be a trifle prickly at times, but he was much respected and nearly all the principals were endowed with friendly personalities.

I remember my first day. I had travelled by train because my car was in dock. I met up with four other chaps and we shared a taxi to the hotel. This would be our meeting point until the set up was established. Then we were called to a more precise location. Who was in the entrance but Kenneth Connor. I wish I could have known him better; he was hilarious. He gesticulated like a manic windmill and yelled out 'through the next village and fifteen miles on'. We in the taxi looked at each other, somewhat bemused – as was our driver.

From somewhere, Kenneth had happened upon a police truncheon. He leapt a low wall, shouting 'I'm the location bouncer, I've been instructed to move you on!' (He was 5ft 5inches tall, with a slim build). He then collapsed laughing, as did we. All except the taxi driver. He muttered sullenly that his fare had already accelerated by £5!

Both *Hi-De-Hi* and *Allo Allo* were shows where it was extremely difficult to be awarded 'walk-on' status. The directors were OK, but they expected extras to be as accomplished as the principals, without the rewards. I only managed 'walk-on' fees on one occasion in these two shows. I was a named German soldier (Kurt) in a scene where efforts were made, yet again, to get two British airmen back to Blighty. They were disguised as the front and back legs of a cow, in a field filled with the real thing. I was a part of a small contingent of

German soldiers who had marched towards the gate enclosing the cattle. Our brigade was called to attention. On the other side of the gate stood actor Jack Haig giving the impression of being a cow girl!

In our brigade was a German soldier who had lines: 'Kurt, bring me your helmet. We need milk, and I shall squeeze some from their titties'. I arrived front of camera and handed my helmet over. After a couple of seconds' hesitation, our principal German intoned, 'These titties seem out of milk!' (How much closer could we have got to the British airmen.) 'Kurt, your helmet. Put it on, and get in line', and then in German, 'Quick March!'

Repeats or not, this truly was an enjoyable time. I could sense my mental and physical well-being were so much improved.

Like *Allo Allo*, the principals on *Hi-De-Hi*, with one rather sad exception, were very friendly mixers. On one of my 'working' days, August 1985, my wife Judith came down to Dovercourt to visit relatives. She met the *Hi-De-Hi* crowd. We had arranged for her to be back around 4pm so we could drive back to Ipswich (actually Bramford) together. The *Hi-De-Hi* team really took to Hannah, our first daughter, 16 months old, and were all really lovely with her.

I never, in five seasons, made it to 'walk-on' in *Hi-De-Hi*. They were crafty on their own locations. One time there was a scene in the ballroom, when I was deputed to be Sylvia's dancing partner. Timewise it took the best part of a morning. (The 'powers' knew I could dance, because when we applied for work, it was a question the agent would ask). I knew exactly where we were placed on the dance floor. But their money merchants hadn't missed a trick. The only things showing were my arms!

I felt sorry for Sylvia, who was on the point of forty. As some cruel wit once said, at that particular age a woman has the face she deserves. Sylvia was good in that particular role because she was frayed around the edges. It was pointless trying to talk to her, although we had close on two hours to endure. My daughter: 'What a bore'. My Tudor house built in 1499 'How awful! How could you live in it? It's only got a small garden.' Perhaps I should have said nothing, but I tried because there was absolutely nothing forthcoming from her. Suddenly, despite the fact that she had probably been disappointed in the recent past by a *Hi-De-Hi* VIP, she had the life she deserved. If that sounds harsh, I'm sorry.

Before I grow beyond the day when my memory stands up to scrutiny, I should not forget *Lovejoy*. Not only did it survive successfully for so long, but it was based close to my own Suffolk doorstep – Debenham. I was in so many episodes, all as an 'extra' – Hey ho! Every now and then I see myself for the first time; literally blink, and you would miss me!

A circumstance I had to remember was a 'Vintage Doll Auction' in Debenham. One of my agents telephoned me to ask if the family could be available on such and such a day - 'The fact that you have three young daughters would be perfect'.

It was a wonderful day, I think in 1989. We were settled in the front row, and just had to respond (without acting). This was the second part. The episode started with the girls walking through the door of the hotel, to be welcomed by Ronald Pickup. He was in fact the villain of the piece, but lovely with the girls, as was Phyllis Logan, the lady of the manor. She appeared as the housekeeper in Downton Abbey. She was sweet, and so patient. (Mine could be demanding, to say the least.) We were placed in the front row, and as the auction progressed the cameras panned from left to right. The girls were delighted when they watched the transmission later in the year.

One of the other episodes, in 1987, was set on a cricket pitch in Hadleigh – in a roundabout way between Debenham and Ipswich. It was a hot summer's day and Hannah (who was just three), had learnt the song 'The sun has got his hat on, hip hip hip hooray'. I was asked by one of the agents if I would play the part of a cricketer. I jumped at the opportunity and said that I did play for my house Second Eleven.

'Can you bowl?'

'I'm a bit of an all-rounder.'

They gave me the job. I dashed into town to buy a David Gower sun hat. What I had forgotten was that I had not played cricket for thirty years! I returned home, wearing my sun hat. Suddenly Hannah burst out laughing and pointing to my hat shouted, 'Mummy, It's Daddy's hip-hooray'. I had that hat for fifteen years. It retained its title.

I arrived and found my way to a changing room which had been pointed out to me by a steward. The rest of the group, some of whom I knew, were all donning their 'whites', as was Bigelow, a category actor, who was cast as the umpire. He worked for 'Charlie Gimbert', Lovejoy's nemesis, played by actor Malcolm Tierny, in a servile situation. His master was batting – no chance of an LBW decision coming my way. That's what I was asked to achieve by the agent. I had spent too long thinking about it, and my first ball was a leg side wide! I put my hand up towards the Director's chair. He probably didn't expect the first effort to end with a 'wrap' (job done). But then I over-compensated, and the second ball was well wide of the off stump on the opposite side!

I heard the director shout 'One more'. It worked; the ball would have taken Charlie's middle stump. But then I spoilt it all. For only the second time in nearly fifteen years I really over-acted, jumping up and down like a demented drongo rather than just making an appeal. The director shouted 'OK, thank you', but I knew. How could I have been so foolish? In the fullness of time the programme was transmitted – without my LBW.

I now return, in brief, to the Vintage Doll Auction. Because the aim of the *Lovejoy* directors was to encourage as many children as possible (especially for obvious reasons girls), they advertised locally, stressing the fact that all would be most welcome. The management hired a merry-go-round and an ice cream van.

I suppose because they had been featured 'inside', my girls were invited to take the first roundabout ride, which was duly filmed. Later they were asked to be filmed again, while eating ice-cream as well. I can only think it was a sound decision. It seems later, the roundabout had cause to be used again with that second filming.

For some reason, I missed these at the time. I can only think I turned the television off as the programme ended and the credits rolled. I can remember the girls talking about it, but it slipped below my radar. Then last year, nearly thirty years on, I was watching repeats, and for the first time, I saw them. The next week I saw the second one. I must admit I shed a tear or two.

* * * *

On one of the London calls, there were two coaches waiting to transport us to Berkeley Castle, our location for the day. It was quite a long journey, but the weather was perfect and the scenery along the way looked exquisite. We were directed into the grounds.

It may be remembered that Berkeley Castle had a bloodthirsty past. In 1327 King Edward II was imprisoned there. His quarters were the equivalent of an open sewer. (His principal boyfriend, Piers Gaveston, had already been executed.) It was considered that his situation would kill him off, but it was not to be. It was imperative to make sure his dead body had no visible signs of violence. I think most readers will have heard of the red hot poker...

An actress I had not heard of called Helen Cherry had a major role in the production. She was married to the esteemed actor Trevor Howard. Some may remember the film Brief Encounter in which he co-starred with Celia Johnson, all to the wonderful Rachmaninov Piano Concerto No.2 in C Minor. Mr Howard was not involved in the filming that day, but was there for company and support. Several principals had their own trailers parked for convenience. I don't know what they would have done with the rest of us if had been pouring with rain!

Coincidentally, Malcolm Tierney had his trailer close to where I was parked. I mentioned the cricket match in Hadleigh and he remembered it well, for different reasons. This was something of a relief to me. 'The chap who staggered onto the ground and promptly collapsed dead, bringing the game to a halt, stopped me reaching my fifty!' What a wicked sense of humour.

Back to practicalities: they did provide a ladies Portaloo in the grounds, but we gents were told 'it was easier for us!' After lunch, and just before our extra scene, the moment arrived when I had to see how 'easy' it actually was. I was able to get behind a sturdy oak, and duly re-appeared 'zipping up'. On the other side of the esteemed oak appeared Trevor Howard, also zipping up. He roared with laughter, gave me a wink and said, 'At least we didn't get caught together in a bloody Portaloo!'

Trevor is remembered as a hard-drinking, cricket fanatic. Filming schedules had to work around his presence at matches, particularly Test Matches at Lords. He could 'command' because he was a very highly rated actor. Soon after this, he was featured on television celebrating his 70th birthday. I am sure he knew his days were numbered. I was able to add him to my esteemed list of VIPs who over a period of years, were doing the same thing at the same time: Harold Wilson, Michael Hordern (actor), Ray Clemence (England goalkeeper), Lance Percival and Georgie Fame. None of these involved an oak tree!

* * * *

One day I received a telephone call from London, fairly late, offering me work the next day on *Till Death Do Us Part*, starring Warren Mitchell and Dandy Nichols. I had never worked on that programme before, so this was a bonus. I was pleased to accept.

'Arrive 8.30am BBC,' he said. 'There will be a coach waiting to take you to the location. You will be one of about twenty'. I thanked him and promised to be well on time.

I never met 'Mr Alandar', although he gave me a fair amount of work. He, like so many other agents, would advise us to telephone the office just after 5.30pm. Some work did come in to the agencies quite late. This was a very useful source of work. It was one telephone call for us; it may well have saved him twenty. I felt this was both wise and fair.

On one occasion, I remember telephoning at the suggested time. He was sorry, but it was very quiet. I just said OK and it was worth the call. Next came his pet phrase - 'I shan't forget you', followed by 'Who's that speaking?'

We were on the coach for no more than half an hour. The first thing I noticed was Warren Mitchell's Oxford accent. I didn't get the impression he spent much time talking to extras; why should he?

By now Dandy Nichols, his co-star, was very frail. She was quite obviously gently grateful for the attention she much deserved. During the lunch break she was helped to eat, and then Warren Mitchell took her out for a long walk in her wheelchair. He showed a genuine essence of caring.

The arrival at the suburban location chosen for the morning had, so it seemed, been well organised. The scene was of Alf Garnett walking along a pathway, passing house after house. All the residents (we extras) had to act as if we wanted to avoid him at all costs. On the call of 'ACTION' he first passed a house which was ostensibly not involved in the scene. He reached my domain (house #2), while I was clipping 'my' hedge. At the first sign of Alf I ducked so I would be out of his vision, leaving my shears on top of the hedge. At house #3 were ladies in conversation at their gate, who surprised by Alf, all dashed back inside, again wanting to ignore him at all costs. When it came to house four, children were involved. They were all in high spirits as they came from a side street, and noticing Alf, they all scurried back down the same side street (they did well).

This was fully rehearsed and all of us were prepared for the first take. The director, Johnnie Speight, who wrote the series, called 'Action!' At the very moment 'Alf' started walking along the road, out came a stern-looking Rastafarian, not an extra, from house #1. Warren Mitchell responded by defensive avoidance, and then carried on with the shot as if it was a genuine part of the scene. Mr Speight motioned for the cameraman to carry on filming, I saw the director's 'orders', which occurred just before I ducked. The filming at house #1 was exquisite.

There was quite a long delay while all and sundry in the technical teams poured over the film. Eventually the call came, 'It's a wrap for lunch'.

Months later I watched the episode. I doubt if, in the history of motion pictures, this had ever happened before (except for dubious reasons). Mr Speight came over and said he liked the idea of the shears left on top of the hedge. 'I'd have left that in if I needed a retake'. He then said he thought he knew me from somewhere.

'Mutual membership of the Eccentric Club?' I ventured.

'That's it. The next time I see you there we must have a couple of beers.'

We shook hands. It never came to pass, but it was still a very good moment.

A similar thing happened during my 'starring role' as Kurt in *Allo Allo*. As already mentioned the British Airmen were the front and back legs of the 'Pantomime Cow' in the field behind the gate. Filming of the shot involved was finished, but one inquisitive cow was not. It spent nearly a minute sniffing around the disguised airmen. It was so funny, but... 'It is crass, too burlesque!'

The difference between the cow and the Rastafarian gentleman was that the latter could have joined us on the bus that left the BBC to transport us to the next location.

* * * *

I had the most walk-on work offered to me from 1985–1989. One, particularly, was most bemusing. We were filming at one of the esteemed Oxford colleges, a programme set in the 1930s starring Edward Petherbridge and Harriet Walter and titled *Gaudy Night*. The author was Dorothy L. Sayers. It was a time when ladies were beginning (very reluctantly) to be accepted on degree courses. But these times were not easy for females who had to establish themselves in an area which for aeons had been a masculine preserve.

I don't remember which college was involved in our 'walk-on' day, but if the reader would imagine 'Dreaming Spires', they would be very close to the real thing.

I hadn't been long out of the coach when a person who left me to imagine his status told me he would like me to play a character by the name of Cedric who was a resident non-official pastor. He said I looked the part, and when I was called, it would be to place me facing the camera with Harriet Walter (the principal), facing me with her back to the camera. Everybody else was to be positioned by the Stage Manager. This for me was a first – and a last! To have so many others positioned around the two of us was something special. (As you can imagine, many stars had a 'stand in' for this situation.)

The Director hadn't given me any indication of dialogue, so I didn't provide it. I decided to indicate that I was listening (to Harriet).

The episode was transmitted faster than most. I was apprehensive, but then relieved with my 2–3 seconds of screen time, which I can honestly say must have been what was required. I had only 'listened' to Harriet. At the time the director seemed happy; it only needed one take. I was certainly pleased. After all, if I had not proved satisfactory, the director could have replaced me, saying something like 'You're too tall for this shot'. What did I do wrong? (An explanation is on its way).

I never thought beyond the next week's work. It was at least six months later, when I had a day's work in SW19 on *The Bill*. The Director was there and as soon as he saw me exclaimed, 'I can't use that man in any capacity whatsoever. Get him off the set!'

Even the Assistant Floor Managers were dumbfounded. Why had this disaster not been revealed? After all, the Director receives the script and list of players ahead of filming.

A couple of months later the same thing happened again. I was booked for a day, and when this Director recognised me, he looked as if he was going to have a fit. I was demoted for the day, then reinstated, though only as far as my walk-on 3 was concerned!

I never established what was in his mind, but I am hypercritical of my own shortcomings – this was unlike anything that had happened before. I can only think that when I quite reasonably claimed my WO3, and was paid (with repeat fees) for *Gaudy Night*, it was up his superior snout.

Around the same time, I was on location at London Victoria Station. My position happened to be on a wide platform on a very cold day. My porter's garb was very thin. I was waiting to do a scene in which I was extremely secondary to the principals, Robert Powell and Sharon Maugham. If you don't remember the latter as the wife of Trevor Eve, you must remember her coffee adverts of the 1990s, made with an incredibly good-looking paramour (played by Anthony Head), both of whom exuded sex appeal.

I felt hypothermia was about to raise its freezing head. Before my teeth gave the game away, Sharon had already realised my problem. She was so kind, and immediately called the Director over. 'This man needs thick, warm clothing and a hot drink before anything else,' she said.

'After this shot,' said the Director.

Sharon said to him, 'No. NOW! I'm doing nothing until he has a hot drink!'

And bless her she didn't.

* * * *

In July 1986, when my middle daughter was six months old, one of the Norfolk agencies telephoned to ask if we would bring her to the location of *Double Helix*, a play about the discovery of DNA, set in 1953. The cast were excellent, although the female actor obviously had no knowledge of babies. Judith had carried Vicky to a small studio, where she as good as grabbed her from Judith; Vicky screamed volubly, and nearly rent the rafters. I could hear her ranting forth from some distance away. Eventually Alan Howard took responsibility, and the 'take' was completed satisfactorily.

In good time the Nobel Prize in Physiology or Medicine was awarded to Crick and Watson. The lady scientist, Rosalind Franklin, could not share the honour. She had died from ovarian cancer five years previously, aged 37. The rules of the award stipulate that you cannot be bestowed a Nobel Prize if you are deceased.

* * * *

Another day on location, I expected to be part of a crowd. I was one of about forty reporters listening to Martin Shaw (acting as Inspector George Gently), giving an update on a murder enquiry which remained unsolved; at the end of the dialogue, he had to use an absolutely awful joke. The technical chaps were having all sorts of problems; 'hairs in the gate', a 'cracked lens' and 'lighting difficulties' such that Martin Shaw broke into his script and changed the joke. I couldn't resist it, and said in a loud voice 'At least it was better than the first one!' It proved to be a belter, the timing was good, and Martin Shaw nearly corpsed. I thought I was going to be sacked there and then. I got a right dressing down, but it was worth it. When I eventually saw the episode, I had been picked for a 'solo' (where you are the only one on the screen).

* * * *

My family and I were about to set out on our annual holiday when the telephone rang. I answered it while Judith was bundling the girls into the car. It was Mr 'Shan't Forget You' Alandar. 'Eddie, could you make Thursday, George Gently for a scene with Martin Shaw?' I swallowed hard and got into the driving seat.

A call from Norfolk enquired the age of my eldest daughter Hannah. At the time she was nine. I was told that would be perfect.

'How do you think she would respond at a funeral when the camera pans?'

I said I was doubtful if it would pose her a problem.

'That's good; she will be filming with Helena Bonham Carter.'

She did the first part – what can I say? Jump forward four years and she was performing professionally. She was never 'pushed'.

Towards the end of the day the Director asked for Hannah to do a different take, but the Floor Manager told him 'Sorry, Hannah has passed her optimum work period'. No exceptions. She was mortified and we had a few tears.

When Hannah had dried her tears, it seemed sensible to be homeward bound. As we walked along the drive of the country house towards my car, something sparkled in the gloaming. It was a brand new £1 coin. I settled Hannah into her car seat and showed her the 'sparkler'.

'I'll add another one,' I said, 'and we'll stop on the way home and get some sweets'.

'Thank you Daddy'.

I did find the responsibility of three children in three years demanding. I was forty-one. I still love them to bits, to the extent that if they needed every penny I own I'd only ask them to wait until the next day. (I would need to sleep on it!)

Moving briefly back to lunch; Hannah and I had been told we could collect our food. A voice suddenly awoke me from my reverie.

'Hello, I'm Helena Bonham Carter. And this must be Hannah.'

I was tongue-tied. Pathetic, isn't it? Instead of completing the introductions by introducing myself, I waffled a lot about the film *Nine Day Queen*, the sad story of Lady Jane Grey, in which Helena played the title role while still a teenager. She was, so she said, pleased I had remembered. Most readers will recall, (or at least have heard of), the film *The King's Speech*, starring Colin Firth as King George VI and Helena as his wife, Queen Elizabeth the Queen Mother.

CHAPTER 10

CONFESSIONS AND TEMPTATIONS

N ow I need to return to the state of my alcoholic intake. I continued to drink more than I should have done, although the difference was (and I only comprehended it later than I should have done), that at sea everybody drank more. I would think nearly 50% of officers drank more than I did. Shoreside of course, over 50% didn't drink any alcohol during the week, with the exception of the odd glass of wine with a meal. But I was used to drinking every day. I was actually drunk on just five occasions. Apart from my 21st birthday (when my drinks were spiked), I felt ashamed on the other four occasions.

Most (maybe all) species of animal/bird/marine life, not to

mention multifarious species of dinosaur, are programmed for a life of 'duty'. As, it seems, is a proportion of the human race. But certainly not all. We have yet to catch up.

I am one of the worst – a serial womaniser who 'moved in', 'moved out' and 'moved on'. A chancer with a love of leisure. When I did marry, I had been closer to Judith than anybody else, both mentally and physically. I thought even for me, I could commit myself to her, and our life together. She provided me with a wonderful family. And I was faithful.

But I had not realised that Judith was not 'programmed' either. I got older, and to be fair she was thirteen years younger. She found a younger replacement.

An example of programming of which I had no comprehension whatsoever, appeared when I was a teenager. I had left school, and obtained a sinecure as a filing clerk. I met a couple who worked in the Accounts Department. He was seventeen, as was I; she was sixteen and had joined the British Steel Piling Company straight from school. The word soon spread that they were 'walking out' together. He was very good looking (I despaired); she was sweet, with a calming personality. She was pretty rather than attractive.

I often used to say to her, 'I expect you two lovebirds will be enjoying a night out together'. On one occasion when I naively repeated the mantra, she said 'not tonight – it's my night off...'

I thought 'Is this really going to last?'

They married. At the time most of us lived locally, but though I saw them on several occasions I never knew if they had a family. I hope they did. It would have been a happy household. Anyway, they came to the Bramford Cock from time to time. He would have a couple of pints of bitter and she a Babycham. I remember them in the 1980s and through until the turn of the century. I never saw them *not* holding hands.

* * * *

During the period post P&O, I found that unlike my working colleagues in the Bramford Cock I had developed the taste for strong lagers and ciders. I blame Winston Churchill for the 'Special Brews'. He accepted them from the King of Denmark at the beginning of the 1950s. This was similar goodwill to that shared with Malta.

On holiday in Portugal, I was introduced to a memorable drink and brought some bottles home. It was 55% proof! What an idiot I was; no fool like an old fool.

At the age of sixty, I collapsed with a throat haemorrhage. The diagnosis was cirrhosis of the liver. I had a long journey in front of me.

* * * *

I had been invited to stay with Chrissy, who I had met in 1978, with her mum and new husband in Fresno, California. Chris and I had been something of an item, and we had both hoped something would come of it. She was working in the property market as a seller. In California, when people were interested in a property (and it was part of the Companies Portfolio), they would work on the big sell, having done their own research into the potential home for a prospective buyer, rather more than just 'showing them around'.

On one particular day, I had been invited to see one at work. (In California this business is known as 'escrow'.)

The lady involved was doing her best, to bring the best, of a property valued at $1,400,000. She was superb at her job, and never had to give any semblance of exaggeration. Mind you, the house was the most amazing I had ever seen. It was like a palace, though not as gaudy, and it was matched by the land, the panoramic views, the stables, and horses (which would remain if the buyer would wish it). The swimming pool must have been Olympic sized.

The escrow lady then chose what seemed to me the perfect moment to 'bow out'. 'It really is about time to leave you to weigh things up. Please do feel free to call me back, if I have been unclear on any point. Just knock on the door'.

We were waiting and hoping on her behalf (I think I was deep breathing). The excitement was intense. Eventually the buyer called out to say that she had made a decision. She wanted the property. Our 'Miss Escrow' said she would be there whenever the purchaser might need her advice. She provided the legal advice as part of her job specification.

When all had been completed to the high levels of professionalism required, and the lady buyer was fully assured that all was as it should be, this special lady began jumping up and down in a frenzy. If she had wanted to 'jump over the moon', I'm sure she could have done. In one afternoon's work she had earned 25% of the deal – $350,000!

The company could not complain. They had done nicely too, thank you. How? I really don't know how!

* * * *

A few days after this, it was decided that a trip to Las Vegas for a weekend would prove enjoyable (if decadent). I'd always fancied Reno, down the road for two or three hundred miles more. It was part of a song Ginger Rogers and Fred Astaire bestowed upon their adoring public.

Talking of them reminds me of way back thirty years, when there was the most devastating fire the United States of America had ever experienced. The Fire Chief for the whole of the US was one Red Adair. Someone asked for his autograph. His reaction was 'Why me? I'm only a fireman'.

The response was instant. 'I did so enjoy you dancing with Ginger Rogers!'

We arrived in Vegas, the 'world of no time'. It was packed. In Caesar's Palace the band was playing; I say was, because suddenly they stopped. Everybody stopped. Even the slot machines ground to a temporary halt. That takes something special.

The special 'something' turned out to be me!

Barry and his band, the Bunny Austin Quartet, were unsurprisingly in top demand. P&O were able to enjoy them onboard in California, for two or three cruises before I left the next year. We had many excellent bands while I was working for P&O, but The Bunny Austin Quartet was by far the best. They even invited me to sing with them. Everyone has a blind spot!

They insisted that I should join them ashore as their guest. They took me to the major studios in Hollywood, in one of which I met the Harlem Globetrotters. Then I was invited to dine with them. It was hard enough to persuade them, nay insist, that I would buy the wine. All because I treated them with routine respect.

I gather they had one really bad experience which took the gilt off a cruise (not P&O). This was a quartet who could have played successfully anyway in the world. Inexplicably, they were told, they must not, under any circumstances, converse with the passengers. Can you believe it?

'Ladies and gentlemen, a young man we know has just joined us in Caesar's Palace. He was our boss last year. On behalf of our quartet, I would like to welcome him and his party. He was the best cruise director we ever worked with. Put your hands together in welcome.'

I raised my hand; I was determined to enjoy this. I received a standing ovation – only, I hasten to add, because they were standing already!

Dancing, and particularly the 'slots', resumed with a vengeance. One lady was on her last dollar, but had no luck with it and had to 'resign' with nothing. The next lady's first dollar won her $2,000. The scream from the losing lady would have been heard in Reno!

* * * *

Chrissy and I left it that she was welcome to come back to Ipswich (her sister still lived there), and we could judge if we felt we had a future. As earlier mentioned, she duly returned about six months later, but soon made it clear that she would never have chosen to live in an old house (something I never anticipated). I did think it was deeper than that, so the best thing for me was to drive her to her sister's in my new car (I had bought this run-around as the house was finished). I had just enough room for her and her suitcases.

* * * *

I had only been back home from the States for two or three

days before I was back at Heathrow for the arranged trip to Sydney, Australia, together with my book of postage stamps. Annette's parents had bought my flight. All this has been mentioned before in detail, so no more than as with Chrissy, it was the end of the road with Annette. With neither situation was I aware of animosity, or ill-feelings. Maybe Jude in my mind had priority.

It took at least two days, maybe three, to recover from jet-lag. In those days forty years ago, the journey took twenty-eight hours (Sydney to Heathrow). As soon as I was home, I thought to myself it was time I had a good rest. I turned over in my four-poster bed and was 'slipping away' when the telephone shrieked. I had a telephone extension in my bedroom, so I picked it up. It was Judith, in what sounded one hell of a state.

'Oh Eddie...' then she burst into tears. I gleaned from her that 'coitus interruptus' had not worked, and that she had found herself pregnant, with no way of contacting me. Had it been anybody else, I would have doubted the truth this statement, but I had no doubts with regard to Judith. I said I would contact her soon after I returned from my travels. For some moments I was speechless.

She said she hadn't known how to cope. Her knowledge of her mother's resentment came in advance of any semblance of care. The doctor didn't handle things particularly well; I gather he was frightened of her mother. They had not been able to agree over a termination. One day yes, next day no.

Why hadn't I given her a forwarding address? I take the vast majority of blame for her situation, although as I remember, it was an 'immaculate conception'. She said that all things considered, a termination was the only sensible choice. Judith was bereft.

Before concluding our devastating call, I belatedly gave her my address and telephone number, and said I would be in touch very soon, and that I was deeply sorry. I told her I had had two experiences of feminine entrapment already, and that she was the first woman I had not doubted after the first five seconds of her call. I suddenly felt very close to her, and despite 'vicissitudes' I never wavered.

That afternoon I ordered a dozen red roses, to be delivered to her at St Hugh's College, Oxford, with a note informing her I would be at the Randolph Hotel, at such a time and on such a day, if she still wanted to see me.

The next day the telephone rang. I really did hope it would be Jude (as I would call her for the next twenty-six years). It was, and a happier voice said, 'the flowers are lovely, but don't go to the Randolph Hotel, meet me in London. I'll let you know where & when'.

I failed to skip around the flat (on both its levels), but I did look forward to seeing her, and being with her. I was soon on the correct platform at Paddington in good time.

In the period of time before we came together, Jude told me of her mother's seeming hatred towards me. One complaint was that I didn't drive a proper car to justify my so-called status! Jude had a sense that she was attracted to me. Oh surely not? For a start, I was hardly attractive, and there was almost a generation between us. Her mother, beyond my status, suggested I was probably of a 'lower class'. To be fair, her father was a hairdresser with a small but successful business. Her husband worked for an insurance company.

I am proud to acknowledge myself as 'lower middle class'. My mother's family were 'middle class'. I have already described my grandfather as being a master cabinet maker, with his father's established business. Their reputation was renowned.

My father was a delightful artist, from an early age. His mum, my grandma, had a pencil drawing of Ginger Rogers he had accomplished at the age of eleven. She had found a simple but intuitive frame, and it had pride of place in her lounge.

Returning from the war, my father was persuaded to join the emergency teaching organisation, which required only a year for those who had the aptitude. He taught perspective, for example. The deeper the student painted into the distant hills, the more colours fade. For example, green becomes (in the distance) pale green/blue. I observed him several times, and he knocked my grammar school art teacher equivalents into the veritable 'cocked hat'. There you are; nobody's all bad!

* * * *

The Paddington train from Oxford arrived, (unlike nowadays), on time. I had to wait for a short while, but then before I had a chance to panic, Jude appeared. She was smiling, she looked very small, but we had a really nice hug, which I hoped would give at least some minor relief for her appalling experience.

I led her to the taxi rank, where I asked our driver if he would take us to a reasonable hotel. Something between the Ritz and a 'double bunk' and its menu of rissoles and chips! He didn't let us down. The hotel chosen was smart, clean, and comfortable (with all that was required).

I hadn't booked a hotel for any other reason but our convenience. I made no moves. Jude however, had her own agenda. She made it clear, (despite what happened), that she wanted a 'full' relationship. Like millions of others, she was now on the pill. That side of things was very special for twenty-five years. I'll very rarely mention it again.

When the time seemed right, I suggested that we should go up west, have a nice meal, and 'take in' a show. I telephoned from the room and booked a Chinese restaurant. We mutually chose *Evita*, with, I think Elaine Page. It was a very happy evening.

The next day, before we set off in our different directions, we had noted a matinée performance of Oscar Wilde's *The Importance Of Being Ernest*. It was very good, as anyone would expect. We caught a taxi to Paddington, and I waited on the platform until Jude was out of view. I was hopeful everything that could be mended. Within a day or so, I telephoned her. We had a lovely chat, and she invited me to come to St. Hugh's for a long weekend. I was in the process of my new move, which would not restrict me in entertaining Jude, when she was available, and chose to do so.

CHAPTER 11

motors, money matters and marriage

In the early part of New Year 1980, I saw an advertisement in *Stage* magazine for a compère/organiser at Holimarine Caravan Park, between Lowestoft and Great Yarmouth. I had passed it several times, and decided to apply for an interview. This 'not employed' lark was for millionaire pools winners! It was close enough for me to take my day off at home as in days of yore.

I drove to Holimarine reception and found a young lady who said I was expected, and she would let me know when the Manager was ready to interview me. This duly took place, and seemed quite relaxed. However, we were diametric opposites in every way. I thought the interview went well, although I was perhaps more laid back than in years of greater necessity. But I was accepted and stayed for three consecutive seasons.

We only had one altercation, when the Manager criticized something I had done, for dubious reasons, in front of caravanners. I was incensed; I had been a P&O Cruise Director less than two years before. To a large extent it ended '15-all', and a little mutual respect was important for both of us. In the third season, he said that he was amazed I was still working there; after all, 'You did a dreadful interview for the job!'

In 1981, the year of the Botham/Willis Test Match against Australia, one of the local workers volunteered to try and patch up my car. It was kind of him and he did his best. In truth she was falling to bits. There was more rust than there was car! I thanked him, put a few quid in his direction, and drove this small car, which resembled a circus banger, to the nearest garage.

In the days when I still lived in the family home I had almost bought a yellow Lotus Elan from our next-door neighbour. He had a small legitimate business at the back of his property. I was really looking forward to that, but then he called me over the fence to say that the Lotus had a potential serious engine problem that could cause irreversible damage. He said he would feel guilty if he sold it to me. As all garages say when you bring in a car for exchange, he added, 'It's worth a little for spares'. He asked me how much I had to spend. I said to him, 'about £2,000 less £250 for the spares'. He looked at me and suggested I was pushing it. I smiled, and was told he had a real 'special' which would be a snip at £2,300 (taking into account the spares). He told me it had done less than 1,000 miles and had been an exhibition vehicle.

He pointed towards the back of the garage, and there she sat in subtle splendour. A 2 litre Colt Celeste Sports Coupé, coloured gold and as new. We fell in love with each other at first sight. I paid by cheque at the agreed price, took the keys and drove her back to Holimarine. It felt terrific, and I never felt an apologist with regard to Jude's relations. That was my car for nearly five years.

In due course, I couldn't resist the temptation to drive her at over 100mph. I only did that twice. It was a strange feeling, but up to 90mph I felt in complete control, beyond that, it felt as if the car was in control. I'm surprised I risked it a second time.

I cannot fully remember the catering arrangements at Holimarine, but from early doors I used to drive the half mile from the holiday park to a little 'all-day eaterie'. I used to have a mini fried breakfast, toast and tea. It was a perfect start to the day; I only needed to be back at the park just before 10am to be in time for the morning competitions – table tennis, actual tennis, snooker, and darts (not to mention the swimming gala), depending on the day of the week.

On my first breakfast visit at the end of that first week, I was met with big smiles. 'Are you Eddie from up the road?' said one. I reluctantly admitted to what felt like an indictable offence. In fact there were three enormous toothless grins from behind the canteen.

'They've really taken to you, haven't they!' I was a little perplexed, as I had only just started.

'We're the first to know', came back a toothless canyon. They were regulars who had been coming since 'before the war', so it seemed they made quick judgements. I was obviously very pleased. Ever since Butlins, fifteen years before, I had been determined to at least give folk the opportunity to 'take to me'. Every time I went to the eaterie, I was made to feel like a long-lost relative who needed sustenance!

* * * *

On the 21ˢᵗ June 1980, just before I bought the Colt, my sister (oboe), and companion John (cello), married at Bramford church. It was a lovely occasion. I managed to hire a 1930 Austin convertible, together with a chauffeur, which added a little to the proceedings.

At this time, I was very much involved with Jude. I had been invited to her home for Christmas 1980. This was the first time I had seen her mother since their Thorpeness holiday. I was given the full indictment, and it soon became clear that she had no idea we had been 'very much in touch' over the period which encompassed the first hotel, her rooms in St. Hugh's and my double bedroom at Holimarine. I dropped a faux pas when I mentioned number four, my new Tudor home near Ipswich!

I was not made to feel particularly welcome, with the exception of the vicar (a close friend of the family), with whom I found myself in a respectful theosophical discussion (albeit very absorbing). This was soon broken up by the mother as if we had our fists going. The second person who made me feel at home was her father, Jude's grandfather, who was gay (married 51 years – sexual relations with spouse, once!) When I was as good as booted out on Boxing Day, he was incredibly sympathetic. I would not criticise him in any way. Despite the fact that there was nothing like that on my family side, yet two of my three daughters are gay!

I remember crying all the way from Buckinghamshire to Suffolk. I had to admit to myself that Jude was something special. Despite the Christmas, she hoped we could 'carry on' as was. This was just before I had bought my Colt; no doubt my small car was still being sneered at.

I enjoyed the pace of Holimarine. Apart from the band, who were willing, played for all dancing tastes and backed the cabarets efficiently, the only other thespian was the children's entertainer. He always wore flowing robes and looked like Rasputin. When I first saw him, I thought the children would be frightened of him. I had lost the plot; children smell fear. He had nothing of that to offer. They all loved him and the cuddles they gave him spoke volumes. He was not a good organiser, but everyone rallied round, and all was well.

I was expected to work in the mornings and evenings, while Steve (Children's Entertainer) worked every afternoon with his shows, and I started competitions again at 4:45pm with the bingo sessions. I always arrived in the Club Room well in time to introduce the band at 8pm. I gave the band leader some leeway, but he began to turn up later and later. In the end I had to take a stand. He went ballistic!

One of the guests came down on my side, saying 'Come on Joe, It's nearly 8:15'. He ignored that and gave me another 'side swipe'. At the end of that first year, I was told he had driven his car onto the heath, together with a hosepipe. He was found the next day. We were told he had an incurable brain disease. Having no comprehension of this, I didn't feel I should have a sense of guilt, but I did.

I had worked with the band, introducing the different dances, adding a suggestion of comedy, and did my own act once a week when there was no cabaret booked. One cabaret,was booked at the last moment, because the 'regular' was confined to bed with Asian flu. What a malady to succumb to in the summer!

This guy was quite well established (as a magician) and I was quite prepared to give him an encouraging introduction. He sort of shook my hand, and said that all the entertainment 'assistants' (I gave him a withering look which was lost on the guy), helped him with his act. 'Everybody else is pleased just to help me,' he said.

I told him I was not 'everybody, but I would be pleased to assist him for a tenner. 'Now, are you working or not? I don't mind which'.

He said he would report me to the agency. I retorted, 'if you've got the number, we can telephone them now'.

I can hardly believe Mike and Bernie Winters would expect me to perform for nothing. On second thoughts...

One of our cabarets, a delightful chanteuse, was suddenly cast adrift from the show. She sang the songs from *Evita*, a smash hit in the West End. As many readers will remember, the Argentine Junta declared war in the Falklands! She was a good professional, all 4ft 11in of her, and the guests understood.

* * * *

Jude who (as previously mentioned) was reading history at Oxford (major part architecture), was (as all others were), challenged mentally. The sleepy seaside environment proved to be a necessary contrast. The Manager was very happy for Jude to come whenever she wanted, or even needed a break. I'm still grateful for his understanding at that time.

I still had my day off, which coincided with bridge in the evening, and a temporary return to my cosy home. My large car was even acknowledged.

Back at Holimarine, during the week, you may or may not believe it, but I did reintroduce the 'Mussel Shoot'. It was ideal because behind the reception area were the caravans, and at the end of their line, and just beyond, were the cliffs where steps led down to the beach and breakwaters.

* * * *

The dear old harbourmaster was as usual deputed to bring his 'lugger' into the deepest breaker, which would enable the caravanners to step aboard and choose the left or right handed guns. It was both nostalgic and pleasing that the success rate was as good as in the past.

Only on one occasion was I slightly concerned. I wore a polo neck shirt, with the right arm inside at rest, with my elbow bent, and the sleeve flapping. I said to four big lads to please leave the pool out of proceedings, because I'd sprained my wrist. 'I'm sure the holiday guests would feel recompensed if you stripped me in the ballroom!' I said. They seemed quite happy with that and made the most of it. They lifted me shoulder high and raced around the ballroom, while I was waving my fist (with the good arm) complaining how unfair it was (I had been stripped down to a pair of tight red shorts and a yellow top). I looked like a traffic light that never changed to green!

When it came to the second season, there were many 'returners'. I decided to organise a 'Boggit hunt'. Readers may well say to me 'you've got a nerve', but I explained that Boggits were a different species from mussels. I patiently explained to our guests that Boggits came from both sides of the channel; the males were unhappy in their singular situation around the Calais area, and the English female Boggits were also frustrated and hated Dover. Instinctively they performed a 'volte face' with regard to their geographical differences and both sexes burrowed themselves halfway between Dover and Calais, met, had a few dates, and then settled down into monogamous relationships.

I pointed out a sepia photograph (on the noticeboard) taken in the 1930s after a so-called hare shoot, with my 'grandfather', and several colleagues admiring their booty. Most people thought they looked nothing like hares. Many fellow sportsmen were convinced they were Boggits. They had to endure the hunting season during the month of June. July was the time of their annual Boggit beano. They always took this holiday, fluctuating between Dover (one year) and Calais the next. They thought it only fair to share between their original habitats. Boggits are excellent swimmers; it is within their annals that one or two of the fittest males had actually swum non-stop between their two original homelands...

I found it hurtful and untrusting that nobody believed me!

* * * *

I was now drinking about four or five pints most days. I still didn't think I was damaging myself. I was in denial: for me it seemed to be the norm.

During my third season at Holimarine, Judith's visits were not so numerous. For obvious reasons; her finals were becoming too close for comfort. The pressure was exceptional. She nearly broke. One day I was called to the office to take a telephone call. It was Jude; she was in a dreadful state. Finals were after the weekend; it was Friday afternoon.

'I've got to get away,' she said. 'I've worked out trains and I can get to Lowestoft at 9:10pm'.

I checked with the Manager that it would be ok. He seemed to understand. I also informed the band leader. I should by now have introduced this man; he was part of the original band, and had taken over after the tragedy of his erstwhile leader. His name was Andrew and he played the piano well. He was reliable and laid back, without seeming to make any effort, he was always on time, and made sure his sidesmen were as disciplined.

Coming to our sleepy seaside was the best thing Jude could ever have chosen. She needed a break from the mental demands. In fact she wasn't too far from a breakdown. Our time together for three nights helped her (in her own words), 'over the line'. She scored a high 2:1. I take no credit. I just happened to be in the right place at the right time. She had done all the work.

I went through one of my doubting periods at this time. I had always found it difficult to commit, and although Jude and I were on a very similar wavelength, I still doubted myself.

We had booked a long weekend in Paris. I was never into photography, but Jude was good and took quite a quantity of pictures. We did the usual things. Paris, with a trip (to the second top platform) of the Eiffel Tower was breathtaking. I can't imagine how far away the horizon was. We also visited Notre Dame Cathedral on the Sunday, which was open to the public, even if they were not attending the service. We reached a position close to the choir just before the Communion. The choir stood and sang the Cantata (Motet) *Ave Verum Corpus* by W.A. Mozart. At the end I was in tears.

We also booked a late berth on a river cruise along the

Seine. We were served an excellent dinner with wine, and enjoyed the lights of the great city and excellent music.

On our return I hailed a taxi for Jude, who would pick up the underground east, which would take her close to her present flat in Barkingside. I left it that I would telephone her within a week at the very latest. I had overcome these doubts before.

Two days later I was on duty with the Ipswich Samaritans; my session finished at 16:30. I waited for my 'swap', and left by the front door. Jude was sitting on the brick wall opposite! I was not sorry to see her. My doubts were fading. She said the photos were really good, and 'I did so want you to see them'. I offered her my hand, and she gently slid off the wall. I suggested she came back to Ancient Lights. 'Tomorrow we can go to Barkingside, and get you packed up and put your notice in. I also think we should come back to Bramford, get yourself settled in with your own goods and chattels, and we'll shack up together.'

That's how it was for the next 22 years.

* * * *

Jude had very recently obtained a job in London, high-powered people organising major media events. Obviously it was easier to get to the offices from Barkingside than Ipswich, but the main line terminus from Ipswich was Liverpool Street, just five minutes' walk away. She had a bicycle, as it would be quite a while before she passed the test to drive. The bike ride to Ipswich Station was just over ten minutes. It would be an early start, but she never complained.

We settled well into being together. Jude's alarm was set

for 6am. She took a shower and had a coffee. She usually had a snack on the train. The routine continued; she phoned me from the office (about 8:50am).

I went back to sleep soon after she left. I was back in the realms of the Not Employed, until I started my final, awful summer season at Gunton Hall. I believe I was set up before I started. I couldn't believe what they offered me: £6,000 for a twenty-week season! That was a great deal in 1983. I only stuck it out because I had a large tax bill looming). More of that later...

Judith and I had both talked about having a family. She was the first person I had thought of seriously for this direction. I was to be so lucky. We decided we would get engaged, and when the time seemed absolutely right, to reject 'precautions'. This was mutual.

I mentioned seeing Gunton Hall through to the bitter end because I needed the money. Towards the end of 1981 (second season at Holimarine), I was attempting to fill in my tax form, and discovered I couldn't do it without telling out-and-out porkies. This involved non-declaration of monies invested in Jersey and Ireland. I had the tax form which coincided with my new investments, and I had declared the first amounts and these had not been assessed. This allowed for some mitigation, but that was all.

I telephoned Mum to explain my predicament, wondering if, having lived in Ipswich all her life, she knew anyone she could recommend with regard to my plight. Not for the first time, she came up trumps. A gentleman who was a contemporary of her late brother still had an accounts concern in Ipswich, despite the fact that he was well beyond retirement age. Her advice for me to make contact immediately was sound. Two days later I was admitted into his chambers in Ipswich Town Centre. The upshot was that Mr Eric Leathers told me I might well have reached him just in time.

'I'll send off for an interview with the tax inspector tonight,' he said. And so it started. It travelled back over five years! I have to say 'my' tax inspector was a delightful guy. When he enquired about me (very politely), and discovered I had been in the entertainments business for nearly twenty years his response was 'did you tell jokes?'

I had to admit to another misdemeanour.

'Tell me one,' he said. I thought I'd better humour him, and told one of my favourites .... would you like to hear it? If not ignore the next three or four lines...

Couple on their honeymoon night – happy after a wonderful day. Groom suggests his new wife should get ready for the bedroom. 'I'll just have one more drink and join you in no more than ten to fifteen minutes'.

He arrives; she has a sheet over her, and is crying. She told him, 'We've had a burglar'.

'Did he get anything?'

'Yes', she sobbed, 'I thought it was you'.

The reader may well think my tax bill should have been increased!

Each joke I told was commanded by this 'state burglar'; I thought he might go easy on me. The final demand was not established until 1984. I shall provide the final denouement later.

* * * *

Jude and I settled down very well together. We would dine out once a week, usually Saturday, which seemed only fair. Her earnings at that time went into our joint account. She would cook for us, usually on the Sunday.

Gunton's horror season started in May. Jude had been offered a 'sinecure' in the camp shop. It added to the coffers, for which I was grateful. In late-ish July, she confirmed that she was 'with child', as previously described. This was not unexpected, and we had made arrangements to apply for a Bishop's Licence. This arrived without fuss, and we immediately approached our local (Bramford) Rector, who conveniently was able and willing to provide for us. The church gates were twenty-five yards from Ancient Lights.

As you will imagine, Jude's mother was incandescent. We both wanted a quiet wedding, and this was it – four of us and the Rector! We asked Sue (Haywood) from the Thorpeness days, and Iain (a university friend of Jude's). Iain stayed overnight with me. Sue and Iain were soon mutual friends.

It was a fine day in high season August 24th, and everything proceeded smoothly. After we had signed the official documents, my car was waiting to take us four to Hadleigh, a picture village seven miles from Ipswich. It boasted a luxury hotel, a fine restaurant and excellent 'fayre'.

We had only one photograph taken, but we were lucky. It was as good as we could have hoped. For some strange reason, with one exception, I find a woman wearing a hat diminished! The 'pill box' was the exception. And that was what Judith was wearing. She looked stunning. Sue Haywood had taken responsibility for Judith. It was clear that she had given her all; Jude's dress was exquisite.

When we entered the restaurant it was quite full, and our

party were accorded a generous round of applause. When it came for us to leave, the same thing happened again! It was quite touching.

Next, Sue annexed Jude to help her change. She then drove Iain to the station for his journey back to Godalming in Surrey. She had done so much for us. In the fullness of time we treated her to dinner in an established restaurant, where we could truly thank her for everything.

Jude and I led the way back towards Southwold, where we were booked for bed & breakfast at the Red Lion – our honeymoon night – before the return to Gunton Hall, where waiting for us was a lovely present from the manager and his wife. We had already booked our real honeymoon, a ten-day 'extravaganza' over Christmas and the New Year, to be expounded upon anon.

I think the two weeks I enjoyed at Gunton Hall were during Dave May's indisposition (he had expected my job). This helped uplift me for our wedding day. The band's reaction of hatred had been a marvel to behold.

It is right, and fair, to come back to my alcohol intake. During my three seasons at Holimarine, I had consumed four or five pints of bitter a day. I did not drink spirits, except on the odd occasion when they arrived unannounced. I saw myself as half a bon viveur, with no apparent problems. Even at this stage, it never entered my head that I was a problem drinker. But here I was, back into universal hatred. The band were excellent at doing Dave May's bidding when he wasn't in the ballroom to do his own.

It was at that stage, early September that I bought myself a bottle of Scotch, which I hid in the dressing room. The first time I thought to take a swig was the moment the lady band vocalist suddenly appeared from behind a curtain. She pretended she hadn't seen, but who could do that with a leer on their face?

Within days of this, Jude had a scare; an unexpected bleed. Everyone at the camp (apart from the aforementioned) was sympathetic and caring. A lady in reception telephoned Gorleston Hospital and declared an emergency at Gunton Hall. The ambulance arrived in less than five minutes, and she was taken to the hospital for complete rest over a three-day period. Before leaving, they were able to reassure us to a large extent. This was not rare; there was an excellent chance she would quickly stabilise.

This was how it was, and fortunately we had no further scares.

* * * *

The season came to its natural conclusion. Jude had said very little, but the shop manageress had apparently taken every opportunity to belittle me in front of her. This was extremely unkind and hurtful. It had something to do with the fact that the manageress did not have an Oxford degree.

At the end of the season, in fact in the last few days, a gentleman approached me and suggested that in the immediate future summer seasons would probably be difficult. He told us he worked for an insurance underwriter called Confederation Life. He thoroughly enjoyed his work, and had acquired financial success beyond his expectations. He then said he thought I would make an excellent underwriter.

I was taken in by the rhetoric; after all I had endured a season which had made me doubt I would ever again make a success of anything! Melodramatic, and an awful exaggeration, yes, but when you've been made to feel useless over a five month period, anything must be better. Wrong again Scott!

I tried to do the job to the best of my ability. The first month was ok. One was invited to 'tap up' relatives and friends. After that, all the encouragement I had been given was as ash in a promised fire. Most potential customers were 'out'.

I watched others working; one was a chap who was taken on at the same time as myself. One evening, when I had nothing planned, after so many cancellations, he asked me to join him and to see how things went. He was useless! This must sound like sour grapes, but he was a guy I knew who had endured, with his wife, the loss of a child in a freak accident. That was for life.

The best was when he told a prospective buyer he had the contract for him to sign. The cost was £2,000. Suddenly, he snatched the contract back away from his prospect, saying he had reckoned it up wrongly. It was £4,000.

'That's all right, I'll sign for that!' said the prospect.

The nearest I got was when a gentleman I had spent hours with held the pen above the contract and asked 'Is this where I sign?' In came his wife. 'Oh no it isn't, you don't sign anything anywhere! I need a new washing machine!'

It was interesting to learn that the most successful underwriters were Mormons. I suppose they were so used to being dismissed from a doorstep with an expletive that their thought patterns were just 'it's ok, on to the second' and so on, confident that by number ten, one would have shown an interest. So on with the next ten. Maybe there's something to be said for most things...

For me the downward trend moved inexorably toward its

nadir (making pretend calls in the office was the pits). I felt myself moving deeper into depression, not truly knowing if it was reactive, or clinical. It felt like a bunch of both.

Just before my downhill spiral, our first child was born. It was at a time (April 6 1984) when parents were not told the sex of their child, but most fathers were present at the birth. It seemed to be all systems go, and the midwife (she was so good) was expecting things to happen quickly. Our child had other ideas. Having started to be born, she decided to fall asleep in the birth canal! The midwife insisted this was no problem as she would soon awake and come along to enjoy the party. She did wake up, but for poor Jude the labour was to last for nine hours. It was only when the surgeon threatened forceps that 'little one' decided to make her appearance. The lovely midwife should have finished her shift two hours before, but she declared her desire to stay: 'This one's mine', I remember her saying.

When the baby was two minutes old, she was handed to me. They say new-born babies cannot focus their eyes. This one could! Her message to me was 'Well this is it! I'll just have to make a go of it!' She was named Hannah Catherine.

Poor Jude was exhausted. I gave her a big hug, and kissed her goodnight (it was after 11pm). I telephoned mum to let her know that at sixty-three, she had become a grandmother for the first time. She did better than me. In August 2019, I became a grandfather for the first time at seventy-three.

As our new, and very much changed, lifestyle developed, Jude and I soon adjusted. She took control of our lovely home, and responsibility for the family. She did the shopping and cooked very nicely for me. Because she didn't drive yet, I drove her to the supermarket, and collected her at an appointed time. I took responsibility for our earnings, and also for our accounts. Jude didn't have to worry about that. I did! I think it was a fair division of labour, taking into account that Jude could not find an occupation commensurate with her qualifications without a year's further study. The time was not right for that, we both agreed.

One morning, I found her looking a bit strained. Her 'get up and go', had got up and gone. We knew a lady in the village who was happy to come and do some cleaning. She was very reliable, and it took just a little pressure off Jude.

Hannah slept in a rocking cot on my side of our four-poster bed. When she was ready to be fed, she let us know with a vengeance; I lifted her and handed her to Jude. She breast-fed her. I was pleased I never had to shell out for a dummy!

Hannah had her own routine when it came for me to settle her back to sleep. It started with a loudish protest cry, followed by a short hesitation. Then came what sounded like the end of the world. The first few times this happened, I speedily removed her to Jude. She rather liked that, I noticed. After I had put her back, there would come a small 'grumble' but it almost said, 'I've had a good run for my money!'

After a couple of these outbursts, I persuaded Jude to let me leave her in the cot. That time she subsided. There was a tiny little moan, but that was it. She slept through, and was in good form in the morning. Jude thought I'd been cruel.

'Give me one more chance,' I said to her, 'Hannah's too clever by half'. She didn't demur. It was one of the only times I ever got the better of her.

From a year onwards, I was able to lift her at about midnight and she would instinctively 'perform'. Daytime was not so easy. When the 'potty' was suggested it was always 'Hannah soon'. It all came right when her favourite doll Emmy 'performed' in the bathroom. We had filled her pot with water and sat Emmy down over it. Hannah was asked to check if Emmy had 'performed'. It was a big surprise to her, but she wouldn't be beaten by her doll!

This may all sound fine, but as previously mentioned I was sinking into depression. It was not usual for me to feel unable to cope with a new chosen career, but I was not coping. Jude had noticed me struggling physically. It took a great effort to lift Hannah so that she could sit on my lap. My doctor gave me a certificate to pass on to Confederation Life. At the same time I was diagnosed with ME.

Thirty-five years later, I found I had passed on a genetic condition to my youngest daughter. Although different to ME, the symptoms, particularly lassitude, were very similar. A rogue gene fights against muscle competency.

The Confederation Life manager visited us and said I had made a very promising start. He obviously hoped my present state was a 'blip'. I knew deep down that this was unlikely. The next thing he suggested was to give it two weeks and he would come once more, in good faith and accept however I felt at that time.

Meanwhile, I remembered my insurance underwriter explaining to me that if I had health problems, I should contact PHI with the official notifications. There was nothing to lose. I heard from the company two or three days later. It was a polite letter, acknowledging the facts and with a desire to meet me in my home. They suggested a date and time which was convenient for me. I was reassured as their letter continued to say that the company would take responsibility for my medical situation.

I really cannot remember how much they subsidised me,

but it was more than I expected or even hoped for. It enabled us to pay our way. We were also in the fortunate position of not having to find the money for a mortgage.

I return briefly to our belated honeymoon, when we spent five days over Christmas in Ullswater, in the Lake District. Then we went north and took a car ferry to the Isle of Arran, which was quite a contrast – what a lovely place. We celebrated Hogmanay there. It was my first, and to the present day my last. Jude enjoyed the experience. I did not. It was self-inflicted misery! It turned out to be my worst drinking spree since my 21st birthday at Pontins, and this time around, my drinks weren't spiked! We were with a group of 'young indigenous', who were also feeling no pain (at that time). I can still remember persuading them to sing 'Maybe it's because I'm a Londoner'. I also recall the manager of the establishment coming over to make sure we had enjoyed ourselves. I reached out to shake his hand and missed!

I offered to drive Jude back to the hotel. I couldn't believe it; she refused! I insisted I could drive better than I could walk.

If only I had made myself bring things up, but instead I rested my weary head and allowed myself to sleep. I woke at five in the afternoon, still feeling quite violently ill. The upshot was a month with no alcohol, not because I felt guilty, which I did, but because I just couldn't face the thought of it.

Jude had spent many holidays in the Lake District with her parents, and like them enjoyed climbing. She persuaded me to have an attempt at one of the least demanding climbs, known as Stickle Tarn. It took a supreme effort to climb just under 1000ft, but I got there, exhausted but triumphant. I now know how they felt on reaching the summit of Everest. Jude, as ever organised, produced her camera. 'You'll be able

to show this to your drinking buddies; they'll never believe it!'
At dinner that night she said, 'Oh, we've had a bit of bad luck;
I forgot to put the film in the camera!'

* * * *

This was just before my ultimate visit to the taxman. I knew I
had a fair amount to pay, but for a start, I had all my earnings
from Gunton Hall tucked away. He went through everything
we had discussed, and he said that at this stage I had to sign
a guarantee, saying everything had been discussed. Before I
signed, he noted I had one sum of money that still had not
become inclusive to the package. I was lost. My taxman
found some figures which 'looked about right' and said he
would accept them, so I signed. I thought I'd have to pay
about £10,000. I had forgotten compound interest! Despite
my declaring what hadn't been assessed, my bill was £21,750.
The taxman was sympathetic. He realised it was a blow for
me, but he said, 'Had we got to you before you came to us it
would have been in excess of £50,000'. I would have had to
start again.

As it was, I found another kind side of this 'destroyer'. He
said he knew it would take some while for me to co-ordinate
my finances. 'Give me a ring in six months, and I'll give you
a date future to that when I would expect your payment,' he
said. I acknowledged my gratitude. This really made a big
difference to me.

Jude had come into town to give me some moral support.
I had 'parked' her in the Great White Horse Hotel (of Dickens

fame in Pickwick Papers) in Ipswich town centre and ordered her a coffee. When I returned to her, I rued the time I had estimated £8,000 to £10,000 pounds. There was no point in hiding the fact – we were a team now.

'I'm sorry Jude, I had forgotten compound interest. The actual bill is £21,750,' I said.

She gulped a bit, but I insisted she shouldn't worry. I quickly told her that the taxman had been extremely generous and given me in excess of six months before I needed to make payment.

It was four weeks to the day after that Hogmanay on Arran. Jude had a second coffee. I decided I needed something stronger to raise me above the perils of compound interest. It was seven weeks before I joined Confederation Life, and ten weeks before the appearance of Hannah. The late, great Tommy Cooper died on stage the week after her birth. I ordered a Special Brew...

By the end of the month of May, the General Manager of Confederation Life Insurance had made his final visit to Ancient Lights. We showed him all the medical assessments, including the diagnosis of ME. He was very sympathetic, and was now certain the job was not for me. He wished me well.

The ME diagnosis was nearly right. As already stated, the malady was genetic. Jude remembered times in the past when I had had little energy, and found it hard enough to climb the stairs. I also remember at the time describing symptoms to my GP. He said 'it sounds like ME. Everyone seems to have it these days, so you might as well'. He shrugged. I was not impressed. It was pleasing though that after so long, I could feel justified in having not made things up. That's how you can be made to feel.

I began to feel I should make an effort to contribute on the work front. The PHI insurance was a godsend, but not to wallow in. The first place I approached was the Mecca bingo hall in central Ipswich. I enquired in the reception area if they had any time available for bingo callers. I explained that I had been a full-time professional caller in London with the Top Rank Organisation. In those days the bingo caller was the doyen of the hall; not any more. A reliable cleaner now earned more than the 'front man'. This was no problem to me; I was just trying gradually to return to some sort of employment. I think I understood what would be helpful from my confidence point of view. The Manager told me that Saturdays were presently a problem, and I was only too pleased to offer my services. Not only did they pay the going rate, but I had tax returned in proportion to recent employment. I hope it came from the back pocket of my taxman!

After Hannah was born (with a touch of jaundice, which disappeared within a week), I had a telephone call from the Carl Adams Norfolk agency asking if I would do three weeks' work, five days a week, in Nottingham. They were prepared to put up 'walk-ons' very cheaply. This was at the time of the miners' strike. I told Carl Adams that I considered myself available, and would confirm within an hour. I immediately called Jude to ask her what she thought. I told her I would only go if she was happy she would cope alone at such an exacting time. She asked me how I felt about it. I just said it was worth over £500 for our coffers; this would be at least £1,500 in 2019. 'I'll be working with no pressure, and will phone you every evening,' I said. 'If there's a problem, I'll just come straight home'.

We were well into springtime; the weather was warmer, and the *Darling Buds Of May* were on their way. Jude said she was happy I should go. I returned Carl's call, informing him I was up for it. He said he would put all detail into the post.

We were actually on a film set. It was called 'Jenny's War', starring four times married (including Cary Grant) Hollywood star Dyan Cannon, best known for being difficult. She had a massive caravanette on the dreary set. It reminded me of a carriage from the 'Orient Express'.

It rained almost unceasingly. The director decided he would film the extras (we were railway workers) on our own. The loose Cannon refused to appear in the rain. In a way it was a woeful time for us all, but I met a chap about my vintage who very soon became a friend. Steve had been booked by a London agency. There was nothing unusual about this; often on set we met others who had been booked by a variety of agents.

Steve, without any prompting, found pen and paper and wrote down all the necessary contacts for four London agencies. (One was Mr Allander – Mr 'Shan't Forget You'). We spent many happy days together. Every day on location with Steve was a good day. We met mainly in London, but not infrequently in the 'sticks'. We were at Thames Television the day Benny Hill lost his 'life blood'. I was returning from the Green Room as two fellows arrived through the main door – Benny Hill and his agent. Benny was within moments of being told his time with Thames Television was at an end. The shock hastened his death.

I returned from Nottingham, and told Jude I was glad I had done the job but I wouldn't do it again. After all I really missed Hannah – oh, and her!

I continued at the Mecca Bingo Hall until the early part of July. We had already spent time out with Hannah, as much as possible (on the good days) in her push chair. Like any child, she had her moments, but she laughed a lot (though not at my jokes). We sometimes went to Felixstowe on the coast, taking in the wonderful fresh air and visiting the playground where, hanging tightly on to Hannah, we introduced her to the swings and roundabouts.

We had also discovered a delightful 'Bluebell Wood', three miles from Bramford. Talk about being 'closer to God in a garden'. It was so peaceful. We went dozens of times as the family grew.

In October the weather was still good. Judith had come by a travel magazine which was advertising North Norfolk caravan holidays and holiday breaks. She had stayed in Blakeney just once with her family, but she quickly said we didn't feel it was any less good as a holiday venue, it was just that we were all in love with the Lake District.

Jude had already proved to me that she was not only an excellent mother, but with a little help, she could keep a large Tudor property spotless, and look after me, the most undomesticated person in the world, or not far off. She thought a four-day break would be a change for us. She also said she was happy to do the food if we had the odd meal out. We had more than an 'odd meal' out. Jude did the booking and made sure it was a caravan with a cot.

The idea Jude had, for the break could not have worked out better. We did a mini-shop in the precinct, so we had breakfast sorted. It was fine, but a trifle chilly, so we put our 'warmers' on, except Hannah! Mum made sure she wouldn't be cold.

Jude suggested a trip to Holkham Hall, which was only about eight miles away. It was a splendid place architecturally. I noticed a cricket pitch, albeit closed off, but I made note of it for the future.

Directly opposite was the road which enabled holiday makers to get to the beach. It was said that if the car-park was full, each person will be left with just one acre of sand to themselves! We were happy to put 50p in the tin, when told any contribution would help to keep the summer season costs to a minimum (we'll believe anything when we're enjoying ourselves.)

We did get close enough for me to observe the whole vista of Holkham Beach for the first time. Jude had stayed with Hannah, who was due a feed, and unless the oil in the car was going off, a change!

We took a detour via Walsingham and noticed a narrow-gauge railway which ran from Wells directly to Walsingham. We were lucky to find an open door, which showed me for the first time the ruins which were left at the time of the Reformation. We also noticed that further down the road was a Thai restaurant – another consideration for the future. Both Jude and I thoroughly enjoyed oriental cuisine. But it was now time to get back to the caravan, and to settle Hannah down for the night.

CHAPTER 12

OF BRIDGE AND BABIES

At the beginning of 1985, the time when I was trying to overcome clinical depression, with my failure at coping with Confederation Life, yet managing the familiar bingo-calling and walk-on work, I saw an advertisement in the *English Bridge Magazine*. Its essence was to encourage players who might have the ability to teach. I decided to make contact in the hope that it might give me an evening class. I had taught several disciplines; perhaps I could add to them?

The deal was to apply and request a written exam regarding knowledge of the game. You were expected to score 60% before proceeding to an 'oral' in front of an expert who would ask questions, give you a challenging example of play and choose a subject out of six that needed revising in advance, which you were expected to lecture on in front of the expert.

My letter, showing my enthusiastic interest, was posted

before lunch. The response, which included my written exam, landed on the door mat on the second day after my request. Jude knew about it, and thought it was a good idea. I settled down to the theory. I have to say all limitations were such that I consider myself, at nigh on seventy-four, a better player than I have ever been. I hasten to add at a 'usual competitive level' than the 'also rans'. Having done my best, I returned my exam paper. I felt the same as I did when I handed in my 'O' Level efforts.

The results came back, with a date to confirm for my oral in London. I had hardly covered myself in in glory with the theory (at best average + a bit). However, I was reasonably happy with 75%. By return I accepted the date and time for my oral.

I travelled to London from Ipswich, as ever enjoying train travel. On arrival, I caught the Underground to the designated place, which just required a five-minute walk. I reached my destination just as a previous lady had been called into the 'lion's den'. As far as she was concerned it was just that. I sat waiting my turn to the sounds of shouting, screaming and what seemed like crying. Finally she stormed out shouting and swearing, looking purple, and with tears flying from her eyes.

As the clicking of stilettos faded, I wondered what I had let myself in for. I needn't have worried. He and his remarkable wife welcomed me. They were Mr and Mrs G.C.H. Fox; he was the bridge correspondent of the *Daily Telegraph*, and an erstwhile international player. He welcomed me in with an inviting smile.

'It's Eddie Scott, isn't it?' I responded in my usual way to such a situation, with a very slight head bow.

'Yes, sir!'

'Don't call me 'sir' Eddie. It's Geoff, and this is my wife'.

I'm ashamed to say I don't remember her Christian name, but in her own way I was made to feel welcome. It was August 15th. He asked me quite a lot of questions, most of them general. If you've stuck with this from the beginning, you may remember that at the age of three and a half I used to climb onto the gate at the front of the house and instigate conversations with anybody who walked by. I think this was something that grew with me, rather than something I grew out of. I answered his questions with careful confidence.

Next, he dictated a hand onto the convenient blackboard, and asked me to find a way of making ten tricks after the opponents had led the ♠ KING. I tried one way and stopped. A second attempt was not working; then I saw the line I had to take. I asked Geoff if I could have one last try.

'Yes Eddie, go ahead.'

I managed to get it right, just in time.

'Well done, it was tricky. We'll take a short break'.

I have used the word 'stentoriously' in the past, but only for a description of the male voice. Mrs Fox was the first lady I had met for whom the word was appropriate. In the depths of her basso profundo she announced her wares. 'Do you take tea?'

As it was, I didn't, but I told them I'd happily wait while they had theirs. That wasn't strictly true, but £2.50 for a cup of tea in 1985 seemed a bridge too far. Yuk!

We were soon back with my test, and Geoff asked me what I would like to speak on. You'll probably remember that I was originally told I had to 'gen' up on the six subjects enclosed with my letter. The Director would choose one.

Geoff finished his tea, and noted that there were six choices. He smiled, and just asked me which one I would like to talk about. I moved on quickly before he had a chance to change his mind. I chose 'Stayman'.

I am acutely aware that many readers have no knowledge of bridge. Why should they? Some of us don't come from card-playing families. Others might have done, but simply didn't enjoy the game. Some love fishing, some run, some swim, some love football, and/or cricket, rugby or hockey. Some enjoy playing chess. And some enjoy scuba diving. Bridge became my profession for twenty-five years. In an autobiography, I can't ignore this.

I will endeavour to make bridge detail clear to the general reader. I really will do my best.

'Stayman' is the name of a convention which players (partnerships) use to try and get the best possible contracts (the amount of tricks – four cards one from thirteen, fifty-two cards). When one of the partnership uses a convention, the other partner has to alert it. No secrets allowed!

I presented the subject to the Foxes. They looked at each other and nodded. Geoff then thanked me and said that he couldn't give me a decision today, but they would be in touch as soon as possible. I thanked them both for their forbearance. 'Thank you for coming' he said, giving me an encouraging wink.

As I left, I thought of the lady in front of me. Whatever could have happened to elicit such a reaction? Perhaps she was flippant? I know that would not have gone down well, or maybe Mrs 'stentorian' Fox didn't take to her and said something derogatory? I'll never know.

I felt OK about the morning, and returned to Liverpool Street for the next train home. It was lovely to be back just before Hannah was settled down, and Jude and I shared a bottle of wine over dinner. We talked about each other's day.

The next morning, just as we were finishing breakfast, the telephone rang. I answered. It was Chris Chambers. Chris was both an old friend and an old adversary – he was one of the best Bridge players in Suffolk. He was also an established bridge teacher. He was one of two at that time; the other was now an elderly gentleman, whose wise counsel created many competent players to add to the Suffolk contingency. (Sadly he was to pass away at the end of the year).

'Chris here Eddie, I need your help. I've just registered at night school class at Copleston' (a very good secondary school in Ipswich). Term time ran much in line for the school, and the adult bridge classes. I asked Chris what we wanted me to do. He told me that forty-one people had registered for the classes! He couldn't take on that figure on his own. He felt it would be hard on him, and perforce, it would be hardly fair on those attending the classes.

I told him I had sneaked through the written paper, but was still awaiting results of my oral.

'Confound you Scott! Please help. I know you can do it. I implore you.'

'Ok Chris, but just in case, I trust you will come to my defence if I am accused of false declaration!'

As agreed, we met at seven in the pre-ordained room. I was directed to the classroom reserved for me. It didn't happen that often, but the entire group of forty-one arrived on the actual first day of the adult education term. Chris took the odd one, leaving me with twenty. It was decided on the last day before the Christmas break that we would have a mini competition.

I enjoyed every moment of that first experience. Added

to that, a letter from London soon arrived with a positive reaction to the result of my oral. I felt I was on my way.

When it came to the last Thursday of the autumn term, we all gathered in the room where Chris had done his teaching. He had set it out for a 'first friendly competition'. It would often be questioned how you divide forty-one by four; perfectly understandable. You can't! But in classes, an odd one can easily be involved. Take a table of five, everyone sits out for just one hand, and the one sitting out can briefly can take advantage of watching. This in itself adds to the sum of learning.

The competition was close, and much enjoyed. It came down to the last three hands. Chris's team won that 2:1. Everybody left happily, looking forward to the spring term. Chris and I took ourselves out for a quick pint and a natter.

I like to think that the only reason I lost the competition, was because all term he had one extra brain; so Chris had a distinct advantage. I think the reader will already know something of bridge and consider my expostulation 'sour grapes'. If I had honestly meant what I said, they would be right!

The year after, Chris, because of more pressing commitments, was unable to teach bridge. I was on my own! I was invited to take, if possible, five classes, in my second year, and in the third nine classes! I still suffered from my demons on and off, but medication, which took about twelve days, eventually kicked in. What a relief. I still managed somehow, (I don't remember how), to take every opportunity of walk-on work. During this period it was mainly *Hi-De-Hi* and *'Allo 'Allo*.

I regularly sent the PHI Company details of my part-time work, but it was not until 1996, on one of several visits, they considered me 'able', and on completion of the benefit, added £500 to help cope with the change in circumstances. I thought they had been very fair, and yet I wish the genetic problem had been isolated by them rather than 'ME. Everyone seems to have it these days, so you might as well...'

I shall briefly return to bridge (boring, I hear you say), but there is much more to indulge the reader.

* * * *

I feel it's time to share with you the greatest happening of my life (the second greatest was my promotion to Entertainments Director in the P&O Fleet). The greatest, shared with Jude, was the birth and raising of three very special daughters. I've already touched on Hannah, but she was followed by Victoria and Katherine, all born within a period of three years and three months. Jude was a brilliant mother. We did without dummies, and she breastfed throughout the period before weaning.

Hannah was twenty-one months old when Victoria was born in January 1986. She wanted to be at the hospital, and Jude and I agreed she should come for an hour. Sue Haywood had kindly bought Hannah a nurse's uniform, which she changed into at the hospital. She really looked the part, and amused the nursing staff as she 'took charge!' After the hour, Sue took her home to Ancient Lights and stayed with her until I returned.

Jude was convinced she was having a boy. Since the first kick, the kicking had hardly stopped. She was certain he would play for England! Her labour was easier than with Hannah, and the birth was straightforward. We had decided on 'Megan' if it happened to be a girl. She weighed in at a healthy 7lb

11oz. Everything seemed set fair; when I returned to Ancient Lights, Sue had made me her speciality Welsh Rarebit. I was better off than I deserved to be.

It is now the moment to introduce Auntie Read. She lived next door, in the 'fourth part' of the old house. She was about sixty-five. She had one daughter who had duly married, and one granddaughter; our daughters became her surrogate granddaughters. She was absolutely wonderful with them. She had offered to come and sit with Hannah when 'Auntie Sue', as she became known, returned home.

As promised, I returned to the hospital to visit Jude. As my short journey was wending its way hospital wise, I began thinking about the new arrival I had held and looked at for the first time. She was lovely, but to me the name 'Megan' seemed wrong for her.

I arrived at the ward. Jude looked cheerful and well. I gave her a kiss and she said, 'All seems fine. That is, except her name. I hate to bring discord on such a wonderful day, but I don't see her as 'Megan''.

'Jude, you may not believe this, but it's true; I've been wondering how to tell you. I don't think she's a 'Megan' either!'

We both breathed a sigh of relief, laughed together and then she asked me if I had an alternative in mind. I told her my choice would be Victoria. She thought about it for a short while, then asked me if she could 'sleep on it'. I suggested she should, as after all I didn't expect to have the last word! When I visited the next day, she told me she liked the idea of Victoria very much. We sealed it with a kiss.

In the meantime, sister Cathy and John were also going through the process, and a healthy boy was born on July 15th 1986. Cathy, however, came out of labour frighteningly ill.

John for a while despaired of her life. She didn't know who she was or where she was, and didn't know John. It must, for him, have been the most harrowing time.

She was gradually nursed back to normality, but despite the fact they had hoped to have two, he decided, on behalf of them both, that they had a healthy son (Paul), and that next time Cathy might not be so fortunate. What a guy to have as a brother-in-law! I think Cathy thought she had let John down, but he said to her with a smile, 'I'd rather you stayed alive'. He was absolutely right.

Paul turned into an expert swimmer, just missing the Commonwealth Games (in the early part of the new century) by around 0.2 of a second. His best friend – they had both been involved since youngsters – made it to the games in 2006, and in the free-style, won the Gold Medal. Was Paul envious? Not a bit of it. He had invited all their swimming friends round (with a few eats and drinks), and all cheered him home.

It was several months before we saw Paul for the first time (hardly surprising, considering Cathy's malady), but by then we were expecting number three! It was a difficult time for Judith, because Vicky had already started behaving in an extraordinary way. Talk about Dr Jekyll and Mr Hyde; she would be fine one moment, and the next like a wildcat at bay. It was frightening for both of us, but as mentioned, I had resigned with regret from The Samaritans, explaining that it would be totally unreasonable to be absent from home all night during one of the coldest of winters. Jude was becalmed in our bedroom with two little ones, one with what seemed to be, unfathomable problems. I used the word 'regret' because I had spent invaluable time with unassuming people. Today, it seems, they might have found a way around our situation with regard to nights, but that was then. We all had the same disciplines to adhere to.

When we first took Vicky to the doctor's he said, 'she might be a coeliac, or have other food allergies. I'll recommend she has an appointment at the hospital'. All we got then was an example of lip service. Eventually we persuaded 'Mr No one' to at least provide us with an appointment with the Head of Paediatrics at the hospital. Between us, Jude and I had written a long paragraph about her symptoms, how she was affected, and what we in our simplicity found it difficult to explain. He took it, never looked at it, and put it on the edge of his table. Can you believe it? He then said, that this was beyond his comprehension, all with a shrug of his shoulders. He said he would make an appointment for us at Great Ormond Street, in London. Nobody seemed to realise that all we wanted to know was how to cope with her. Eventually we received our appointment.

If you can imagine how long all this took, it might help if I say that by this time our third daughter was to be born on the 8th July 1987. I was booked for an all-day bridge seminar through the Suffolk College that day. Our number three behaved conveniently (just).

Jude said her waters had 'broken', so I got her into my car and drove her to the place that now seemed like a second home. She promptly went to sleep. The midwife said to me 'About four hours. Now you're here, would you like to stay?'

Auntie Read had been seconded for the night.

This aspect of the hospital had been wonderful. Three different midwives, all superb. Their attitude, exceptional. They provided me with a 'put you up' bed. I was woken at 5am, and told that things were about to happen. The birth was quick; Jude stayed calm. The midwife informed us we had a healthy baby girl. She was 6lb 15oz, her name Katherine, to be known universally as Kate.

Hannah had said that she wanted a brother. When I arrived home, I had time to let everybody know before final preparations for my day's work. We had told Auntie Read that this might happen, and she loyally stayed until the early evening, when I returned home.

Hannah was at the top of the stairs, behind the safety gate, with Vicky at her side.

'Well you two,' I said gently, 'you have another sister.'

Hannah's face drooped, but only for a moment. She had a tear on her cheek, but lifting her blonde locks she said, 'I really wanted a little sister'.

Vicky was eighteen months old at this time. The process towards help had lasted just over a year. Great Ormond Street sent the time for our interview. We were told it would be ideal if the whole family were together. It was a rare time when I had to apologise for a day off work.

Jude and I had once again provided 'pertinent paragraphs' regarding our observations; once again, they were tossed aside. There were some toys on the floor, so the girls did at least occupy themselves. We got absolutely nowhere with the specialist at Great Ormond Street. When we were ushered out of his esteemed presence, we discovered this 'specialist' did not even know which one of our three was Vicky!

We were offered a follow up appointment, but Jude was adamant it would be a waste of time. What were we to do? And this was when we enjoyed an extreme moment of serendipity. I was speaking to a friend, and erstwhile bridge partner, Mike Malin, and by chance mentioned Vicky's plight. Mike was Polish; he had travelled with his parents as a very young boy, before the war, and stayed. He told me that years before, he had been very unwell, surviving on coffee, and had got to the stage when he was about to lose a leg. Someone mentioned a Dr Nelson Brunton, a homeopath who had a practice in a place called Witham, about forty miles from Ipswich. He was a well-qualified doctor who had chosen the holistic route to healing. As Mike said, 'He not only healed me, he saved my leg!'

As soon as I got home, I told Jude we had a lifeline. She was as excited as I was. I phoned the number Mike had given me and made an appointment there and then for just three days hence. This was a miracle for us. Jude and I rewrote our experiences of Vicky as we saw them, much as we had when they were ignored by two specialists.

We were called into Dr Brunton's surgery. He was an Indian gentleman, and I felt I was surrounded by an aura of goodness. Jude felt the same. We tentatively handed Nelson our notes. What a difference; we sat in silence for at least five to ten minutes while he inwardly digested them.

This, he told us was reasonably rare. 'But I'm sure it's a multi-allergic reaction to many foodstuffs'. (That figured, because it was only when she came off breast milk that the situation had reared its ugly head). He described the likely sources and talked of the foodstuffs to be avoided. He understood this would not be easy, but Jude had always been resourceful. Vicky, who was nearly three by now, was also very good about the situation. She never complained. On one occasion, when the others had chocolate (after they had finished their dinner), Vicky said to Hannah, 'Do you think I could just smell it?'

Vicky did however have a special treat. Nelson had given us the address of a sweet company which provided anti-allergy alternatives. They came in the post about once a fortnight. There was always a special day for Vicky. Whoever went to collect the post would shout that there was 'something special here for someone'. Vicky arrived from wherever she was causing her usual mayhem and it was lovely to see her so delighted. I must say, much as her sisters were concerned, they were genuinely pleased for her.

Dr Brunton drew our appointment to its end. He asked to see her again in two months, unless the problems became worse. His final words to us were 'the raging storm will come to an end in six weeks'. He was one day out!

We continued to visit Nelson for several months. We are eternally grateful for all he achieved for us. I was always grateful to Judith. It must have been demanding work for her, but she never wavered. I fell in love with Vicky that day.

* * * *

In September 1988, Hannah started school. We attended the local church, twenty-five yards away. Alternatively we went to St. Thomas Church, two miles from Bramford, where I had been a choirboy since I was seven. At the age of twelve I was awarded the prestige position of Top Boy. This was for the two years until my voice broke – nay, smashed!

The girls, in due course, joined the choir in Bramford. Jude and I had decided we would continue while they wanted to be there. After a few years, they began to drift away. After all, we could do no more than show them an alternative, and leave them to decide for themselves.

I remember Hannah's second day at school. I watched her through the window, and when she felt settled I would move on. But on this morning, her desk had disappeared. Hannah was already 'compartmentalising' her life. This was not part of the scenario. The poor little thing burst into tears, and they flew, just like the bridge lady in London.

The school had a brilliant headmaster and he said to Hannah, 'Just give me two minutes. You wait there, and I'll come back, and we'll go on a desk hunt!' I couldn't stay long enough to know the full result, but I'm sure his reaction couldn't have been better. Hannah thrived.

Vicky started at the school in 1990, and Kate in 1991. Mr. Sharples, the Head, put his life's blood into St. Matthews School. The trouble was, he wanted to teach as well. He was often not leaving the school until 10pm. He never gave the impression of being hardy, and he had a serious nervous breakdown. In the fullness of a long time, he recovered and returned to teaching, without the immense responsibility of 'headship'. We were given to understand that he was happier now.

In the meantime Hannah was pushed forward a year. Unlike her sisters, she was hardly affected by the massive difference with her change regarding Mr. Sharples. She passed an exam to be admitted to the Ipswich High School for Girls at fifteen, passed 'O' Levels at seventeen and 'A' Levels at nineteen. At twenty-two, she graduated with a 1st Class Honours Degree in 'Modern Languages' at Durham University.

The others had to put up with a left-wing acolyte (I hasten to add I have the same repulsion for the right-wing). His policy was that not one child was permitted to move on until the last one in the class had completed the 'course'. This was brought home to me when Vicky climbed into the car one afternoon. Judith's time would come, but for now she had enough on her plate.

'Daddy, it's great at school now,' she said. 'The work is so much easier than last year.' I couldn't expect her to understand politics, but it was obvious even to a simple soul, like myself!

Within a week, we had been accepted by a 'sister' church, St. Margaret's, for Kate, where she thrived. She won the Drama Prize. They just had no legal space for Vicky. We decided we would pay for her to attend Junior House at the high school where Hannah was studying. We were able to attain a part-paid place, dependant on income. Vicky also flourished. She was the most sports orientated of the three – hockey, netball, long distance running. I often wondered if her enforced diet had something to do with that.

In time the three were reunited. It was a happy period. (I just had to present my accounts and pay the required amount.) It was tight but manageable, and very fair. It was an outstanding school with an equally outstanding Headmistress.

When Vicky was eight, I was asked by the Head, one Miss MacCuish, if I played chess. I said it was my game before bridge. She said to me that eight was the ideal age to learn. Coincidentally, my three daughters could all play bridge (to a basic level) by the age of eight. I was invited to teach chess for two hours, once a week. I enjoyed it. I stayed for five years.

* * * *

Away from school, we liked to get 'out and about' with the girls. Our nearest resort was Felixstowe, little changed from its heyday about 1880–1910, despite the enormous docks. The girls knew they could expect an ice-cream, money for the 'slots' on the pier and a bracing walk along the promenade. In the summer months there was the added stimulation of swings, roundabouts, train rides, crazy golf, and a helter-skelter. There was also an excellent swimming pool, and, in season, bowls. A day at Felixstowe was always a good day.

I have mentioned the 'Bluebell Woods' before, but a visit there was always special. When the girls were very young, 5–10 years old, Auntie Read made one visit every week. She taught them to cook, to knit, to weave, and to bake. She was a sheer delight with them.

I remember every Saturday morning, one little but loud voice: 'Is it my turn with Auntie Read?' This was the time I went to the 'Cock' in Bramford to prepare my 'bridge hands' for the next week. This was a two hour labour, three Special Brews. The beginning of my problems. I was really ignorant!

Sunday was 'British Legion' day. Jude came along sometimes, but it wasn't really her scene. It was not a question of 'just a drink, and a packet of crisps'. It was games and cards, squares and shapes, snakes and ladders, cokes and crisps, and after the fizz, a quiz! As the girls grew older, it was pool. When I thought they were ready, I checked at the bar if they could play. We all played.

I enjoyed about 2½ pints of lager, but never left them for male company. Obviously I enjoyed 'banter at the bar' while I ordered repeats and essentials.

When Hannah was twelve, I went to the bar and asked if she could play snooker. Again they said, 'If you take responsibility, that will be fine'. Over a two-year period, with the logical gaps, we played 95 frames. Hannah won 48! 'Twas ever thus.

* * * *

I will return to the family on 'their holidays' soon, but I should now remind you that I had started what, much to my enormous surprise, turned into a new career. It lasted until I retired, and I celebrated a bridge silver marriage just before I hung up my cards.

As previously mentioned, I completed my first year with Chris Chambers. He was supportive throughout, and I was indebted to him. The next year, 1986, Chris had important commitments which precluded him from teaching. When approached, he passed my name on, and as mentioned, I was invited to 'front' five classes. This was hardly a money spinner for a man trying to keep a family of five afloat, but my instinct was to stay with it. I was of course still receiving my National Insurance payments, for which I was grateful. I still had to battle bouts of clinical depression, and I don't know how I would have coped without the backup. I had though, along the way, passed my oral, with kind words from Geoff Fox. I felt properly qualified.

In 1987, I was invited to do nine classes. Somehow I still managed to get, without double-booking, my television 'walk-on' work, which was always a pleasurable day with a few pennies to come.

One of those days in London, early in 1987, before Kate was born, one of the students and his wife approached me, and introduced themselves (I had to call a register at the beginning). The gentleman was Max Newport. He owned his own printing works, and suggested, as bridge books were quite expensive, that I put together a basic manual on our learning for the year. He would happily print it for £1 a time.

I agreed, saying I would enjoy the challenge. The next day I wasn't teaching, but was offered a day's 'walk-on' in London. I had got into the habit during this period to take preparation papers with me. On this occasion it was my good fortune that I had not forgotten.

I arrived on location after a 5am start, to be told that they had had problems the previous night, and the scene I was supposed to be in had been cancelled. The lady was almost embarrassing with her apologies. She handed me a £10 note, which she didn't have to do. She was insistent, and said, 'Your full fee will come to you in the normal way'. She put out her hand with a tinge of discomfort, but I grabbed it, saying she 'had been most reasonable under difficult circumstances'. She said 'at least stay for a coffee'. I stayed for two!

As I was 'poured out' of the building that could have been the haven of my stardom I came to the realisation that the car (my second Mitsubishi, a Colt Lonsdale, an excellent replacement for the Celeste, was parked in Redbridge on the 'East Side of the East!' I was in the Portobello Road.

I wandered along the street, full of antique stalls. They were like people; sometimes happy, sometimes lonely, animated in a temper, animated with a sense of peace. Failing, succeeding, flying, falling, being ....

The clocks had already wound on to 11am, and the doors of the hostelries opened. I took a direction, but it was a while before I found a bar. As I walked in, I sensed one of the worst atmospheres I had ever encountered. It felt like a posse was coming towards me. The barman, who was the only white man in the building, ordered me out in a most threatening manner. This was the first of very few experiences when I was racially discriminated against.

I sought out another public house, where my money

was considered to be as acceptable as those already in situ. I ordered and paid for a pint of bitter. I took out of my case, lessons 1-12, which I could transfer into book form. This was only my second experience of writing per se, and I enjoyed it. I have since written a total of nine books, one of which was published. I am determined to publish this one, my memoirs, and although I may well have my head in the clouds, I do think it deserves consideration. Only time will tell.

I managed to detail in book form ten lectures, with the oiling value of two more pints of bitter. During the rest of the week (I'd got the bug), I completed all twenty. It only provided a bridge pamphlet plus, but that was the idea. Max was delighted, and by our next class, we had a hundred copies to offer early students. Max made it an attractive little 'early learner' from which we made £50 each!

At the end of local classes in 1987, in excess of thirty students had stayed with me through 1985-1987. This, to clarify, was 1985 Beginners, 1986 Improvers and 1987 Advanced Improvers. I knew the majority could take their game to an even higher level.

Close to the end of their year one, Max lost his wife,. They were so close; I mourned for him. I was very fortunate in that he helped me with three or four projects which turned into moderate successes. He wouldn't take a penny.

CHAPTER 13

SINGLE-PARENT FAMILY

In 1980, my first season at Holimarine, I had met a family from Billericay, Essex, and we 'hit it off' straight away. There were Grandma and Grandad, daughter and son-in-law and two sons. Gwen and Bob, Patricia and David, and their sons Ian and John, who were eight and seven years old. The lads were delightful. I wasn't sure if Dave and Patricia were that 'close'. Although Bob was on a second marriage to Gwen, Pat idolised him, as did the boys. He spent hours with them, teaching, showing them ideas, encouraging and caring for them.

It was a dreadful shock, when the next year, in only his late fifties, Bob collapsed and died from a massive heart attack. It cast a pall over their lives. I didn't have the chance to get to know him well. Enough though to feel his welcome, and kindness.

We kept in touch; Judith met them (during the second year), and felt as fond of them all as I did. She even once said to me that if anything happened to her, she would be happy, if the circumstances were right, that I should settle with Patricia. We were close. Had the circumstances been right, who knows?

But I had some unusual things to cope with, particularly just after Hannah was born in 1984. Within a week I had been propositioned three times!

This reminds me of something said by Peter Crouch, (Ex-England, Stoke and Southampton goal-scoring frontman). He played over thirty internationals, and scored over twenty goals. I'm not sure proportion wise, but I would be surprised if any player who has represented England at least thirty times will ever have scored a higher percentage.

Peter Crouch is about 6ft 9in and hardly George Clooney, but I can see him making for himself a successful career in the media. He already writes a good column (not ghost written). When interviewed he was asked what he would have been, if he hadn't played professional football. He said, 'a virgin!'

I have digressed; I apologise. We (Billericay and Co.) kept in close touch. We followed the boys' progress, and they the birth of Hannah. We next had a lovely letter inviting us for Christmas 1984. By return, we said we would be delighted, but absolutely insisted on contributing. In fact, I drove down on the 23rd with a hamper and several bottles of the 'good stuff'. They still had a cot, which was ideal for Hannah. We arrived about 8pm and settled ourselves in. It turned out to be a wonderful Christmas. A little supper was perfect, and we were soon ready for an early night.

There were a few Christmas rituals, but no one was put out by them. On Christmas Day Dave always used to go to his chosen local, which was about three miles away. Several of his buddies would be there, some of whom, had also gone to Holimarine for their family holiday. We had three 'tinctures' over an hour and a half. I bought the first and third, as I felt more comfortable with that. Dave wasn't an easy conversationalist, but as the nectar hit home it became easier for both of us. Dave was quite a heavy smoker, and succumbed to lung cancer about five years on. I did wonder if he had some premonition.

We returned for Christmas dinner, Hannah taking everything in her stride. After that, my goodness it was as good as the Ritz, we worked together to clear everything away.

Next, it was time for presents. Someone came up with the idea that it might be fun for Hannah to open hers first. This fitted in with Jude's routine with our eight-month-old. By then she would soon be in need of feeding, changing and sleeping. We could enjoy ours a little later.

It was hilarious. Hannah did much the same as most infants her age. By far the most interesting part was the coloured paper that enclosed the gift! Unlike some who just let the gift drop, giving themselves even longer to examine the contours of the paper, Madam H decided to hold onto each for a few seconds before flinging whatever it was over the most convenient shoulder. Rather like King Henry VIII discarding his bones at a banquet!

We played games, we played cards. Something on the television might grab our attention, but that was the exception, rather than the norm. We were soon already for the trip to 'Bedfordshire'.

Christmas 1985 and 1986 were just as enjoyable. Of course, during the former Jude was a big girl, being eight months pregnant. The family were lovely; whenever Jude offered to help, she was firmly told to sit down and relax. *I was told I was to do all the washing up etc etc!*

Hannah's reaction to presents was similar now she was nearly twenty months old. The wrapping paper was of no further interest, but what was inside was given a tad more consideration. Once decided, over her shoulder it went. She was ready to concentrate on the next mystery.

We seriously felt that to stay any longer would be to outstay our welcome. It would have been most unfair on the boys to have the two girls (Vicky would have been eleven months) riding roughshod over their treasures. John was understandably worried when Hannah had a small posset on his new mini snooker table. Wouldn't any child? Trish persuaded him that there was no permanent damage, which was right, and nice lad as he was, (and is), he didn't pursue it.

We had been extremely fortunate to spend 'quality time' with genuine friends. We remained so. We met over the years at various family functions. The most recent was the time Gwen passed away, at the age of ninety-five. Even this was a celebration of a life so well lived.

* * * *

Christmas at home was just as Jude and I hoped it would be. We must remember that Hannah was by now over three and a half years old. However, our traditions in Ancient Lights, (including visiting Father Christmas), was special. Whether she had any memory of Christmas in Billericay is somewhat dubious. She was in the throes of a new beginning with her sisters. Vicky was nearly two years old, and Kate close to six months. The visit to Father Christmas was the high point. A roundabout ride in the town centre was another part of the build up towards the big day.

This was close to the first time when Dr Nelson Brunton worked his miracles for Vicky, and it was so joyful for Jude and me to look upon a happy, cheeky, jokey, high-spirited little girl. She had suddenly become the life and soul of the family, as Hannah always could be. There was never envy between those two.

Each year, we went to a farm close to Bramford to buy our Christmas tree. We had bought lights and decorations for Christmas 1983, forgetting we didn't need them, before the advent of the girls. Hannah and Vicky joined in the dressing of the tree with gusto; never mind the fact that it could have been done in half the time.

When it came to Christmas Eve, we had to remind Hannah and Vicky that we didn't have a chimney on the house, and that was Father Christmas' usual access to deliver presents. However, to reassure them, we said that these days, many houses didn't have chimneys, so Father Christmas looked out for a board which would tell him the way in.

Finally, Jude said 'It would be nice to say a big thank you to Father Christmas by leaving on the table in the hall a glass of sherry, and a mince pie for him, and a nice big carrot for Rudolph'. What did they think? They were entranced by the idea. When they checked the next morning, they were thrilled to see the sherry glass empty with a little left at the bottom, the plate with a few mince pie crumbs, and a small section of carrot!

All families have their Christmas traditions, and having been a store Father Christmas for three years, it was easy to tell how many differences there were. It really didn't matter what ideas people espoused, as long as they were able to keep alive the 'legend' for as long as it was sensible to do so. Hannah was seven when she gently challenged us. We agreed that she was right, and re-assured her that Mum and Dad were also seven when the penny dropped.

Before we had the chance to say how much *we* had enjoyed the five years, and hoped she had not felt cheated, she said it was her 'intention', her word, to keep it a secret from the other two. We just said, ' Well done' to her, and got on.

As it happened, the reaction of the other two was a complete dichotomy. When Vicky was ten, going on eleven years old, she still believed. She was being teased at school by all her class mates, and yet, she managed to weather the storm. She was one of those who were concerned that admitting the non-existence of Father Christmas would leave them with no presents! Vicky was not alone. Up and down the country a proportion of children take to that 'mind set'. Kate, several years before Vicky, took the opposite view. Even Vicky had promised she would not let on to Kate, and we were certain she hadn't.

Having left the sherry, mince pie, and carrot in their traditional places on the table in the hall, I waited about ten minutes and crept into Kate's bedroom. Her stocking was ready to be filled and I was convinced she was asleep. I was in the process of 'posting' the first into the empty stocking, when suddenly:

'Put them in. Now Daddy.'

'But Kate, I'm just straightening the stocking so Father...'

'Put them in NOW!'

* * * *

In 2004/5 two of the girls were already at university, with number three on her way. Jude was now a qualified driver, very much with my blessing, and had worked hard for the year she needed, on top of her degree, to establish herself as a teacher of history and much more. After a brief spell at a comprehensive school, she applied for, and was accepted at, one of the distinguished schools in Ipswich. I was thrilled for her, not realising this would be the end of our 'togetherness'. It was sudden, but looking back, I'm sure I must have missed a few signals! She had found someone with whom she was very much in love.

Jude hadn't seen her mother for nearly twenty years when, just into the new century, she graciously asked if I minded her paying a visit. I wasn't completely happy, but it would have been churlish of me to deny their blood-tie, and again I gave her my blessing. I knew that because of our marriage, Jude's mother had cut her out of her will. What had been an enticing sum divided by three was now divided by two, Judith's two brothers. I learnt Jude's mother had changed her will back. It's likely that Jude's 'prodigal' return was enough to have the situation divided by three again!

I hadn't gained any 'brownie points' when Hannah was born. We both decided Jude's mother should hear it from us. Back came a vitriolic letter with regard to the child: 'You can hardly expect any congratulations from me!' With Jude's blessing, I answered: 'We don't remember asking you for your congratulations on the birth of Hannah. We did however consider it an orthodox move to inform you of the event!'

I have much sympathy for Jude. She was thirteen years younger than me, and very fit. She still played an excellent game of squash. I was coming up to the age when most people these days have already retired, and still suffered from the genetic disease which interferes with 'muscular generation', mis-diagnosed as ME. (Sadly the problem passed on to my youngest daughter, Kate.) Neither of us could have anticipated where we would be over twenty years on.

Jude suggested we should have a trial of our possible future with a family holiday abroad. It fitted into everyone's responsibilities. She suggested Portugal. We all agreed.

It was a lovely holiday. I particularly remember swimming with dolphins. Mine was called Luna, and I shared her with four others in the pool. I happened to be number one in the line. Luna came and gave me a dolphin kiss. She then went and kissed numbers two, three, and four. Number five would not play ball. He turned his back on this lovely creature. After a moment's thought she came back to me; I got a second kiss!

When we arrived home, Jude said she owed me an apology. 'I'm sorry but I didn't have the intention of changing my mind,' she said. I found this hurtful. But we all change. She had still been a good wife, and remained an excellent mother.

I had been invited to join a British Legion friend for a holiday in Thailand; he was going at some stage during the next year. I readily accepted the offer to join him. (He was married to a Thai lady.) I obviously, am not. It was not a success.

The Portugal holiday was the last part of my father's legacy. The rest went on education fees, which I was delighted to provide.

I gained little satisfaction when Jude's 'yearned for', decided he could not leave his wife of many years. This must have been devastating for both of them. There was some ease for this massive disappointment when another 'paramour' came out of the cloisters.

It was Christmas Day, and I had been kindly invited to Jude's new home so that I could share the day with our daughters. At some stage, Mike said that he loved Jude very much. I never doubted his sincerity. I could hardly feel resentful. He hadn't broken up our marriage. I just realised that from then on Mike was likely to see more of my daughters than I was. That truly was excruciating.

They stayed together for over ten years, but his complicated baggage, and a long period of ill health, changed his personality. (I know this from my daughters.) And, in the end, Jude understandably couldn't cope. He was living in *her* house, so it was an amicable decision that he would move out. I had no negative feelings towards Mike; I hope he soon enjoys better health.

We sold the Tudor house for £250,000. By then I had bought up two more sections of the property, first the downstairs (the building had been broken up into five dwellings in the 1960s), which turned it back into a house, and secondly a few years later, an addition to the downstairs, which had been provided for the mother of the owner. He was in his mid-eighties when his mother passed away, aged 106. He survived her by five weeks.

We received planning permission to remove some 1960s rubble from between four of the inside beams. When the second part was examined, hidden beneath concrete we found Queen Ann brickwork. This really was a wonderful find, and a superb feature. In this enlarged room I was able comfortably to have eight tables (32 people) playing bridge. Previously I could, at a struggle, cope with just six tables.

Jude always said that the only way I would leave my beloved home would be feet first. She was right of course, but not for the right reasons! In 2005, she moved out. Ancient Lights was desolate. She had found a house to rent during the period before future decisions would be made. I was living in a forlorn dwelling, with much of its furniture stripped out.

During this period, I was continuing bridge at Ipswich Sports Club, while the Woodbridge section continued as it was. I coped as best I could, but one evening, I arrived back to my single domain with a handful of lightbulbs. There was only one (of six) working in the house, and as the ceilings were eight feet high I needed to stand on a chair to achieve some semblance of light.

Having achieved about four lightbulbs, I had to stretch for the fifth. The chair decided it had already done its bit, and thoughtlessly went one way as I was endeavouring parity to achieve the other... I remember little, except crawling to the telephone and dialling 999. I knew it was a bad one.

I don't think I was conscious for much of the time, but I remember a loud knock. I shouted out loudly. How they managed to get in, I never found out. They saw me, and saw the chair. It looked as bad to them. They edged me towards a stretcher, and gently balanced the angles. We all arrived at the front door, and I was gently removed – feet first. I never returned. It was exactly the twenty-seventh year to the day since I had moved in. My right leg was broken in four places below the knee.

I do not intend to dwell long on the procedures. Suffice it to say, the leg was plastered by an eighteen-year-old medical student, reading out of a manual what he should be doing! On repairing, it was out of line by 28 degrees! As bad was the bolt and screw inserted below the 'angle of the ankle' to support the leg above. When it was time to remove it, the nurse, instead of pulling it out from the screw end, decided to pull it from the other side, so the screw went through my flesh from start to finish! It will come as no surprise when I say it was like a Tudor torture.

The upshot was that family & friends said I must take the NHS to court. After all, I was now a semi-invalid. I am not a litigious person, but I did agree with their entreaties. I consulted solicitors, who placed the case from me as second of six levels. It was no win, no fee. The proceedings took four years. This, when they were found responsible, had failed to engender any support for re-breaking the leg!

I was offered £20,000 to settle out of court. I said I would accept £25,000, which they offered. Several people said I should have asked for £30,000 but I remembered my chances were second out of six, not first. I immediately paid my remuneration into my small private pension, which with 'drawdown' of £4,000 annually will last until I'm 82. That's it.

Jude was now able to afford a mortgage. She bought a 'des res', quite recently built, three bedrooms I think, and a good choice. The sale of Ancient Lights had provided us with the statutory half and half, which amounted to £125,000 each.

With her teacher's salary she must be comfortably off, but I realise this takes hard work, something Jude is prepared for.

Because I was close to retirement I really couldn't cope with her ambitions. I was able to purchase a two-bedroom leasehold flat in sheltered accommodation, which only stipulates you must be over fifty-five. The company is good, the warden is there if you need her, and it has a lovely garden, good views and very tolerant associates. It suits me well.

I am in regular contact with my daughters; my youngest lives in Ipswich, and I see her most weeks. The other two are disparate – one London, one Cambridge. But we speak every week, and I see them as often as possible.

When, just having moved, I had a throat haemorrhage caused by cirrhosis of the liver, I was looked after better than I deserved. Jude kissed me goodbye when she had visited me. It was something of a surprise, but a pleasing one. Over a period of three years, I totally abstained from alcohol for 11½ months in two of them! On both occasions I just missed the full year. During one of those situations, it would take the best part of another book to describe how I was overwhelmed!

I do feel that we drinkers get a raw deal. For smokers who suffer from emphysema, or lung cancer it is simply such 'bad luck'. I wonder if it's because King George V and King George VI suffered through being chain smokers? For us it is not just cirrhosis of the liver. It is alcoholic cirrhosis of the liver, caused by drink abuse – charming! It's bad enough being there, without every adjective available to press home the point!

* * * *

I remember one lunch time when I had taken Hannah to the

Angel Inn. It was a lovely day in midsummer, when she was just two and a half years old. She chose a small orange squash and a packet of Monster Munch. 'Are they nicer than crisps?' I enquired, and she nodded.

Mum often recounted the story that apart from 'Mum and Dad', I said very little. She thought logically that the two of us alone in the house was not conducive to conversations (Dad was away on the post war emergency teaching trainees course). I suppose it was similar for Hannah, with me at work. Vicky was only five months old, so feeding, cleaning, changing and sleeping were no more conducive to esoteric conversation than my mother and I forty years before.

Anyway, 1986 was a year full of ladybirds and aphids. My mother said that when I first spoke it was a complete sentence. An aphid landed on the back of Hannah's hand. With the other she decided to be brutal, and swished it off her. I asked her why she had done that.

'Oh Daddy, I just wanted to get it out of the way!'

Jude thought it was special. I didn't tell her that my first sentence was one word longer! How did I know? The truth is I didn't know, but it was at least a sentence!

In the early spring of 1988, a time when any child is special, Judith suggested it might be an idea for me to take Hannah to Felixstowe for a long weekend.

'You're obviously on a downer,' she said. 'I think it would help you. Hannah will look after you, wouldn't you Hannah?'

'Oh yes. Please can we go Dad?' I have to say I thought Jude's idea was brilliant.

'Get your case packed with Mum's help, and I'll set up the bridge room,' I said. We had a session on Friday evening, but

I knew that if all was laid out for them, the members would manage between them on the odd occasion, and Judith said she would (as usual) pour the teas and coffees at the interval. (I apologise for moving back).

As booking a hotel at this time of year would be unnecessary (it was more likely to be full in the summer), I just packed and when Hannah was ready, and after we'd given Vicky and Kate a big hug and a kiss, I said 'We'll be back soon, and be good for mummy'. I strapped Hannah into the front passenger seat of my car, and we waved as we set off for the seaside.

We chatted all the way there, and I asked her if mum had packed her swimming costume. It transpired that she had; as had I mine. That was already a lovely thing to look forward to.

I remember, many years before, 'the folks', (Uncle Ken, Auntie Judy, and our cousin Peter), came to Felixstowe for a week's holiday. Certainly on three of those days they travelled up to Ipswich (twelve miles) to take Grandma Scott and our family out with them. They stayed at the 'Melrose', which they considered a very good family hotel.

I told Hannah, and she said she would be happy anywhere like that. We were able to park close by, and duly rang the doorbell. A lady answered, and I introduced the pair of us and asked her if we could stay for three nights with an early start on Monday morning. (I had a class in Woodbridge but not until 10am.) If we could have an early breakfast, I could also get Hannah to pre-school on time.

The lady who answered the door said she would be delighted for us to stay. Yet she felt the need to say, 'This is your daughter?' Hannah had one of those rare moments: 'Yes, and he's got two more at home!'

It's a sad state of affairs for all concerned when a question like that has to be asked and addressed. It took Hannah, in her innocence, to 'clinch the deal'. But I hasten to add, throughout our stay, no one could have been kinder than this same lady. She showed us the lounge, with a television and cupboards full of toys and games to help keep families occupied if the weather was really bad. She showed us the bird table, and asked Hannah if she would like to help with scraps of food. 'I usually do this about 9:15am' she said. 'This should be in time for when you've finished your breakfast.'

I asked if they could provide a double room with single beds (still walking over red hot coals), and this was provided. A bell rang at 8am. Breakfast was served from 8:30 – 9:45.

It was a warm evening; the days were longer, and after shepherd's pie, followed by apple crumble, we were replete. I asked Hannah if she wanted a shower and an early night, or perhaps a walk along the pier. She decided on the latter. The night was only just beginning to draw in and the pier was a good start to our 'mini-break'.

When we returned, we had one way out – via the slots! Hannah's eyes almost popped out.

'Did you bring your pocket money with you?' I asked. The eyes told me she hadn't. I said 'It's a good job I didn't forget'. She giggled. I found £1.50 in loose change in my back pocket.

'Will that do?' She giggled again.

It must have been nearly an hour before she finally ran out of money. I said to her, although it was my money, 'it was worth every coin, watching you make that last so long'. I can only say that if everybody else made their pennies work for so long, the 'pier slots' would soon be out of business!

It was getting darker as we made our way back to the

hotel. I put my arm around her so that she didn't get chilled. 'Nice start Hannah?'

'Thank you Dad.'

We arrived back and walked into the hotel. It was about 9:30pm, so not too late. I helped Hannah get undressed (where she needed it), and simply left her to her independence when she felt capable. I said to her, 'We'll sort out your shower after the 8am bell'. I wished her good night, kissed her on the cheek, and said 'I'm looking forward to tomorrow'.

'And me Dad, good night.'

'Good night Hannah.'

****

The bell, as promised, was rung at precisely 8am. It was not loud, just enough to wake you, but if you wanted an extra half hour, you would not have been jolted out of oblivion. Jude had packed all the toiletries any four-year-old could possibly need! I said I would help, when I could. Hannah washed her hair, then I left her to her own independence and asked if she could do the rest so I could have a good wash. I did dry her hair and her back.

We were down to breakfast in good time. It was first class. Hannah and I chatted about the day in front of us.

I chose half-board (breakfast & dinner), which gave us the choice of staying out while the weather was good. We had a really nice walk on the promenade, and I pointed out to Hannah the rusted remains of the old Victorian bathing machines, the fishermen on the pier, (there were only two or three left last evening), and told her that fish that live in the sea are very different to the fish who live in rivers and lakes. I mentioned some examples of sea fish, like cod and haddock, which would just die in rivers or lakes, known as fresh water, just as fish like trout, which thrive in fresh water, would not survive in sea water. Bless her, I could tell she had taken it all in.

We walked partly on the beach, a pebbly affair, so we could try to skim some stones. There were a few visitors swimming, but when I saw her looking longingly towards them, I suggested we had a paddle. I told her the water would be very cold for swimming, but that I had planned for us to go swimming tomorrow morning, and we could stay as long as we wanted. This sounded all right for Hannah.

We took off our socks and shoes. I pulled up my trouser legs and she her skirt, until it was above her knees. We dashed to the water, where she found how cold the sea really was!

'Sea or swimming pool?'

'I think I'll settle for the pool Dad'.

We walked back over the stones, and I espied a bar/restaurant across the road. The road was busy, so I held tightly to her hand until we reached the other side. We went through the door and I checked with the bar manager if it was all right for Hannah to come in with me; he nodded with a ready smile. 'My you're a bonny girl,' he said. Hannah looked up at me. I told her just to say thank you to the gentleman. She added, 'We're staying at a hotel!'

Suddenly her head dropped. She was close to tears. 'Oh Dad, they have got penny machines, and I've forgotten my money.'

The manager obviously overheard what she had said. He came to our table and said to Hannah that he had just found something. Then he placed two piles of 25 2p pieces on the table.

Hannah looked at me; she obviously didn't know what to say. For a second or so, neither did I!

'It is kind Dad isn't it?'

I pointed to Brian, the manager, as I walked to the bar. I asked him for a pint of lager, an orange squash for Hannah, and a packet of cheese & onion crisps. Then I said to him, 'That was a lovely gesture, but I feel I can only accept if you have a pint with me. Or whatever your choice!'

'You don't have to...'

'Please,' I said, 'We're enjoying our day, I must insist so that I keep enjoying it!'

So he had a pint of lager with me. I returned to Hannah with drink and crisps and said to her that a word of thanks to the manager would be appreciated. 'You go up to the bar, I'm not moving from here. There's no need to be shy.'

I don't quite recall what she said, but she made him laugh.

And there the dichotomy; I need to prove my innocence, while the bar manager needs no such mention. For him every little association with Hannah was natural, normal, and within my sight!

This won't surprise you: Hannah said, 'Can I play the machines Dad?' It was only just after 12 noon, so we could enjoy a snack a little later without having to keep more space for dinner. As usual Hannah had good value from those two pence pieces. She had at least three profitable drops in her favour, but eventually the last 2p dropped with nothing to show for it.

'I really enjoyed that Dad'.

I said to her that if she forgot her pocket money tomorrow, I'd pay for my swim with it!

Brian provided us with haute cuisine cheese and tomato

toasties. As we had enjoyed ourselves, I asked Hannah, if we made a prompt start for our swimming, whether she would like to have a snack and a game of cards with Brian. While she was thinking, I suggested that if she remembered her pocket money, we could share what was left at Brian's slot machines, with those on the pier.

'Yes Dad, this is being something special'.

'And for me Hannah.'

I gave her a gentle hug. She reciprocated. That was very special.

She said 'I'd prefer to have a shower after swimming tomorrow', so after dinner of roast lamb, we finished with chocolate sponge and ice cream. We popped into the lounge, where the television was showing a comedy programme. We watched until the end, and settled for an early night. It had certainly been a busy day. We both had a good wash, having decided to shower later.

We settled after I gave Hannah a little kiss on the cheek.

'Good night.'

'Good night Dad.'

* * * *

We slept well and when the bell whispered, we were up quickly to make the best of our day. Hannah loved scrambled egg, which she had with toast. I rather fancied an 'English Breakfast'; I knew I couldn't eat a full one, but I had sausage, bacon, hash browns, beans and fried bread. The hotel didn't half look after the 'inner man' (and his daughter).

In our own good time, we pointed ourselves towards the excellent indoor pool, of which residents are proud. It had a wonderful water chute, and Hannah took full advantage. We stayed in the pool for over an hour. I helped Hannah dry and dress after she had taken a shower.

'That was smashing' she said. 'Oh Dad, I remembered my pocket money, so you mustn't pay for your swim out of it!'

We drifted towards the bar we had enjoyed the day before, but Brian wasn't there.

'I'm his daughter, Vicky,' said the woman serving.

'That's my sister's name' piped up Hannah.

I bought drinks and crisps and persuaded Vicky to have a drink with us. Hannah wanted to know if Brian would be coming back. Vicky told her he would only be about half an hour, then said, 'You must be Hannah?' She smiled and nodded.

'My Dad Brian said you were very well behaved. He gave me some pennies for you.'

While we had our drinks, I suggested to Hannah that we should count up how much money she had brought with her. She had a £1 coin, five 10p pieces, six 5p pieces, twelve 2ps, and eight 1ps. That's £2 (quite a bit thirty years ago).

'I'll keep the pound coin for now with me that will be a pound to spend later. Would you like to have your toastie first?'

'Pennies first Dad, in two p's please.'

Vicky was able to set up 50p for her, and once again she made the most of it.

We had ordered toasties when Brian came in. 'I've got a sister called Vicky,' Hannah told him.

'Do you love her?' he asked.

Hannah thought for a couple of seconds, and then said 'Most of the time'!

'Come and see us again when you are here next,' Brian

offered. I think we both knew we would. I helped Hannah into her jacket and we waved goodbye.

We walked along the pier, which was now quite full of fishermen, then popped into the machine room. I told Hannah she had been very good. 'I will keep your pound safely and give it to you when we arrive back home,' I told her. 'In the meantime, I've got just over a pound in change which you can have now'. It was worth more than £1 just to watch her operate!

We enjoyed dinner; steak and kidney pudding, followed by treacle tart and custard. We watched television briefly before retiring. I had a quick chat with Hannah about the next day.

'We will need to have an early breakfast. I've spoken to the lady, she is prepared for us just before quarter past eight. The bell will wake us. I'll pack now; another job will be done. I'll drop you off at home.'

Having collected my bridge boards, and lecture papers, I thought I should be in time with about ten minutes to spare for my appointment in Woodbridge. This was just before Hannah started school. She chatted nearly all the way home. Thanks Jude, it was a brilliant idea; and kindly. Hannah reminded me that I was still holding on to her £1!

We were nearly through a place known as Trimley, about four miles from Felixstowe when we saw a large board resting on a chair. I noted the words 'PIANO FOR SALE, please ring..... I asked Hannah if she would like to learn to play the piano. Without hesitation she responded 'Yes Dad'. After that moment, we just chatted until we reached Ancient Lights.

'I've only a few moments, but I'm sure Hannah enjoyed it, as I did,' I said to Judith, 'Ring this number?' Now I was more established, I would encourage Hannah, who responded in the positive instantaneously; when the time comes I would automatically support Vicky and Kate.

I gave Jude a hug and said 'I'll make it with five minutes to go. I'll phone you usual time'.

* * * *

The next day we drove to Trimley. We bought the upright piano for £75. Because we didn't haggle, the owner who had a lorry, volunteered to deliver it.

Very close to the mini-break with Hannah, we were invited, en famille, to Sanderstead in Surrey, where my only family members lived. The reader will remember when I last made mention of their holiday hotel in Felixstowe, the Melrose, many years before. After Hannah and I enjoyed it so much we realised how astute their judgement was.

Peter and I were both born in 1946, he slightly younger than me. My sister and I relished the times we spent with the family when they came to stay at Grandma's, just half a mile from where we lived. Arrival and departure seemed so close together. I have to say that Uncle Ken was my hero. Now I'm nearly seventy-four, he still is. When he passed away in 2001, at ninety-three, Cousin Peter said to me, 'I've not only lost my father, I've lost my best friend'.

I gently envied him. When I was younger, I was not flavour of the month, but Catherine was. It didn't last. I remember as an early teen moving in the direction of comedy, and sitting opposite Auntie Judy, I decided to tell a few jokes. She was one of the best 'audiences' I would ever have!

When Jude and I married, we had an early invitation to stay at Sanderstead. I don't think the folks had ever actually met Judith, but I was humbled by their welcome. They had given up their own bedroom. There were cups of tea delivered at 'waking time' and I could tell they made every effort to make sure Jude was totally included. It obviously didn't fall on stony ground. We were, on both sides, a mutual appreciation society.

Returning to our invitation for lunch a couple of years later, nothing had changed. We arrived close to 11am. This was the first of four visits; on only one did we have to cope with an element of bad behaviour. Fortunately it was not the last visit.

We were shown into the front room, which was filled with surprises all wrapped up. It was like Auntie Emmie all over again. This struck home. I knew Auntie Judy would have wished Peter had married (he was an only child), but it wasn't to be. Lesser people might have resented it, but our folks were not lesser people!

The girls were thrilled and almost overcome. I cannot remember now exactly what they were given. They were certainly as good as one's main Christmas presents!

We had a lovely lunch, and walked it off in the park at the bottom of Cranleigh Gardens (Peter was just as lovely with the girls). We had a light supper, and well satisfied, we set out for the journey not knowing that within months, the visit would be reversed on a sad occasion.

* * * *

As already mentioned, a hospital telephone call informed me my father had collapsed and was in intensive care. I was in the middle of a private bridge class. It was pointless leaving it, but on completion I drove to the hospital. Within six weeks he had passed away, suffering from secondary brain cancer. Whether it was a bad fall or working with asbestos, we will never know. It was June 2nd. He was sixty-seven.

I organised the funeral, and then I invited the folks to stay, at least overnight, until obsequies were finalised. Jude and I were able to reciprocate their kindness to us by giving up our bedroom. Peter and all of us were soon sorted with elemental comfort. The next day Auntie Judy said to me, 'You're a lucky boy'. I agreed, but did say I had worked very hard for it. Her smile and nod were appreciated.

I think there must have been a semblance of competition between Peter and me in Auntie Judy's eye. There need not have been. From an early age, he had had a fascination with everything First World War. Having left school, he had already been employed at Betram Rota, an antiquarian bookshop with a highly established reputation. He wrote many articles for reputable publications, and in fact, for about three years, he published his own magazine. He sent me some copies, even though the subject was not in my domain. They were very professional and interesting. He is an established historian, something I would love to have been.

Towards the end of his long life, I had my most special association with Uncle Ken. We phoned from time to time, and each found some time together during the three or four visits when our family were invited to Cranleigh Gardens. He spoke of his memories as a schoolboy of six or seven, of the sounds of World War I reaching from across the Channel, the bombing, the gunfire, the shelling, and he told me his first memory when he was only two and a half in 1910, and was visiting his mother's bedside. She died a few days later, succumbing to cancer at the age of thirty, leaving Uncle Ken, two, and a daughter of four and. I gently looked away. I knew he would shed a tear.

A little while after our fourth visit, Peter phoned to say uncle was in hospital. The day before, he couldn't get up. It appears he was 'worn out'. He remained conscious, and on the 19th May it was his ninety-third birthday. He passed away on the 24th. (He had worked until he was over eighty). That was Uncle Ken.

* * * *

I should not ignore my greatest area of income; so many people ask me: 'How do you possibly make a living out of playing cards?' The truth is, I don't! For one thing I am not a good enough player to compete at a high level, and most of those who are have trolley loads of 'bunce' to cope with a run of bad luck, however long it may last. I have written five books. I just started within the confines of teaching, managed to pass a written exam, and as already mentioned, an oral face to face with an expert. I was lucky, because after my first year with one evening class, I was the only qualified bridge teacher available in Suffolk.

At the end of my third year, I had one class of very promising players. They were thirty plus in number, and had come to the Beginners' class in 1985 (my first year), in 1986 to Improvers', and in 1987 to Advanced Improvers'. At the end of that class a voice piped up, 'What can we do next?'

I suddenly had a special moment; I told them I could use a part of Ancient Lights, since I had purchased the downstairs section, to provide room for six or seven tables and play three or four times a week. I added, I meant *play*, after they had endured so much theory.

I had just started teaching in the small garden town of Woodbridge. It was absorbing as Ipswich had been, and after the same three years of theory progress, they were keen to continue with the same enthusiasm as Ipswich.

I retired in 2011, but both bridge schools are still busy, Woodbridge especially, with over forty members.

* * * *

I had the idea of 'Sunday Seminars' in Ipswich, and for those I needed Jude. She was superb. Her catering was such that I thought of changing the name of our lovely Tudor house to the Ritz! She produced a hot and cold buffet which entailed being up at 5am on the morning to be certain everything would 'come together' at the right time. We had more of these seminars, which were a very useful source of revenue as well as value for money. And the bridge? What bridge?

I was pleased to be asked to write a bridge column for several magazines. It all helped towards our forthcoming education expenses. I was also asked to do bridge seminars through the Suffolk College. It didn't entail catering, but it was now a full-time occupation. I was still finding time for the occasional 'walk-on'. How? I can't remember!

I was not popular with the English Bridge Union when it espoused 'Bridge For All'. This was around the turn of the century, when after thirty years of growth, the playing of the game took a countrywide drop. During its 'salad days' the EBU had employed extra staff, and come what may they were determined to keep them, justified or not, even if it meant an extra levy on the clubs. I refused to be involved. After all, mine were schools, not clubs. Some members moved onto a higher level. I would shake hands, wish them well, and follow their progress with interest. Some who were competent enough for the upward change often still found time to come and play at Ancient Lights. I was fortunate, as I did not, as such, suffer from the down-turn as many did.

* * * *

During the year, we often visited Martin and Robin, their wives and their growing families, and we reciprocated. Judith also had close friends (already mentioned) from Oxford University, and it was exactly the same with them. I did really miss those happy days. To stop seeing the children when they were half grown up was a genuine loss. Hey ho!

I did enjoy making the most of the Directors' Box at Ipswich Town Football Club, the opportunity presented to me by the late Sir Bobby Robson. A holder could take a guest. Jude in our day came, as did John Cooper, Vicky's Godfather, and Martin in the village, who helped me get my bridge book published.

I have no regrets, having chosen to retire at 65 in 2011. I'm enjoying every minute of it. Even hammering myself into the ground trying to put this book together!

* * * *

Two of the most remarkable things that could happen to a family (well, I think so) happened in consecutive years. 1995 and 1996. Our local theatre, The Wolsey, was opened in 1978 by Sir Trevor Nunn, who was at Northgate Grammar School in Ipswich, about five years before myself.

My mentor, Neil Salmon, was his English teacher, and I understand they have had a constant friendship throughout the years of his wonderful career.

The Artistic Director, Dick Tuckey, chose to have a change from pantomimes, and in 1995 the Christmas production was *The Railway Children*, to be followed in 1996, with *The Secret Garden*.

Vicky and Kate chose drama when they decided not to continue with the piano. We gave them every opportunity, but although the lessons were good fun, the practice was non-existent. We decided the next week that they would pay for their lesson – just the one. They duly resigned, but they did work hard at drama, so we happily continued to underwrite their lessons. Jude and I both thought they were good, but we watched others who were as good. That was not important, their enthusiasm was!

I apologise; I have digressed. An advertisement in the local paper asked for children between eight and twelve years of age to attend the theatre at such and such a time for auditions for The Railway Children. The principals had already been cast. A young, and delightful, actor named Maeve was to play Bobbie, played in the 1970 film by Jenny Agutter. Because working times are restricted for children, they needed two teams to share the juvenile roles.

Hannah, who had had little to do with drama before now, was chosen to share the role of the younger sister, Phyllis (played by Sally Thompsett in 1970). The other smaller parts were for the Perks children (the stationmaster, played originally by Bernard Cribbins). Vicky was given the part of Victoria, the only one with specific props and dialogue, and Kate was delighted to be cast in the small role of another Perks child. They were all absolutely delighted, having attended with no expectation, and Dick Tuckey put the three of them in the same team. Family, friends, and bridge members were all delighted for us. Several times I heard, 'You must be so proud of them!' Not a word I like, but deep down, I knew they were right.

Naturally, outside of bridge nights, Jude and I watched as many performances as we could; some together, some alone, depending on our commitments. Hannah, who as previously mentioned had had little contact with drama, was hard to comprehend. She was eleven years old, and yet so laid back. She performed without acting. Dick Tuckey said to Jude and me that she baffled him. In rehearsal time, he had to give her some quite complicated instructions. He despaired, as she didn't even give the impression that she was listening. But when it came for Hannah to work to his instructions, she had it 100% right.

I should say the girls did not just 'walk out' of school. Jude and I wrote a carefully drafted letter to the Headmistress of Ipswich High School for Girls, asking for permission for the girls, (Hannah and Vicky), to take part in the Christmas shows at the Wolsey Theatre. We wrote: 'We can guarantee they will keep up to the education demands that may be missed during day-time rehearsals, by catching up in their own time'. A similar letter was sent to St. Margaret's, where Kate would normally have been in attendance, and received an equally sympathetic positive.

Next year was far away, but they were to be given the same privileges, as long as this was the last time. I think the heads were aware that it was. We made it clear to the girls how essential it was not to get behind with schoolwork. We told them that this was perhaps the most important time of their education. They didn't let us down.

In the meantime, Kate, before leaving her Church of England school, won the Drama prize. Vicky won the esteemed prize for singing outright, and later Hannah, when she was about to start at Durham University reading Modern Languages, was awarded the German prize.

Once again, I digress, although what I have written was all happening at about the same time. This certainly was one of the most exciting times of my life, and Jude's.

The Wolsey Theatre Management during this time were encouraging variety, and giving Suffolk people choices. It is now forty-one years since it opened with a Restoration comedy and an Ivor Novello musical (*Perchance To Dream*). How's that for variety?

The Railway Children was very well supported; very close to full, throughout the long season. Adding to Dick Tuckey's words regarding Hannah, I sat and watched during a mid-term meeting of all the principals. That was the adult actors and Hannah. I am sure he had the same meeting with the other team, which had its own Phyllis.

While I cannot help my sheer delight, I can be brutally honest. At that meeting, Hannah had more than her share of the flak. All the principals (except one) had one or two reaction improvements. Hannah had four. Dick Tuckey, for whom I had very high regard, did his job so professionally that he treated my eleven-year-old as if she was no different from the professional actors. Where improvements or adjustments were required, he informed everyone in the same tone. I think Hannah was more stimulated than upset.

According to Dick, Hannah always responded to criticism in a positive way. *The Railway Children* was a wonderful experience for our entire family. The girls did what was required to justify the Artistic Director's faith in them.

The show finished well into the festive season. Where there was a suggestion of feeling lost, we told Vicky and Kate that they should keep up their drama classes, always doing their very best. There was next year, at the Wolsey Theatre, *The Secret Garden*. Maybe they might be considered to audition for that? It was just about enough to take their minds off the stage and into Christmas. We had traditionally booked ourselves into the Westerfield Swan on Christmas Eve. This year, 2019, will be the 22nd anniversary. When Jude and I went our separate ways, I continued the tradition. I did invite her, but I spent most of Christmas Eve preparing for Christmas Day. In the past, I had always seen it as the day she ate out with us all together, so I had extra time for Christmas Day. But lives change, and there was never any animosity.

* * * *

The next year, 1996, continued with the same educational situation with which Jude and I felt most comfortable. I had been teaching chess for two years at Ipswich High School to children who started the game at eight years old, the age at which juniors are recommended to learn bridge.

Hannah was moving steadily up the grades for the piano; Vicky and Kate were the same with their drama grades. I can honestly say they were never pushed; school hours are long enough without trying to force other disciplines on to them.

However, they were thrilled when Dick Tuckey phoned to say that he hoped the girls would be coming to auditions for *The Secret Garden*, with a date I can't remember, probably mid-September.

I drove us all to the Wolsey Theatre, on the date and at the time requested. Obviously the girls were extremely excited, and it was difficult to say anything more than, 'You're not alone!'

The family that arrived home were ecstatic! The evening was such that everything fell into place. I would still say the girls were fortunate. A different Artistic Director might well have made different choices. As I mentioned before, the girls, in my eyes, were quite talented, but there were many others I watched whom I considered just as talented. (After all, I was fortunate to have held an Equity Card since 1967). This suggested a modicum of judgement.

The Secret Garden also required two teams, with three younger players. The ideal age for the production was 9–13. Hannah was twelve, Vicky 11½ and Kate 9½. The eldest character was 'Dillon', a complete natural within an un-established garden. Plants, animals, birds, wild fauna and flora were all part of a magical experience, especially for children. Two who were interviewed came through comfortably, and totally justified inclusion.

When Dick Tuckey happened to bump into Hannah, he asked her if she felt up to being a 'Mary', and she nodded. He said to her, 'I don't think you need an audition'. A bit naughty? He then told her there was much work in front of them. A different director might well have had that conversation with another just as worthy. In defence of Hannah, Dick Tuckey did say to us, 'She's never let me down'.

Vicky joined the audition for the second 'Mary'. I imagine it was 'nip and tuck', but Dick came down and gave her team two. She was thrilled.

Before we left, our esteemed Artistic Director thanked everyone for their support in numbers. But the character of 'Colin', the invalid boy in the story, still had to be cast in one of the teams.

Up went Kate. She managed to get Dick's attention, and said to him, 'Mr Tuckey, I know I'm not suitable to be a Mary, but you have seen my short hair, and quite a few people have said I look quite boyish; could I audition for the 'Colin' that's missing?'

Dick did a quick double-take worthy of the late Kenneth Williams! 'You've really put me on the spot, Kate. I'll think about it and let you know'.

A week or so later, the telephone announced its importance. 'Dick Tuckey, message for Kate Scott. We'll give the part of Colin a go.'

I will briefly move on a month. Rehearsals finished, production under way, with 'Colin' spending much time languishing in bed. It was the interval, and there was a coach-party which had block booked. The full theatre was privy to the following shout from three rows back: 'Oi, Elsie! Could you see that poor little boy in bed? He really didn't look too well to me!'

Overall Kate did OK. I remember a performance Jude and I attended; we were actually in the front row, (and before readers scream 'NEPOTISM!', we were in the last two seats on the left, the hardest to sell). We were within inches of Hannah 'gardening' in that corner. I think it was harder for us to cope with than Hannah! At least she couldn't move around.

According to Dick, Hannah and Vicky 'did the business'. About two weeks before the end of the production, I walked through the stage door to hear Dick talking to Kate. She had suddenly dropped the necessary quality of performance, acting when she should not have been, and fidgeting when others in the scene *were* acting). He said to her he was thinking of 'resting' her. I said to Dick, 'Give me a moment, and if there's no improvement, I will obviously support you all the way'. I took Kate to one side, and without being brutal, I was firm. I knew she would be devastated to be dropped. I asked her if she was content to be taken out of the production because she had proved not good enough to continue. For one of the few times in her childhood, she did respond to me (Jude was the one they usually agreed with, whatever the circumstances).

I was pleased that Kate took my words to heart. Dick retained her, and even said to me that there had been no further problems.

I drove us all home after the last performance. From the back came the sound of sobbing. It was Hannah. She knew that this was the end, after two wonderful years. In truth it was *an* end, but not *the* end. A few years on, at 14, she passed Piano Grade 8; one below 'letters'. She decided that was 'job done'. Jude and I both entirely agreed. She had concentrated and practised for nearly ten years. The pieces she had to play were awesome. Within two further years she established herself as a 'singer/songwriter' (semi-professional), with which she is very happy. Her high grade on piano has enabled her to teach in London, where her partner Holly is a Landscape Gardener. Hannah went up to Durham in 2001 (aged seventeen), and for the second important time was fortunate. Her Grade 8 piano scored 150, the lowest pass rate.

She was also slightly fortunate at Durham when she graduated at twenty in Modern Languages. To achieve a First, a mark of 60 was required. When the examiners produced the results, there was only one student who had scored 60. In the eyes of the examiners, there has to be symmetry in the results; a top degree is not a competition for one. So all those who had scored 57 or more were raised to a First. Hannah had scored 58.

Vicky had a unique result. I was told by the Headmistress that she had never seen the like of it. Most students achieved the odd A*, A, B+B, with (perhaps) a C. Vicky did not achieve one A*, but she did score nine straight As!

She took her degree at the Rose Bruford College of Drama, in Kent. Jude and I were very proud of her, even when she decided not to pursue a theatrical career. She had her own ideas. She graduated with a 2:1, which considering her start in life, was quite an effort.

Kate was like her father. Getting down to studying was, for both of us, anathema. But like her Dad, she knuckled down at the essential time, and achieved a 2:2 at the University of Canterbury, reading Education.

Things really do happen in strange ways. Having, times past, sometimes despaired of Kate, it transpired that she was a great mathematician. And she's the first of our daughters to get on the property ladder. She was made Head of Department at the age of twenty-six, in an established middle school in Bury St Edmunds, about twenty miles from Ipswich.

My conclusions will largely concentrate on family holidays, and hopes I have for the future. But to fulfil my promise of an 'autobiography', I must conclude the period of my twenty-six years as a bridge organiser, lecturer, and would-be writer, although just one bridge book was actually published. This comes to great bridge players, the ones that achieve publication. And so they should. An interested reader is bound to be drawn to the cash till by a familiar international.

In 2004, I was approached with regard to becoming a bridge teacher/organiser at sea. Perhaps my fame had spread to the 'Colonies'! The deal was that for taking charge of all the bridge on board, (as would be expected in a good club), you were given a free 'full board' cruise for, if possible, two people sharing a twin bed, or one large bed, (depending on the situation of the travellers).

On board, the Director/s were expected to front two morning classes from 10am until noon at sea, one for beginners, the other for improvers. In the afternoon, we were expected to direct 'duplicate bridge'. This was the means by which every pair eventually play the same boards. This gives greater kudos to winners, rather than luck. My first cruise in this capacity was with P&O.

In the evenings at sea, it was the same as the afternoons. But, if the ship was in port, bridge was not expected, nor advertised (except once, more of which soon).

For the first four cruises I was able to take someone with me, (male); the cabin did have twin beds. They were able to help a little, and put a few bob my way, rather than just take a free cruise; I was grateful for that.

Usually directors came in twos, most likely a married couple. The other configuration was two ladies, who were probably co-directors at their regular club. All the work is thus halved.

As I travelled alone for the last six cruises, with Fred Olsen, Cruise Maritime and P&O, I had no respite, and

I was beginning to feel it was too much hard work. I was sleeping in port just to catch up. The last straw came when P&O invited me to direct a six-week cruise with them. When I arrived on board I discovered it was not a cruise, but a 'leg' of a world voyage. The classes were just manageable, but in the afternoon, eighty-eight (yes eighty-eight!) turned up for duplicate bridge. We needed a spread of three public rooms to accommodate them all. I found myself working all morning and all afternoon, followed by scoring. I just made it to dinner before the evening session. I slept from midnight until 4:30am, when I set my alarm to score up the last evening session. I did just make it to breakfast for a bowl of porridge.

I am convinced that in my original time with P&O I never treated a team member so harshly. But that wasn't all.

People, (including myself) talk of 'bucket lists'. If you have never enjoyed the spectacle of transiting the Panama Canal, it would have to be top of the list. Learning the history, and the miracle, of one Ferdinand de Lesseps' achievement (between 1889 and the opening in 1914) is awe inspiring.

I have been through the Canal at least ten times, eight of which were before the end of 1978. After the first time, when I stayed on deck from start to finish, I invariably took advantage of the break in succeeding transits, and I would certainly spend two or three pleasurable hours out of the office enjoying the experience over again.

Was I given the opportunity for a break? In fact I was deputed to run the bridge classes! Before the transit, I normally had thirty-four 'beginners' and twenty-eight 'improvers', although this varied a little. On one occasion, one beginner, and later one improver, appeared. It was just like Butlins thirty years before, when one monstrous man turned up for a tennis tournament when the court was covered with snow, following a freak fall. (I nearly lost my job over that; he reported me for dereliction of duty.) As I said then, there's always one.

At this stage, the pressure was such that I felt I had to put myself in the hands of the resident surgeon. He was livid. And after he had judged my present state, it was essential for me to be repatriated from the next port (this happened to be Honolulu on Hawaii).

'I shall inform the Entertainments Department,' he said. 'I don't want you to do anything, with the exception of packing. Your steward will almost certainly do most of it.'

I made it home, and a few days later a letter arrived. It said 'We admit no responsibility etc etc...' but it included a small enclosure. I was threatened that if I made mention of it, I would face court action. Come on, P&O! Although this was a sad moment, I look back on all my other times working for P&O with great affection and respect for their unstinting support.

I don't think my regular members of the two bridge schools, (about sixty) were that impressed by my cruises. They might have been right. However, I made arrangements to cover all classes, and took no table money. I think just a very few who were prepared to spread the word gave the impression that because they normally played social bridge (with no expense), they wondered why they were suddenly having to pay. You've heard it all before; back over twenty-five years at Thorpeness, it was the same mantra. 'Do we have to pay?'

I must stress, this was a very small contingent from Ipswich.

I think the smaller the group, the louder the voice! When I

chose to retire at sixty-five in 2011, I was banned from playing at Ipswich Town Sports Centre; only our second venue after Ancient Lights. It was a powerful duo, with the management behind them. The other members were truly bullied, or so I was told by a go-between.

I don't know about the manager, but the other two passed away within three years. One had 'black-balled' me from a possible club membership. Why?) Only the 'bullied' survive! Including the eldest member, in her ninety-ninth year. Onward and upward!

CHAPTER 14

LOOKING BACK

Imake no apology. This is my biography - warts and all. I have not written this with the expectation of making myself popular. However, it would be sad if I lost all credibility because I have chosen to speak my mind. Even if this prophet is without honour in his own country!

The Woodbridge Club (erstwhile school), is thriving, with over forty members, including myself. I look forward to Monday mornings. It involves a fine group of players, and the results, especially mine and partners, point to the fact that the standard is extremely challenging.

In conclusion for bridge, and I again acknowledge the forbearance of readers who have patiently put up with my gobble-de-gook, I have taken the opportunity to go on a fortnight bridge holiday for each of the last four years. Three of these were in Malta, which I thoroughly enjoyed, as I did the one I spent in Rhodes. The standard is very challenging, toppish club level. The hotels were excellent, and very good value. I had two or three successes and three or four disasters!

I've thoroughly enjoyed the company. I'm seventy-four, but I can honestly say I'm still learning this wonderful game.

I suppose I've always been a bit of a loner. I never fitted in when I started junior school, and being bullied from day one exacerbated the situation. It was absolutely no use complaining to the teachers, even for a semblance of understanding, as they 'passed by on the other side'. It was the same when I was encouraged to join the choir, especially from my father's standpoint.

It was actually a 'profession'! We were paid by attendance, and my average *annual* pay was about 15 shillings 75p. I was also, like the others, paid about two shillings for attending a wedding and for the occasional funeral. If I sang a solo, which was often, I would get an extra shilling.

From the age of twelve I was established as 'Head Boy', and when available, I was always expected to sing solo. I don't think it had anything to do with the bullying at all. I just spent the time outside the church, very obviously frightened. The stupid thing was that they didn't actually hurt me. I did not go home with black eyes! I think the best way to describe my situation is that I was permanently 'goaded'.

I mentioned my father. Although he had no faith in anything except Stalin, he realised I was taking the disciples' 30 pieces of silver. When he knew how, my pocket-money dried up for a couple of months. Another victory, another saving.

I just ended up on my own. I have no intention of fobbing off the reader with any suggestion of feeling sorry for myself, it is just the way it was, and I felt comfortable. As I grew older, the unhappy situations were much reduced. But over a number of years, I had become so used to being alone that I embraced it. Had it not been for Thorpeness, Oxford and Jude, it might well have remained that way.

I should say that my first two years at grammar school were thoroughly miserable. It was not so easy to avoid the bullies. But, as mentioned before, Headmaster Norman Armstrong OBE rescued me, and changed my life. The bullying ended, which helped me enormously to concentrate on the work I needed to do to achieve the five 'O' Levels necessary for a professional career.

I discovered at just sixteen that I could do pretty good impressions, particularly Steptoe & Son, Kenneth Williams, Churchill, Peter Cook, Dudley Moore and Peter Sellers. From my point of view, this was extra armour against any further potential bullying. Defensive maybe, but I had been 'Skinny Scott' all of my life, (and within seven months) I had grown to 6' 2', while my weight was 9st 4lbs!

I accepted the admonishment from my master, but didn't change my 'routine'. When he told me off, I sensed the semblance of a straight face, struggling.

He was in charge of a school excursion to Wembley, to watch the Harlem Globetrotters. Their basketball team included the irrepressible 'Meadowlark Lemon', whose comedy on the court guaranteed success. I did represent the school at basketball. I was to meet them fifteen years later in Hollywood Studios, while making a national advertisement. I was being wined and dined by my favourite band, the Austins of Las Vegas!

At the interval, entertainment was provided by a traditional jazz band. I watched my nemesis master. He was entranced. I felt forgiving, and decided that anyone who enjoyed jazz so much, couldn't be all that bad!

* * * *

We had our first holiday at Blakeney, North Norfolk, in October 1984. It was the first year we were to share our Christmas with the folks in Billericay, Essex. Judith had been for a family holiday in Blakeney when much younger, and apparently it was much enjoyed. But the family had fallen in love with the Lake District, where climbing was an activity enjoyed by all. There wasn't too much climbing to be done in Norfolk!

On our first visit to Blakeney, we had a very nice caravan with a cot. Hannah was in her element climbing (well almost); every time she dropped, she laughed!

We decided to visit Blakeney Hotel for afternoon tea, and sat on a large table, where one person was also sitting. It was so busy in the hotel, so we could hardly have been described as intrusive. As it was, we were given a big smile. I thought nothing of introducing ourselves to the young lady, who said, 'My name is Holly Aird'. She was about eighteen. I didn't know her name, and when she asked me what I did for a living, I boasted that I was a 'walk-on' for television programmes. I asked what she did.

Before she answered, she said, 'Could I just hold Hannah for a moment?' Jude confidently handed Hannah to the young Holly. Hannah took to her immediately, and smiled and laughed. They stayed together for an hour.

I asked her again what she was doing in Blakeney, and she responded by saying, 'Much the same as you'. It transpired she was filming as a principal in a television programme, and had already filmed here in a classic; Arthur Ransome's *Swallows and Amazons*. Over the years she has had many leading roles, and that doesn't take into account her theatrical work. When I see Hannah, just over a decade later, with her good fortune at the Wolsey Theatre, I wonder if, when Holly handed Hannah back to Jude, she passed on something of her gifts.

(As I write this today, Vicky came back to Ipswich and I spent three happy hours with her. She was radiant. The 'little skinny rabbit' weighs 13st, only, I hasten to add, because, all being well, she is expecting my first grandchild in two months' time. Her partner is delightful. He seems to have drawn the curtain over her previous 'let downs'.)

By the next time we were ready, and off on our summer holiday, Jude had provide me with a third daughter! I had no regrets. We both agreed to do our best for them, but that we should call a halt! The decision was a relief for both of us.

Kate was just a year old when we went to Holkham in 1988. Everything was fine until it was time to leave. Madam Kate was having nothing to do with leaving. Jude and I tried to carry her out with us, but she just screamed. Eventually we put her down, and walked away without her. She just sat there. When we reached the exit, nearly 400metres away, she was still just sitting in the sand. She had won; we had to go back. She was fed up with screaming, but still had the moral victory. I think Jude and I were left scratching our heads!

Maybe she wasn't quite old enough to remember; we never had an exact repeat. But during her formative years, there existed a cornucopia of very similar actions. It was good that her two elder sisters seemed to understand and cope with her idiosyncrasies better than we did!

This was the first time we had decided to forego the beach (it was a dull day), and we parked the car in legal precincts at the Wells end of the narrow-gauge railway to Walsingham. It advertised for subscription shareholders to help cover the cost of a brand new Bayer Garrett steam train engine, which would cost £37,000. A share of £250, for a minimum of only two years, would give Life Membership allowing you and any number of family members to travel free. I said to Jude that I considered it a good time for us to take up the offer; all things taken into account.

* * * *

I made the pennies, and took responsibility for all our finances. I am sure this was a fair division of labour. After all, Jude was looking after us bell, book, & candle, providing our sustenance, cooking etc and looking after our girls. There is no doubt, she was (and still is) a wonderful mother. On that score, I think I put in a good shift, but I was eclipsed, as I believe any father would have been in my circumstances. However, I think my girls love me as a responsible runner-up!

Jude and I, when she had given me her full support, approached the railway's tiny office at Wells and handed over a cheque for £250. I had no regrets, but I had to acknowledge that my cheque had left my account smaller than their office!

From then onwards we were remembered, and always welcome. One little moment comes to mind. As we left Wells, within two or three minutes in fact, the train seemed to disappear underground. The undergrowth, for that short time, was all we could see. Hannah, four, pointed at it with a slight frown. I said that we were in a cutting. She repeated my word, 'cutting'. This was one of only a very few times when the weather was disappointing, and not conducive to the beach, and I think we took the train probably five times, and each time, at the appropriate moment, Hannah pointed and said, 'Cutting, Dad'.

Over a period of ten years, when the girls made it perfectly clear that summer was Blakeney, we saw no reason to change. Overall, we enjoyed better than average weather. But we did have personal 'insurance'. We decided that if the weather was good, in other words real beach time, we should take advantage of it in case it suddenly changed, and we might have spent quality beach time in a country house. It was a natural thing to aim for the outside when the sun had got his hat on!

If the good weather seemed likely to last, and the girls decided they would like to do something different, at least we would make the most of the early days. Towards the end of the 1980s we had added to the bucket and spade a kite, a small bat and ball, (for French cricket), and a collection of shells, for decorating anything the girls might have built in the sand. It was at this time that they looked towards the sea.

So during the years when we had early good weather, the usual 'first change' was the train to Walsingham. It was a twenty-minute journey, and we arrived at a utility platform, rather than a station, but perfectly adequate to embark or disembark.

There was something about Walsingham. It didn't feel sorry for itself, but carried a great burden calmly. It welcomed the godly and the wayfarers alike. It did not differentiate between the quick and the dead, yet needed both to be aware of the Abbey. Time had not dimmed desecration.

Within easy walking distance of the railway there was a public house which provided ideal luncheon fare. The girl's starter? Coke and crisps! They *were* on holiday, after all. It was the least I could provide. And for Jude, when we arrived at the caravan site, she looked for their mini-supermarket and shopped for all the things we would need for a few days ahead. There was never the attitude of 'You've stopped work; I've stopped cooking!'

I think we bustled about, including the girls as they gradually added to their years. After lunch in Walsingham, we were all, I think, called to the Abbey, where Jude and I felt the spiritual atmosphere. We brought a small ball with us so the children could run off steam without causing nuisance. The scenic views seemed to speak volumes. We had to keep our eye on the time, because even on small gauge railways there is always the 'last train'. Fortunately, over the years, we always made our way back to Walsingham Station in time (with one or two close calls). Imagine watching the train gradually disappearing while getting closer to our becalmed car!

One of our favourite lunchtime spots was very close to the caravan site, in a tiny village called Langham. It reminded me of the village I was in when the police car I was supposed to be driving as a 'walk-on' broke down. You will remember I had to walk back to the set in full police uniform; at any time I could have been arrested for impersonation.

The hostelry, the Langham Blue Bell, had a pool table, which was a plus, and the garden was an absolute delight.

It was enclosed, and was a riot of colour from flowers, plants, and the coloured leaves of the two fruiting trees. Like Walsingham, it had its own goodness to offer.

The Blue Bell offered an excellent selection for a light lunch. It was a venue we usually visited when we had plans for the afternoon. There were several choices. One, for the whole family, was a trip to Sheringham, where there was a full-size railway. You might have thought three daughters would be bored with more trains, but no, far from it. They seemed to enjoy the rides on the 'big' trains as much as the small gauge between Wells and Walsingham. I can say quite honestly that I never heard one of my girls ever say they were bored. Much of this was due to Jude and Auntie Read on a Saturday morning!

The train terminus was Sheringham, and it stopped at Weybourne and Holt, (about three or four miles). I was in my element, as it seemed were the girls. I hope Jude was; she never complained, and did give the impression she enjoyed it, along with all the other activities we made the most of.

We sometimes walked around Holt. It offered quality shopping, and reminded me of Chester. We returned in time to take the return journey to Sheringham. On one occasion in the early years we found a pub/hotel very close to the station with its own playground. There were swings, slides, and roundabouts. Not only those for good weather, but an indoor family room, with a two storey playhouse. They produced food and drink at very reasonable prices. From then onwards, we made it into a whole day, starting with ice-creams on the beach. We must have spent about twelve days over the years, when the children seemed to be entranced by the familiar.

We did try two country houses, trying to add to the variety of North Norfolk, but these did not offer interest to the girls, despite two parents for whom history was an enormous part of their lives, especially Jude, who as previously mentioned, achieved a high 2:1 at Oxford University, reading History. Had I continued my education, I would certainly have become a history teacher.

It was the same at home near Ipswich. The girls were taken to the museum and the Ipswich Mansion. The latter was built during the reign of Elizabeth I, circa 1556. I don't remember the expression 'bored', but Hannah decided she had already had her fill. The other two quite independently gave the same opinion – thumbs down – and they never changed their attitude. Although Hannah was their 'spokes lady', she was never overbearing. She had her views, and left others to theirs.

The first one crossed off any future list was Holkham Hall itself. It purported to give a true perspective on its life and times. I believe I heard Hannah say, 'so does our lavatory!'.

The second was a visit to Sandringham. It is hardly a place like the Canary Islands. No sun-kissed beaches with golden sands, and on arrival it was raining. It still was when we departed.

We visited the church, which was much smaller than I expected, and imagined our Queen and where she must have sat on countless occasions. As I drove out of the grounds and through the gates, I heard a voice saying, 'thank goodness that's over'. It wasn't Hannah. From that moment, such events were expunged from the itinerary!

Just to prove the girls were not total 'plebs', we had been recommended to visit Thursford, a place less than ten miles from the caravan site. Its real modern fame was in its Wurlitzer organ and all its exponents, which gave the venue the same kudos as Reginald Dixon, in his firmament in Blackpool. But

Thursford had much more to offer. It housed a collection of the original roadster steam engines, 1908–1928. It had a veritable cornucopia of old organs, which were 'wired' to play at the touch of a button. There was a tea-room, a souvenir shop, both very reasonably priced, and outside when the weather was good, they had a steam locomotive which functioned on a large circular rail.

I think though, the favourite for us all (except maybe Jude, who liked to wait while we came into view, and wave and take photographs) was a late Victorian roundabout. It was not like the horse ones, which moved up & down, fun as they were. This one, built circa 1899, made you think you were riding waves. It certainly was the highlight for me. Grow up, I hear you say! not likely.

When I speak of Thursford, with its amazing popularity, I can only say that at the time we visited, they held an annual Christmas show (just like, I'm sure, the esteemed Reginald Dixon in Blackpool). Seating was plentiful, about the same as an average sized cinema. There was a four-year waiting list!

There was a variety of lunchtime eateries in Blakeney. The shops were, and their patrons always received willing and helpful responses from the staff. The pubs and hotels in and around the High Street were run in the same fashion, and were very much family orientated. Most provided a playground (or some such facility), and showed an interest in the children. Once you arrived, you immediately started to relax. I can't remember in that decade ever having a disappointing lunch.

One of the hostelries we often frequented had an attached 'Beach Shop'. What a place for children to browse in! A little like a Santa's Grotto, but at the wrong part of the year. It was there that they purchased their first 'crabbing kit'. The gentleman in the shop was pleased to help the girls, especially when he learnt that this was a skill they had not before aspired to. They listened intently, trying to get the drift of what he was saying. He had earned his sale!

They came to crabbing on about our fourth visit, when they were more able to cope with the gear, which could be lethal, especially the hooks. The recommended spot was in the harbour, where the crabs queued up to take the underwater morsels. They had a great life, those crabs; a willing food supermarket above, and nothing to pay! The crabs seemed as if they knew the game. They would, perforce, be thrown back into the shallow water to join the queue for the next meal!

It was around the third year of the girls' crabbing when we all needed to cope with a freak accident. It was not carelessness, although I'd never assume the three were immune. It all happened so quickly. At the time, (I didn't have a clear view), Vicky lowered her head as one of the others began casting. If poor Vicky had wanted her ears pierced, this was for free. But I should not jest. The shock and the pain briefly made her hysterical. A lady unknown to us immediately said she would drive as many of us as she possibly could to the nearest surgery. Jude went with her, while I rescued our car from the undergrowth around the caravan and followed the lady's car, arriving at the discovered surgery about ten minutes later. We were called into the doctor in quick time. He was wonderful with Vicky, and calmed her down considerably. He gave her an anaesthetic. Vicky said it tickled – she was on the mend!

It took a while, but the doctor was gentle and patient, and in time was able to release her. He prescribed a short course of antibiotics, 'just to be on the safe side'. Jude had obviously thanked the lady, and we looked out for her, but it seemed our 'angel' had moved on.

One of the times we went to Holkham Beach, on a beautiful summer's day, we were politely asked if we would wait outside the entrance gate for two or three minutes. After a few moments, the first of at least a dozen horses rode through the gate. Now I love horses, while, at the same time admitting I don't know much about them. But, there are horses and horses. I instinctively assumed these were very special ones. They made me feel as if I was in the company of royalty. I said to Jude, 'These don't have their shoes changed at some local smithy!' She rather liked that (I could not make her laugh very often).

A young lady dressed in riding gear followed the horses, I realised I was 'encroaching', but as politely and subserviently as possible, I begged a second of her time. I said to her that I was convinced these horses were rather special. She just said, 'yes, we're the Household Cavalry'.

This was the first time I had seen horses on holiday. It was at least our fifth year, and we had obviously missed them, because they were regulars like us. This was a genuine holiday. They loved being in seawater and apparently enjoyed wandering along the beach.

The memory of this is an enormous connection for me with *War Horse*, the play which at first playing to packed house in the West End and was then turned into a superb film. I wasn't, at the time, aware that this was an absolutely true story. A horse and master; a team, in the frightful theatre of World War I. The play featured the barbed-wire torture with which this horse was nearly crucified. Amazingly he came through this, and was reunited with his master, who moved to the coast and swam in the sea with him. The horse lived for nearly four more years, dying at the age of thirty-three. Blakeney, the Somme? I cannot think of one without the other.

Our holidays in Blakeney had come to a mutual conclusion. It was like the end of something very special. There was however one other trip that we booked up nearly every year. This was a trip by boat to a very small island in the peninsula which was an all-year-round holiday home for seals.

The trip was invariably breezy, and the crew were cheery. When we embarked on a second trip a year later, the same crew recognised us and chatted away. They also recognised a couple with a son, and I'm sure we were two of many.

The journey was about a half an hour, and you could disembark if you wanted to and take the next incoming boat back to the harbour. There was a single shop which was open for the summer season, and there wasn't much they couldn't cater for. The wonderful variation of ice-creams was why Jude and I were dragged ashore!

And as for the seals? It was really good to meet them! They were inquisitive, in fact they were show offs. They might pretend to ignore you one minute and threaten the boat the next. Many just lay on their backs, happy to be covered in sand so that they had an excuse for another swim to remove it.

Hannah was fascinated by the name of the vessel we used to sail in: *Ptarmigan*. 'I've not heard of a name like Ptarmigan!'

I told her that there weren't many words like that. 'You don't pronounce the 'P'. The 'P' is silent'. And from Hannah, 'Yours isn't Dad!'

We left Blakeney for home, without suggesting anything of future holidays. It had proved once again very enjoyable, and the weather had been excellent.

Jude had a thought about future holidays, and felt that as

Hannah was over ten, and the others not far behind, that we should broaden our horizons. It didn't mean we would never go to Blakeney again (time has proved this to be the case). We have been back nostalgically.

Jude suggested Scotland for next year, Wales for the one after, and Ireland the last of the trilogy. It seemed an excellent idea. The girls thought so too; they were perhaps ready for a change. Jude, was far superior to me in matters of geography, so I suggested that she organised where and when, and I would underwrite it. She settled for a holiday let in Glenfinnan, famous for its viaduct.

* * * *

The time soon came around when Jude was busy packing, I would be tying up loose ends with regard to the bridge schools, and the girls were just excited, as it should be.

When all was said and done, all who needed to visit the lavatory had done so, and all were safely strapped in, we all said our temporary farewells to Ancient Lights and waited for the inevitable punch-line from Kate. I backed up the car and negotiated her in our direction for the next nearly five hundred miles. Kate's innate sense of timing had not deserted her: 'Are we nearly there Daddy?'

I remember making good progress; daughters were well behaved, and Jude's map reading would have been beyond me. We reached Rugby, found a hostelry, and parked the car. We made for an advertised 'Family Room'. The food was good, and French windows gave access to a playground. They knew their family clientele. From our point of view, the fact that the girls had the opportunity to let off steam was a by-product of a calm continuation of our journey.

We hit the road again, and continued north. We had anticipated another one hundred and fifty miles, before a guiding light enabled us to reach a 'stable', for afternoon tea and a petrol station close by. Having filled up with fuel we needed to complete our odyssey, and with the girls asleep, we got close to journey's end.

Suddenly the car overheated, and with smoke/steam screaming from underneath the bonnet, she shuddered to an ignominious halt! I know this is hard to believe, but this happened within three yards of a garage entrance. The last one had been over sixty miles back. I still find it amazing that complete strangers should go out of their way to provide unequivocal generosity, even for these totally unknown to them.

I opened the bonnet.

'Don't worry sir, it's the fan belt. I can provide what you need to drive on a short-term basis, but you must take it to a garage.'

He was true to his word. We made it. His endeavours enabled us to reach our holiday home.

We were all ready to rest our weary heads, and next day we simply had to get to the nearest garage.

* * * *

'Where are you staying sir?' asked the garage proprietor. I told him. 'That's fine. If you leave the key with me, I'll make sure it's back by midday to your holiday home.'

He was true to his word. He handed me his invoice. It was half what had I expected it to be!

I paid there and then, enclosing enough to treat him and his partner to a 'dram'. Before he had the chance to question my small contribution, I insisted his service on my behalf was such that any less would have been unacceptable to me. Sometimes it is really special to shake hands with a stranger.

We soon found our bearings, and aimed to vary our daytime activities. We had to admit that the weather was not special, but this did not seem to affect the midges. I had over two hundred bites. I have visited every chemist in Scotland for quantities of tinctures, medications, restoratives, antibiotics, arsenic (which I politely refused), and bismuth. I might as well have put up with the scratching and saved my shillings!

The weather was hardly conducive to sunbathing on a beach, but on one of the better days we swam in a lake very close to our large room. It was bracing and memorable. I keep wondering why I still thoroughly enjoyed that holiday in Scotland. I think a lot was down to the girls' behaviour. They were stoical in the rain and enjoyed the variety of events we (Jude) organised.

One day we took a ferry from Mallaig to a small island called Rum. (Forgive an old man's memory if it was from Fort William). A lovely steam train ran between the above-mentioned points, and one day, having visited yet another chemist, I kept level with that magnificent specimen. For most of the journey it was parallel to the road, which was not busy. I enjoyed every moment, but still felt guilty about my driving!

One other aspect we all remember was the Glenfinnan Hotel and restaurant, which we assumed was a Scottish preserve (and why not!), where every evening the Haggis was piped in. It was a wonderful sight, and reminded me of twenty years before on Burns Night. The menu was mouth-watering.

The next evening we were early, and were noticed by a Scotsman making his way to dinner. He gave us a big smile and asked us if we had come to watch the 'show'. We admitted that we had, and made an attempt to be sociable. I suggested the menu, was one of the best I had ever seen. He gave me a wink and said, 'I quite agree, trouble is, it's a damn sight better than the food'.

We had an incident-free journey home. The midge bites disappeared. School was beckoning, and of course the girls would have the theatre, something else to look forward to.

As pre-planned by Jude, our next summer jaunt was to 'the Valleys'. Her uncle had bought a holiday home in Mid-Wales and offered us a fortnight's summer holiday there. He refused to accept one penny; Jude shrugged (he sided with Jude against her mother regarding us). Our journey, going almost due west rather than due north, started well, but not for long. The girls' behaviour in the back was appalling. Twice before we stopped for lunch, and once after, I threatened to turn the car around and go back home. Even Jude was annoyed. Had it not been for the fact that we had both worked very hard for this necessary break, I would have done.

For me, the upshot was waking the next morning with severe chest pains. I was doubled up. Jude phoned for a taxi, (at this stage she didn't drive), and I was driven to the nearest surgery. The doctor was a Gurkha, and he covered me with the small circular sticky tabs which enabled them test the heart. He examined the 'findings' for quite a long time. Eventually he said gently, 'I'm 80% against you having had a heart attack. However, that figure in my experience is not quite enough. I recommend the nearest hospital, which will I hope confirm my hopes'.

He picked up the telephone. Within five minutes, I was helped into an ambulance which transported me to Aberystwyth Hospital thirty miles away. (I still think Jude came with me to the doctor's. I'm not sure. Hannah was eleven, so we could trust her with the other two for a short while. I was kept in for two nights, and I cannot remember how many procedures I was put through! The ultimate was having to run on a rubber treadmill.

One way or another, much to my enormous relief, I was given a clean bill of health. I had not had a heart attack! I got the news at 10:30pm, just before my second night. They were lovely people, and this chap said, 'I believe you're on holiday'. I nodded, and he then said, 'we'll give you a call at 7:30am. I expect you would like to take a shower'. I nodded again. 'Right, breakfast at 8am. They will have an ambulance ready at 8:30. One of the orderlies will take your case and escort you to your transport'.

I put my hand out, and he took it. I looked him straight in the eye, and thanked him for their incredible care. It was brushed off, but I was sure it could not have been unnoticed.

'Get your head down boy, tomorrow we will get you home to your family,' he said. And they did just that.

I had plenty of time to get my head around the unusual three days before we found a family-orientated place for lunch. In the afternoon, we found one of the close beaches. It was hot, as it was for most of the holiday. I went in for a swim, and felt an enormous sense of relief.

In the evening, Judith guided me to the hostelry where she had spent the last two nights alone with the girls. It was very welcoming, and as soon as we arrived, Hannah made for the piano. It transpired that in my absence she had asked the owner, who was usually working behind the bar, if she could play it.

'Of course you can, it hardly ever gets played,' he said. I expected something like 'fill your boots', but he was too much of a gentleman.

Hannah, who was at the time, up to Grade 4, played for at least a quarter of an hour, with no music. When she finished, she received very generous applause from the room. We ordered drinks and food, and I worked out, for the convenience of a busy man behind the bar, what I needed to pay.

'Too much sir,' he said. I began to think that if I hadn't had a heart attack, I'd had a brain attack! I soon found out I hadn't .He wouldn't take anything for Hannah's meal. And hadn't for the last two days of my absence! I'm sure Jude would have protested, but it would have got her nowhere!

Jude had discovered (with her map reading) a lovely beach. The trip there was only about a ten-mile drive, and well worth it. This was the year when the whole family was in love with Gilbert O'Sullivan. I had two albums in the car, and he became our permanent companion. We spent about five days on that lovely beach, much of it swimming.

One day we went to Harlech. It was hot, and Hannah, wanting to swim, got stung by a jellyfish. The pain made her cry. I seemed to have bypassed them, and swam even though I had forgotten my towel. By the time I re-joined the family I was totally dry!

The journey home from the Valleys was uneventful. In fact, the likes of our outbound journey were never repeated. It proved to be a one off; never before, and never after. We made the usual stops and chatted about this and that, and the wonderful weather we had enjoyed. The girls would soon immerse themselves into routine, with the theatre to look forward to – again.

* * * *

The next year, as promised, we travelled to the Emerald Isle. South-west Ireland, to be precise. The car ferry had pointed us towards the 'Ring Of Kerry', and eventually to our holiday home for the fortnight. We arrived at the given address and were surprised to find a detached three-bedroomed house, in the shadow of which was a caravan with a large notice, 'PLEASE KNOCK'. So we did.

A woman and a couple of children poured out of the narrow door. 'Mr and Mrs Scott and family?' I acknowledged. She said that she would be pleased to show us around. As she opened the house front door, she explained before we all bundled in that she had been widowed two years before. She was determined to raise her children without the State.

She had a smallholding (the girls were quick to observe chickens and cock birds), which helped her to subsist for about seven months of the year. If she rented the house for five months, she could remain independent. Jude and I had great admiration for her. Not everyone in straitened circumstances is on the 'cadge'.

The house, our brief haven, was absolutely ideal for the family. The girls annexed their own spaces, still leaving some for Jude and me. We soon found a restaurant for a family. (It was the first we tried, and I'll tell you a little more of that anon.) It was a delightful start to yet another superb holiday. The way we were treated by one and all was not as English strangers, but as if we were long-standing relatives who had been away for a while.

When I felt the mood was right, I told them a few Irish jokes. The girls cringed. They didn't. One waiter said, after almost suffering laughter convulsions, 'Do come back soon, and bring some more jokes with you.' All right, he was probably just being kind, or he felt they needed the custom – even worse than that, he felt sorry for me. To be honest, it wouldn't have upset me a jot.

I left geographer Jude to sort out our itineraries; I was happy to drive. The girls were cheerful and well behaved. We'd talked about kissing the Blarney Stone, and Kate said, 'Can we go today?' Jude pored over her plans and said that it would fit in quite well. So, that was the first direction I was pointed in. We reached the top of the tower, where we needed to 'stand' upside down (with help), and, within an open vent only slightly wider than the human head. You could see land nearly 100 metres below. Kate went first, followed by the others. I demurred. Kate had a second try.

Jude had homed in on a lovely beach, as she had done last year in Wales. At the top of the steps was a smart tea-room. There was only one thing against it. It sold ice-creams!

'Please Dad, you said you would buy us one each, I have never ever known you to be mean Dad.' They say wrinkles are hereditary; parents get them from their children.

It was such an enjoyable holiday. We visited several landmarks which proved more popular than museums; some of the scenery was truly memorable. Towards the end of the holiday, we spent the days on the beach. By this time all the girls were swimming, and they were all to become competent and strong, but not competitive, unlike their cousin Paul, who missed representing Wales at the Commonwealth Games by less than half a second.

I digress; the girls were all hungry and I said to them to keep a look out, and if they saw a pub or restaurant we would stop. As it was we all saw it together, a colourful frontage with the name 'O'Neill's' filling up most of it. We had seen these before; the Wetherspoons of the Emerald Isle.

I stopped the car, which was easy to park, and suggested that I should pop in and find out if they could accommodate us all. It was quite full. They seemed comfortable with children. I went up to the bar, and a gentleman approached me with a ready smile; it transpired he was the manager. I said to him I had three daughters and a wife outside and hoped we could come in for a family meal.

'Would you mind three of them?'

This was the second time within recent memory I had been stared at as if I'd had a lobotomy! I have to say that this one came with a 'twinkle in the eye!'

'Are you really asking me if you can bring your family in?' he said. I almost genuflected. 'I'll find a nice spot. We always make room here. By the time you come back we will have your table ready'.

He was true to his word. We all trooped in, and he said to our little ladies, 'Bring your Mum and Dad here.' He pointed to a table which had appeared out of nowhere, and we were hardly settled before a charming waiter appeared with menus. I can honestly say the food was excellent, and the drinks were much appreciated. But for me, the thing I shall never forget was sitting in a large room which was catering for as many children as adults!

All the youngsters behaved impeccably, as (I'm relieved to admit) did ours. They didn't let the side down. For all those children, the impression I got was that this was the norm. I wished I could pick up this wonderful place and transport it to Bramford!

Soon, the sad moment came to pack the car and say our farewell to the lady whose home we had usurped. The girls said goodbye to the chickens and berated the two cocks for waking them too early! When all was said and done (thanks Jude), we started our journey home.

* * * *

Within a couple of months of our return, I had a telephone call from Nadine. I had visited the family near Norwich several times before her father left, and on one occasion she had visited us with her mother at Ancient Lights. She was about fourteen, and we had the added distraction of Hannah when she was one and a bit.

Now we were eleven years on, and after my fiftieth birthday, she was twenty-five. When she phoned she said she was back for a week, and could she come down to Ancient Lights and see us all tomorrow (Friday). I called out to Jude, and said 'It's Nadine, back in the country for a few days, and she'd love to come and see us'. Jude just said, 'Tell her yes'.

I arranged to collect her from the station. It was a bridge day at home, but the times all fitted, and I left the morning class just after the students for the ten-minute trip to Ipswich Station. Once again, the train was on time! After a few seconds, I watched her coming towards me; her arms were outstretched as she reached me. We just held each other for nearly five minutes. This was *the* most cataclysmic experience of my life. When we released each other, the station was empty.

Suddenly, for a very short time, I loved two women. I brought her back, and said to Jude, 'I'm taking Nadine up to the Legion for half an hour, and bringing her back for the afternoon while I'm running the bridge'. She looked at me as if I smelled!

I was true to my word, and spent the afternoon running duplicate bridge. She told me she was staying in the area, returning on Monday evening. I told her that this would be perfect, if she could catch a train back to Ipswich, and I could pick her up at 9:30am. If she could catch the 8:30, it should arrive at 9:34. I could then bundle her into the car, and we should arrive at the bridge venue with at least ten minutes to spare.

I did mention this to Jude, and she said quite forcefully, 'I don't want that to happen'. I nodded noncommittally. I didn't need to telephone Nadine.

I cannot say there wasn't a frisson between Judith and me over the weekend. I assured her my love for her was unchanged and tried to behave in a way that justified it.

I left for Woodbridge at, I thought, the usual time, and all the planning worked out well. Our relationship on the day was, up to a point, intimate. But there was no sordid sex. At first, Jude did not believe me, but I think my daughters did believe me, before her.

However, it was a difficult time for both of us. I can understand the situation from her point of view. As I expected, I was not to see Nadine again. Things gradually got back to normal for me and Jude, and we were together for the next nine years.

These were happy times, and I remember most especially the holidays abroad. After our three holidays around Great

Britain, the girls were ready to move 'onwards and upwards'. We started in Brittany, and next Northern France. This was especially useful for Hannah, who was concentrating on Modern Languages – French, German and Italian. She was already becoming fluent in the basics. I should include Vicky and Kate, who did not follow her path. They were doing well in their own disciplines. Although Vicky achieved a very creditable degree, in drama, she firmly decided she didn't want to go 'on stage'. She went on instead to create her own business, concentrating on everything from one-day breaks to one-week summer holidays. Her Diploma, from Rose Bruford, enables her to undertake supply teaching, which aids the coffers.

Kate, to everyone's surprise, is now established as a mathematician and has been Head Of Department since she was twenty-six, at a prestigious school in Bury St Edmunds. Forgive me if I sound boastful. It's just that the eldest is always in front of the others. I thus feel a sense of loyalty to the others... no, I didn't think you would believe me!

Before I continue with our seaside sojourns south, a brief but incredibly enjoyable interlude resulted from an invitation to visit Nadine's mum Veda and husband Brian at their home in Switzerland, and to meet their friends, who, we were assured, would give us an extremely warm welcome. And so it transpired. Nadine was living away at the time, and she was on holiday on the same dates.

We accepted the invitation with alacrity. When Jude, who took the call from Veda, told me Nadine would not be there, I remember shrugging. One tiny thing was enough to tell me we would have destroyed any vestige of our love for each other within a week! God knows what would have happened if I had 'burnt my boats'.

Veda and I had a platonic feeling for each other. This from nearly twenty years before at Thorpeness. That place has a lot to answer for!

The girls were so excited, and I must admit that Jude and I were feeling much the same. We booked our flight and sent our ETA to our hosts to be. 'We'll be there to pick you up' was the comforting response. They lived on the German side, in a palatial home with wonderful scenic views of the snow-capped hills and mountains. We were introduced to their enormous, yet gentle, Great Dane. This was their third. Sadly, the bigger the breed, as I am sure you will know, the shorter the life span. Their average life expectancy is six years. The sad side of loving such a dog is that the mourning process happening at least twice as often.

They were terrific hosts. Virtually every section of every day was booked up with wonderful times. They were church goers, and we were introduced to their vicar, who we were to meet two or three times during the week, at other events our family had been invited to join.

We visited an Olympic skating rink and watched internationals rehearsing. We travelled on a gondola, affording us wonderful views, and then joined a 'chain train'; a totally different experience. We were also invited to a luncheon party which lasted until 5pm. I was persuaded to 'perform', and, as I still had a fund of stories, I didn't choose to be the lady who 'doth protest too much'. I have to say it was a hoot from start to finish (South Liverpool Football Club eat your heart out!) Kate, then nine, joined me on my makeshift stage, and we led a singalong which in itself lasted twenty minutes at least.

Some readers might wonder how, with all our commitments, we could 'up sticks' and leave Ancient Lights to its own devices. We were fortunate to holiday during the girls' half-term holidays. As for the bridge, my mother was a born organiser, and relished the opportunity to cover for me.

Two other moments were memorable. The friends had heard I played bridge. A gentleman I had already chatted with asked me if I would like to play with him the next afternoon, at the Premier Bridge Club in Bern, (in the German sector). I jumped at the opportunity. He said to me that we were coming in opposite directions, and he knew either Brian or Veda would give me a lift to Bern railway station, which was just ten minutes away. 'I'll meet you there,' he said. He planned the times with Veda.

I duly followed his instructions, and we met just outside the station. We chatted as he propelled me towards our venue. We had time to chat about the systems we played. Fortunately they were much the same. I suggested we took our bidding as 'simple and sound'.

The first two hands settled us, and from then on, we flew! There were twenty tables, which added up to forty pairs. I relished this opportunity and I shall never forget it. At the end of the play we knew we were in the frame. And as the scores were posted, we realised just how close it was:

    1 Pair 4 - 66.82%
    2 Pair 17 - 66.81% - us.

We lost by one trick we had played 624 tricks. It was down to me. I made a lead which, taking all into account, was the only suit not bid against us. And the recommended lead if all else failed. I held KJ109, and led the Jack (top of an internal sequence). So my King never made! It would have done, had

I not led it, and we would have tied. The pair above us were both internationals!

The other memorable moment had been hanging over Brian's head for two years. The banks, like tax inspectors, resent paying Joe Public what belongs to him. After all, if we pay up, we will lose the interest on the capital which we need to pay out bonuses. Why should Joe Public be left in charge of his own money, with which he might well make investments that are neither sound or wise? Better to leave it with us. We'll search every loophole, so you won't have the trouble, and worry, about any responsibility, with which you may be awfully troubled, etc

The sum Brian was trying to protect (and this was in 1994-96) was £20,000,000, all legitimate. For two years, spurious loopholes had been touted, and a variety of accusations made. The Judiciary put a blanket over any further interventions, and said that the courts would make the decision regarding the sum of money involved, taking into account all the evidence and the suppositions). Today was the day (our flight was booked for the next afternoon). Brian was picked up by his solicitor. He turned to us all with a wan smile and shrugged. Veda was in tears.

About an hour later, the telephoned shrieked and broke our silence. Veda picked up the phone, and within moments she was crying again! He had told her that they had found for the plaintiff. A little celebration tonight perhaps? We were pleased and relieved.

Over a two-year period Brian had many times expounded about 'bloody bankers' and after a short while the Great Dane construed his master's displeasure and chased around the room, barking at all and sundry. He had discovered his own 'Party Piece'.

* * * *

In 1997, we moved our holidays from south-west Ireland to the Continent. Our stop that year was Brittany. I have always been a great fan of Jacques Tati. He revolutionised the use of sound, and it was pure genius. In his life, he only made about five completed films. The first I watched was 'Fete de Jour', filmed in 1950; I saw it in 1956. His most memorable film, 'Monsieur Hulot's Holiday', 1952, was made largely in Brittany. On our first day out in this hallowed place, we found a spot close to the beach, but stopped to have lunch 'al fresco'. The building opposite was Hotel La Plage. Surely it couldn't have been the one Monsieur Hulot stayed in? The weather was fine throughout and the girls never said no to a beach. In ten years we never had a disappointing dinner out.

I think I've given readers their fill of my holidays, so I shall conclude with my fondest memories of us five in foreign climes – after all, they do encapsulate a large part of my memoirs.

First, and I must get it off my chest, only one of the holidays was marred by the 'black dog', the clinical depression which had stalked me since 1969. It was easy to diagnose. We arrived at a caravan site, which Jude had planned, in France. I cannot remember where; geography was always my worst subject. It was similar to last year, except the caravan was newer and larger. The swimming pool was three times the size of last year's, and boasted the biggest set of water-slides I had ever seen. The girls' reaction was a joy to behold. We did a small shop, and Jude prepared us a nice meal, which was much appreciated by us all. I kissed the girls goodnight, but the water-slide came across as much more important!

Jude and I had a warm K and C (you work it out!) and I remember nothing until I woke up crying. I had actually been crying in my sleep! I spontaneously recognised clinical depression. I had medication with me, so I started dosing myself immediately, but it takes about twelve days to kick-in. I made myself small, as I didn't want to spoil their holiday. Jude didn't find it easy, but she hadn't graduated in nursing! I shall 'dwell' no longer, and remember over twenty holidays when I was as well as all the others.

* * * *

It was during those early days that a colleague of Judith's at university, soon to be married, became our very close friend over a period of seven or eight years. It matured when we were invited to their wedding. I think it was towards the end of 1984, when Hannah was about six months old. I had to take our 'little lady' out of the service, just once. We had asked to be at the back to facilitate any tantrums! Their names were Guy and Julia and their family soon started arriving at similar times to ours. They had had boy, girl, boy, girl – all very neat.

Guy had gone up to Oxford for one reason only – to become a millionaire! This, he achieved despite being rusticated twice (sent down), or if you prefer, kicked out! He scraped a poor third, the lowest pass you can get, but he achieved his reason for 'going up' and duly became a millionaire.

He filled his rooms with slot machines! He seemed to know how irresistible they would prove, and he was right. His apartments were always packed with young people who already had more money than they knew how to squander!

Guy was duly headhunted by one of the biggest financial institutions. His day would begin when he was picked up from his mansion in Sevenoaks by a taxi or hire car at 4:15am to make sure he was on the Stock Exchange floor by 6am. When this closed, it was back to his office in some penthouse suite in the City, catching up with files on potential customers. This before being picked up at 8:30pm to meet a potential client, whom he would wine and dine in some notable gourmet restaurant. He was picked up by his transport, usually at 12 midnight and arrive back at the mansion at 1am for three hours' sleep, before the whole procedure was repeated the next day.

When Hannah graduated in modern languages in 2001, she had exchanged German for Italian. Guy heard of this, and was pleased to offer her employment in his Italian office in Tuscany, to process a number of properties he had already purchased. Hannah had found heaven, and ever since she has spent at least two holidays there annually. It was not long before she was given the soubriquet 'the White Italian'.

Quite soon after Hannah had established herself, Guy invited us to stay in one of his large properties. He gave us a cheque to pay for our two weeks. It was £5,400, twenty years ago! The grounds were fabulous and the swimming pool large. The main lounge was bigger than any church hall I've ever seen. It was a wonderful holiday that Hannah was able to be part of. I remember one time when they were staying with us, Guy needed petrol. I was up and about, and he said, 'You might as well join me. I'd rather start the journey home with a full tank'.

I somehow climbed into his 4x4, and remember telling him about a bond I had bought which had doubled in value, from £10,000 to £20,000. He kindly nodded and left it at that. His lifestyle was of an ilk I could never have imagined!

The Best Man at Guy's wedding was William Hague, erstwhile Foreign Secretary, who was invited to become the Leader of the Conservative Party. Some may remember him from a wonderful speech he made as a 17-year-old at the 1976 Conservative Party Conference, when Margaret Thatcher was at the helm. His speech at the wedding, in the Oxford Union, was by far the best I have ever heard. As a wordsmith myself, anything I have ever achieved was totally eclipsed by his sheer brilliance and genius. Although he failed to dent the popularity of Mr Blair, and was replaced at an ensuing Conservative Party Conference, he was immediately promoted to the House of Lords, which, like it or not, is a better place for his presence.

I will conclude with a couple of our unforgettable experiences during the lovely times we spent on the continent. I should reiterate that my depressive sensibilities spoilt only one of the myriad holidays. It could have been many more. I have indeed been blessed.

We had walked around a little village close to where we were 'caravanned'. Jude had already explored a bit, and had noted a reasonable-sized supermarket, ideal for our needs. Early the next day she pointed us in its direction. When the shopping was done she noticed a menu outside a building which really didn't look like a restaurant. However the menu was dated 'today'.

'Shall we give it a go?' she said.

Having read the gastronomic enticements, I was all in favour, and the girls must have thought 'They've at least agreed on something!' They decided there was nothing to lose. We arrived in good time, and found the door next to the menu ajar. We entered a small dining area which consisted of a small room with and four tables. Three of them would seat six, and a small one would take one or two.

A French family had arrived just before us and were still discarding coats to their chairs behind. Without staring I was able to identify them as a married couple, and I imagined the children's grandmother. The children were lively, but well behaved. Soon they started a friendly conversation with us, they trying their English, Hannah and Jude participating with a smattering of French. All was well until I decided to butt in. After all, I had passed 'O' Level French thirty years before!

I had worked on my contribution and was sure I would be top man'. I decided to start with 'Je parle français, un petit peu,' but it came out as 'Je parle français un petit pois' – 'I speak French a little pea'!

Hannah was mortified. She blushed, and tried to hide under the table. As that proved to be difficult, under the tablecloth! The French gentleman gave me a commiserating smile, and said to Hannah, 'he really did try'. But that was no salve. The two waiters both had a wicked sense of humour, and I became the butt of their wit. I was mortified and would never forget that pea!

* * * *

On our first time in Portugal, we booked up a jeep ride. It was bumpy, but great fun. We had eaten well, and I had downed a couple of glasses of their 55%. I was feeling no pain. We stopped at a freshwater pool, and Kate and I enjoyed the very best swim we had experienced. It was about 80 metres long, and 8 metres wide. The water was so fresh it took the cold away. I certainly will never forget it.

CHAPTER 15

FINALE AND CURTAIN

I moved into my new flat in 2006. I had spent much of the previous eighteen months under some sort of therapy (at one time sporting a 'moon boot'!) The litigation continued.

Hannah had by now graduated, and Vicky and Kate were at the opposite end of Kent. At the end of term, Vicky stayed with me and Kate stayed with Jude. We both went to their graduations. Hannah was spending more time in Italy, working for Guy, as Kate on graduation also did – I think they enjoyed this very good experience.

As I was sixty and had been diagnosed with alcohol abuse, I decided I wanted to carry on living. I stopped all alcohol (as briefly mentioned) for 11½ months. I continued cruising when possible, and after ten cruises as a Bridge Director. I decided that if I didn't feel like getting up until noon, I wouldn't have to do so. I managed six in 'no capacity' (about one every year). These, as ever, I thoroughly enjoyed.

After a few necessary throat repairs, the surgeon said to me, that I had done well, but informed me that I wasn't yet 'out of the fire'. 'Do you think you could repeat the process of the year before last?' he said.

I told him I would do my best. This time two cruises were a part of my self-sacrifice! The first one was fine, and the second took me again to 11½ months. It was my first visit to Jerusalem. We were taken to see various important sites, ending with the Wailing Wall. We were just a short distance from where we had been booked in for lunch, and I began to feel an overwhelming desire for a drink. I tried, but I could not fight it. We were shown to our seats. At the end of the table were sixty glasses of red wine, already poured... that was the last straw. In mitigation, I had very nearly completed the year and I felt a modicum of success. The wine was awful, but drinking it felt bloody marvellous!

When I attended hospital for a check-up, I was told everything was unchanged, no treatment required. This involved two appointments: one for an ultra-sound scan, the other for an endoscopy, which involves pushing a pipe with a camera down your throat to check the state of affairs there. It is a most unpleasant procedure, but I'm grateful to have the opportunity to know how things are on a regular basis.

Since then, four years on, I no longer drink spirits, cocktails, port or sherry. I allow myself lager, draught Guinness and red wine. I'm quite happy with that, although I will be an alcoholic until the day I die. And *if* I am permitted to pass through the Pearly Gates to meet my maker, I trust he'll pour me out a large double snifter!

* * *

As briefly mentioned, I continued working until I was sixty-five. I was extremely fortunate in that for forty-five years, my hobbies became my profession. At the same time, they were never 'gravy trains'. They also demanded long hours, and I had to remain professional at all times.

In my twenty years of bridge coaching, Jude and I were invited out for a social evening once, and on my own, twice. Wrong side of the tracks? Perhaps that's unfair. We did have three young children, and the members were always very kind to them.

Ironically, it was on the journey home from one of the social evenings mentioned that Jude and I encountered a police car. It was out in the wilds of Suffolk, where there were no 'cat's eyes'. It was, we discovered, the only police car on 'checking up' detail between Cambridge and Aldeburgh. He flashed his lights. I stopped.

'Going rather slowly sir' he said, as if I was the first to be so apprehended.

'No cat's eyes,' I ventured.

'Have you been drinking sir?'

'Yes, we've been enjoying a social evening.'

'Would you mind blowing into this sir?'

I was trapped. And over the limit.

Judith was taken home by the other officer while my nemesis took control of my car and propelled us towards the

Ipswich Penitentiary. In fact he was quite sympathetic, and having recorded the fact that I was over the limit, and that proceedings would ensue, he permitted me to return home in my car, as long as I didn't drive before noon the following day. He could easily have told me that I had to find my own way home, and to return after noon to collect my car. The procedure at the Police Station took in excess of three hours to process. By the time this was complete, I was checked again and found to be below the limit.

The most demeaning moment was when I had to submit to having my fingerprints taken. I was now a criminal for life! I asked if they would kindly put my case back for three weeks, so that I could continue to do the school run for Kate to St Margaret's Church of England School, as there was no obvious alternative. To this they kindly agreed. My next appointment was at Ipswich Crown Court, which was buzzing with journalists. Next to fingerprinting, this was what I had dreaded most. I was reasonably well known in Ipswich, and I could anticipate the fall of a local personality in banner headlines. But once again, I had a stroke of luck. The tableau was all set to await the judge's 'black cap' when one of the magistrates walked away. She said, 'I cannot sit on this panel. The defendant is known to me'.

I had taught her to play bridge!

The court staff were grateful when the Chief Magistrate decided to adjourn proceedings. I was given a new date to attend. At least I had some breathing space. In addition, the journalists had found new headlines!

My case was never reported; an undeserved relief. I was, in fact, banned from driving for three months, which included our summer holiday in Blakeney (we travelled by train, and hired bicycles in situ), and I was fined £100. It was the fingerprinting that hurt me the most. But I have no complaints. As a confirmed drinker, there must have been other times I was over the limit. I feel I deserve no more than to hope for a fair 'rub of the green'.

Along the way, I was pleased to describe events during one of my most memorable television 'walk-ons' – being checked in as a policeman, driving the latest 2.5 litre speed jobs.

* * * *

I refer, as part of this valediction, to a brief mention of the ladies in my life. One of my proof-readers was scathing. He informed me 'a gentleman wouldn't tell'. 'Compare me with King Edward VII,' I ventured. He had a plethora of boxes for 'his' ladies at his coronation in Westminster Abbey in 1902. But he proved to be an excellent King, for just short of a decade. Forgive a semblance of arrogance when I say which choice I would have liked to be remembered for!

* * * *

During the years alone, before my retirement, I remember especially my journey on the Orient Express. It was from London, St Pancras, to Venice. I shall never forget it. At the time we had, I'm convinced, two nights (now it is just one). It must be difficult to imagine the Art Deco opulence, the best service, and quality of food and drink. Beyond my ken! As I remember, the package included two nights in Venice before the return journey. Magnificent!

At this point, I would like to bring the story of *Titanic* up to date, following a recent programme on Channel 4 regarding more up-to-date speculation. It was a good show, but it expounded new, probably spurious suppositions regarding a fire on the forward starboard side. If there was a fire on board, which according to these people there had, it was long before *Titanic* sailed towards New York. No smoke without fire – so where was the smoke? If it had lasted for so long, without anyone but the 'stokers' dealing with it, why couldn't this continue?

I find it difficult to believe this fire had anything to do with the actual sinking. As already related, in 1978, when I was serving on the P&O passenger liner *Oriana*, considerably larger than *Titanic*, we were called, as were all the passengers, to Emergency Stations (the dreaded seven short blasts from the ship's warning signal, followed by one long blast). The next morning we were informed a chip-fat fryer had caught fire. The crew were fantastic, and succeeded in dousing the flames in thirteen minutes. Had it not been out in twenty minutes, the ship would have been lost.

* * * *

As readers will know, my favourite sport is cricket. I also thoroughly enjoy soccer, rugby union, tennis, golf, snooker, athletics and swimming. Not, you understand as a participant these days, but as a keen spectator.

I have had the good fortune to watch cricket in England at Lords twice, at the Oval, Grace Road, Edgbaston, Colchester, and Chelmsford. My first time at Lords, about thirty years ago, was when Graham Gooch, playing for England against

India, ended that first day on 196 not out'. He went on to make 333, and then, in the second innings, another century! In the entire history of world cricket, this was a one-off achievement. England were to end the day on 359 for two wickets!

I was also privileged to watch two days of cricket at the famous SCG (Sydney Cricket Ground). The first of these was a day/night 50-over international, in the very early days of that format. England, and Boycott, hadn't comprehended what a competitive score was, and the Aussies won easily.

* * * *

As you will have already gathered, I am like a schoolboy, with his favourite conker when it comes to 'steam'. You only have to whisper the names: *City of Truro, Mallard, Coronation Scott, Sir Nigel Gresley, Oliver Cromwell* or *Flying Scotsman* and my eyes mist over. My particular choice is one of the Britannia Class; not the last of steam traction to be built, but close to it, plying the rails of East Anglia. This was, and still is, an express passenger locomotive. Around 1954, it became clear that steam traction as we knew it was coming to its end.

Oliver Cromwell was frequently at Ipswich Station Platform 2, ready to speed passengers to London Liverpool Street Station (about 70 miles in 78 minutes). She was also used at the other end of the spectrum, replacing the sturdy tank engines for a twelve-mile trundle to Felixstowe. Why was she so demanded? Well, 1949–1954 was before the time when the majority of families could afford to own a family car. But by then, companies at least gave employees a paid week's holiday. Travel by train was popular. The tank engine was sturdy, but could not, on a July Saturday, pull sixteen packed coaches. 'Olly' could.

On a day I particularly remember, I had arranged to meet my cousin Peter for lunch in the city. It was July 1965. We had both recently left school and had joined the ranks of the employed, he at an antiquarian book shop in, (where he was to stay happily until he retired), and I in a boring office job, where I wasn't. By then I still hadn't even discovered Butlins!

Two years before, we had learned that *Oliver Cromwell* was on a journey to Norwich, and that she would be passing through Ipswich Station, Platform 3. The day, dates, and times were all advertised, and I was there nearly an hour before hand. She burst out of our long tunnel, doing about 25 mph, and in five seconds she seemed dim on the horizon. Five seconds? Absolutely unforgettable!

ODES TO MY FAVOURITE THINGS

In the past I have dabbled in doggerel. These are my favourite things:

To the legend – W. G. Grace, 1848–1915

I was there, I was there.
I must have been there
When 'W.G.' with the broadest of bats
Hit 200 odd before tea.
I can see the great man
With wickets to spare
Lofting a four
Declaring
And leading his side to the square.

His over began
With a wink and a glare

And a monstrous appeal
To the Lilliput arbiter
Who didn't dare
To deny the great man.
I was there, I was there…
I must have been there.
With that bearded Gulliver
Dwarfing the club and the ground;
The players the gentlemen,
Delicate maidens
In colourful crinoline
Parasols nudging attentive top hats.
The smell of the hay in high summer was there:
I must have been there.

For A Steam Locomotive

Remember the giants of iron and steel,
Their carriages above the high tonnage rail
Together they eclipsed the colour of town and dale
As waiters in first class served 'haute cuisine'.
Outside, smoke belching, driving wheels apace
Within, the sorting of tomorrow's mail.

This cosmopolitan Pacific 231,
Propelling rods and wheels a chase
Graced majesty of funnel, dome, and steam.
Through stations, humble halts and fallow fields.
Through tunnel, straight and bend.
Reaching for the terminus on time.
The journey's end.

The Country Club, Thorpeness (because of P&O, it was special in my life)

In Daddy's day, palm court and silver service
graced this genteel folly
Where stately moments lapsed on wicker-decked verandas
And the cordial of summer gratified a clique of Panamas.
Although the passing seasons cast new members
The tableau was comfortably familiar,
And children with the gift of carefree principles
Soon found replacement for a missing kindly knee.
Vistas stretched as far as noble eyes would choose to scan,
Resting on some long cream-trousered dilettante, playing
paramour and tennis.
'Coming two, good serve, good shot!
Game, set, and match'.

But, Daddy's day has gone with that quiet pride of underlings
Who manicured the sequestered lawns
And served with dutiful distinction
Lobster Mornay to their masters.
The clipped moustache has downed his whisky soda.
And all the passing shots have played
Their game, their set, their match.

My Teacher (for teachers everywhere)

Miss?
Is this the way it should be done?
Thank you Miss.
You seem to know just what I need;
You show me how to work
And make it fun.
But when you're not in school, Miss
Are you quite so sure?
If I was old enough I'd see

That sometimes when you close a door
And turn the key, and stand alone
You, Miss,
Ask the way it should be done.
I hope your guide is good and constant
Like you,
Miss.

If you don't think you know me yet, below is the closest to me.
If you don't want to know me, ignore the below!

Man in an Ale House

A clipped moustache and patent leather shoes
were out of keeping with his mug of mild
And welfare spectacles.
A pipe and Oxford accent,
Out of uniform with his grubby collar
And the racing pages of the 'Mirror'.
I wondered where he came from or failed to get to.
He seemed quite comfortable
In his mackintosh and wooden chair,
So who was I to speculate?
I downed my gin and bitters
\And walked my wellies out of there.

I have on my 'bar' three sculptures, soldier, sailor, Spitfire. I look at
them every day, and attempt to remember.

In a Great War Cemetery

Over the tops of blocks and crosses
Soldier sees again those faces
Hears the home fire's crack
And Lucifers with kitbags silenced.

Sky looks faintly at the soldier now.

Once her glamour teased those young dispensables,
Paraded on the nurtured grass, in ordered rows.

Soldier looks at chalk-white symmetry,
Sees the putrid bog turn back to green and khaki;
Etched against the show of green,
Marching through the fog to Tipperary.

I'm not there yet, but I'll keep on trying…

Testament

My spirit moved beyond the cover of mortal life.
And travelling in such brilliance of white,
cast out the agony of missing expressions
I had longed to hold at my departing.
I was carried with such gentleness and reassurance,
the burden of responsibilities dissolved.
I felt as a child given infinite love,
guided to an open gateway into a temple.
A vision of sanctity welcomed me with open arms.
Would this saint become my saviour?
'Have you faith my child?'
'I have honestly searched for God with all my strength
and with undying expectation.'
'Have you been charitable?'
'I have aspired with Corinthian spirit
to value charity above all.'
'Do you believe in truth?'
'I believe it to be the beauty of perfection.'
'Have you cherished beauty?' I hesitated.
'If you failed, was it the fear that Earth's beauty could not last for ever?'
I hesitated. A quiet voice reached out to my soul,
softened into a gulf of sadness.

'Faith, Hope, Charity, and Truth are not enough.

You have spoken, with hesitation your fear
to appreciate the beauty of the Earth.
You are not yet prepared to rejoice in the Glory of Heaven.'
The sympathetic face faded, and the warmth of white turned grey,
and then to chilling starless black.
Where I wait, forever alone and awake until I may answer for
my lack of courage.

In conclusion with a large tongue in a larger cheek....

The Cocktail Party

Bonhomie, camarade
Esprit de corps, the whole façade,
The cocktail party's just begun
With bags of joie de vivre and fun

The host who shakes hands at the door
Reveals this ostentatious bore
And introductions help to break
The pregnant hush and threatened wake.

Hostesses pour out potent drinks
To soak this multi-pseudo-sphinx;
Synthentic gentry, endless thrills
A panopoly of pomp and frills.

Ladies decked in fur and lace
Dripping pearls and painted face
Each a peacock in full flight
Each dusty gown a shade too tight.

Even men are not immune
They do their best to keep in tune
And zealously join in the fray
With after-shave and body spray

OCEANS OF CHAMPAGNE

And as they drinks, ententes are made
And inhibitions quickly fade
The glasses drink the chatter flows
The noise to a crescendo grows.

And from this room of smoke-filled lungs
Of platitudes from loosened tongues,
This tinselled scene drags on and on,
Until, thank God, the dinner gong.

The thought of food, reality,
This funfare of banality,
This pleasure ground of play and pose,
This carousel grinds to its close.

It's one of many social trials,
With facile chat and plastic smiles,
One feigns delight and instant wit,
To entertain some boring twit!

Edwin T Scott 1972

348

EPILOGUE

I began my extraordinary life alone. I attended school alone. I played alone. I remember no friends as such, and until my sister was born, no relatives except much older persons. I listened with mother, alone. When I was three, I had learnt to balance the front gate. I stayed out there, watching people coming and going. If they didn't speak to me, I was in a good position to talk to them.

This reminds me of a little lad chatting at his front gate, but he was crying his eyes out. A kindly lady stopped and asked him why he was so unhappy. He told her his father was a sailor, and had been away for over a year.

Last week, my mum had another baby, and through the gulps and tears I get blamed for everything in this house!

Suddenly in my late thirties, over a three-year period, I found myself as part of a family of five, which lasted lasted for twenty years. It is still a family of four. This has been the most fulfilling part of my life!

To close: two snippets, the first questioning my attitude towards relationships.

To bond or roam?
Surely happier hand in hand.
Than moving from flame to flame
Leaving a lovelorn message in the sand.
The following reminds me of my travels, and how many places had opulence on one side of the road, and abject poverty on the other.

We didn't have the money needed,
To purchase the pegs we wanted,
To hang the clothes we couldn't afford to buy.

If you've lasted the distance, THANK YOU.

BV - #0026 - 170320 - C20 - 229/152/17 - PB - 9781861519580